ATLANTIS AMBIENT AND PERVASIVE INTELLIGENCE

VOLUME 5

SERIES EDITOR: ISMAIL KHALIL

Atlantis Ambient and Pervasive Intelligence

Series Editor:

Ismail Khalil, Linz, Austria

(ISSN: 1875-7669)

Aims and scope of the series

The book series 'Atlantis Ambient and Pervasive Intelligence' publishes high quality titles in the fields of Pervasive Computing, Mixed Reality, Wearable Computing, Location-Aware Computing, Ambient Interfaces, Tangible Interfaces, Smart Environments, Intelligent Interfaces, Software Agents and other related fields. We welcome submission of book proposals from researchers worldwide who aim at sharing their results in this important research area.

For more information on this series and our other book series, please visit our website at:

www.atlantis-press.com/publications/books

AMSTERDAM – PARIS

© ATLANTIS PRESS

Computer Vision and Action Recognition

A Guide for Image Processing and Computer Vision Community for Action Understanding

Md. Atiqur Rahman Ahad

Faculty of Engineering, Kyushu Institute of Technology,
1-1, Sensui, Tobata, Kitakyushu, Fukuoka,
T-804-0012, Japan

Applied Physics, Electronics & Communication Engineering,
University of Dhaka, Dhaka – 1000, Bangladesh

AMSTERDAM – PARIS

Atlantis Press

8, square des Bouleaux
75019 Paris, France

For information on all Atlantis Press publications, visit our website at: *www.atlantis-press.com*

Copyright

Softcover reprint of the hardcover 1st edition 2011

This book, or any parts thereof, may not be reproduced for commercial purposes in any form or by any means, electronic or mechanical, including photocopying, recording or any information storage and retrieval system known or to be invented, without prior permission from the Publisher.

Atlantis Ambient and Pervasive Intelligence

Volume 1: Agent-Based Ubiquitous Computing - Eleni Mangina, Javier Carbo, José M. Molina
Volume 2: Web-Based Information Technologies and Distributed Systems - Alban Gabillon, Quan Z. Sheng, Wathiq Mansoor
Volume 3: Multicore Systems On-Chip: Practical Software/Hardware Design - Abderazek Ben Abdallah
Volume 4: Activity Recognition in Pervasive Intelligent Environments - L. Chen, C.D. Nugent, J. Biswas, J. Hoey

ISBN 978-94-91216-19-0
ISBN 978-94-91216-20-6 (eBook)
ISSN: 1875-7669
ISBN 978-94-6239-058-4

© 2011 ATLANTIS PRESS

This book is dedicated to

my loving mother — Hosne Ara Begum,
my late-father — Md. Amir Hossain,
my Sensei — Prof. Seiji Ishikawa
                                                        &
my lovely wife — Shahera Hossain (Ruba)

for their continued support, love and encouragement.

Preface

The book is about computer vision and action recognition & understanding. If you have a basic knowledge on image processing and would like to study or to do research on action/activity understanding and recognition in computer vision and related arenas – then this is the book for you!

Throughout my endeavor to write this book, I have undergone many discussions with many experts during various conferences and academic meetings, discussed over emails on many challenging issues. I would like to thank them for their valuable time and inputs. Those exchanges facilitate me to build up and mature different ideas in the line of this book.

The materials presented in this book are covered in seven chapters – from basics to methodologies to challenges ahead. The fundamental goal of this book is to cover the important and related issues in such a manner – so that a student or a researcher can find ample of resources and points to go through. Chapter 1 defines action and activity. There is no clear-cut well-accepted nomenclature for atomic action to activity or behavior. This Chapter presents the key issues and I hope that a new researcher will find it very useful. Chapter 2 covers some important low-level image processing topics, which are more relevant for action recognition. If one has no prior knowledge on image processing and computer vision – this chapter can help him/her to build a background in concise manner. In Chapter 3, state-of-the-art action representation approaches are organized for better understanding on this area. It is one of the core chapters of this book that deals with representations, action recognition approaches, affective computing, action segmentation, gait recognition, and related issues.

Chapter 4 presents the motion history image method, as it is one of the most widely employed methods. However, this chapter not only presents this method and its applications, but also digs out various developments at the top of this method, from which one can retrieve essences on developmental issues from an existing approach.

Chapter 5 summarizes shape representations and pattern recognition issues in a concise manner. A reader may need to look into more details on the approaches he/she requires for further study. In Chapter 6, the datasets for action recognition are covered. This is another very important contribution of this book – because no other material is available till-to-date that encompasses the dataset issues in such comprehensive manner, as covered in this book. Finally, Chapter 7 ponders upon the challenges ahead in this important field, through plenty of new dimensions and thought-provoking discussions on present and future challenges.

After each chapter, I put some tasks under 'Think Ahead!' for students and researchers – so that they do some brain-storming based on the materials covered in this book. It is written in a simpler manner, with about 650 relevant citations, so that a student or a researcher can look into those references for further study on that specific area.

None is perfect! Therefore, I encourage you to write me for any comment, criticism or feedback on the book for its future development – to atiqahad@univdhaka.edu or atiqahad@yahoo.com on: What are the areas to improve in future? What topics are left out? What topics should be added? What areas need more attention?

I very much confident that this book will contribute the academia as a textbook, to run a regular course in Graduate-level or Undergraduate-level; and also guide a researcher to accomplish the work in a comprehensive manner. Let's hope that better methodologies in future will lead us towards more human-oriented real-life applications for *better life*. With this high-toned yearning, I would like to welcome you to read this book and inform others!

Best regards,

Md. Atiqur Rahman Ahad
Kitakyushu, Fukuoka, Japan
http://ijcvsp.com
http://iciev.org

Foreword

Humans receive the great majority of information about their environment through sight. Vision is also the key component for building artificial systems that can perceive and understand their environment. Due to its numerous applications and major research challenges, computer vision is one of the most active research fields in information technology.

In recent years, recognition of human actions has become a topic of great interest in computer vision research. Among the areas of potential application are human-computer interaction, surveillance, video indexing, sport video analysis, video games and smart environments. All these applications have their own demands, but in general, algorithms to be used must be able to detect and recognize various actions in real time. As people look different and move differently, the methods should also handle variations in performing actions and work properly in various kinds of environments. In developing novel methods for different applications, it is important to use representative and publicly available test image datasets in order to be able to compare results to the state-of-the-art.

During the past few years, researchers in computer vision have developed various kinds of approaches for action recognition. In general these methods are able to recognize well relatively simple actions, but dealing with more complex actions in varying environments is still a major research issue.

This book provides an excellent overview and reference to human action recognition. After introduction to the problem area, the most common low-level image processing methods for action representations and different approaches used for action representation are presented in Chapters 2 and 3. The widely used approach based on motion history images (MHI) is described in Chapter 4, and Chapter 5 deals with different shape representations and methods for feature vector analysis. Chapter 6 provides very valuable information about different datasets used in research on different types of actions and applications. Finally, Chapter 7 discusses what kind of challenges are ahead in this research area.

The book contains few hundreds of good references of many issues, which are important for researchers and students to look for some more details on specific areas. It is well written and easy to read also for non-native English speakers. The book also covers many research dimensions and anyone can get benefit from these points. The author has made an excellent job in writing this book. It will be a valuable resource for researchers, engineers and graduate students working in computer vision and related fields.

>	Matti Pietikäinen
>	*University of Oulu, Finland*
>	http://www.cse.oulu.fi/MattiPietik%C3%A4inen

Acknowledgments

All praise to *Allah*.

I express my sincere gratitude to my research supervisor, Prof. Seiji Ishikawa, Dean of Faculty of Engineering, Kyushu Institute of Technology, for his excellent guidance and motivation throughout my tenure at Kyushu Institute of Technology, Japan. His sincere and kind-heart always have been a motivating factor for my research works.

Unlimited tribute and veneration to my other teachers of my schools, Notre Dame College, University of Dhaka, Bangladesh; University of New South Wales, Australia; and Kyushu Institute of Technology, Japan.

I would like to show my sincere gratitude to Prof. Matti Pietikäinen, University of Oulu, Finland (Fellow of IAPR, Senior Member of IEEE, Associate Editor of IVC, former Associate Editor of IEEE Trans. PAMI, and Pattern Recognition) for his kind time to write a forward for this book. Various researchers assisted me through materials and discussions in different period, which helped me a lot to bring out the book. Of them, I specially mention Greg Mori (Simon Fraser University), Ramin Mehran (University of Central Florida), JK Aggarwal (The University of Texas), Jeff Cohn (University of Pittsburgh), Leonid Sigal (Brown University), and Ronald Poppe (University of Twente). I am very much thankful to Ahmed Boudissa (Kyushu Institute of Technology), Ashik Iftekhar (Kyushu Institute of Technology), Ragib Morshed (University of California Irvine) and Hafiz Imtiaz (Bangladesh University of Engineering & Technology) for their kind time to review and comment on the book.

I am thankful to many of my friends in Japan for their time and lovely interactions to make my life warm and lively. I would like to mention specially a few of them for providing me the required *mental food* through their love and care — Kenji Kurokawa, Mohin Mahtab and Keiko Matsuoka. I sorely recall my father who spent his life to guide his children for education and better lives. He is no longer here on this earth but my love, my passion, my sincere *duah* for him always. My mother strived a lot for me to bring me up to this stage and her love and pray always motivated me. Thanks to my brothers and sisters.

Finally, I must mention my wife and the best-friend Shahera Hossain (Ruba) for her constant support and her demand to do more & better in my work. She is always inspirational for my development though I failed to follow her expectations!

Md. Atiqur Rahman Ahad
Colorado Springs, USA, 2011

Contents

Preface		vii
Foreword		ix
Acknowledgments		xi
List of Figures		xix
List of Tables		xxi

1. **Introduction** — 1
   - 1.1 Introduction — 1
   - 1.2 What is Action? — 1
   - 1.3 Action Recognition in Computer Vision — 2
   - 1.4 Application Realms of Action Recognition — 3
   - 1.5 Categorization — 4
   - 1.6 Think Ahead! — 8

2. **Low-level Image Processing for Action Representations** — 9
   - 2.1 Low-level Image Processing for Action Representations — 9
   - 2.2 Pre-processing Steps — 9
   - 2.3 Segmentation and Extraction — 10
     - 2.3.1 Feature Detection from an Image — 11
     - 2.3.2 Edge Detection — 11
     - 2.3.3 Corner Points — 11
     - 2.3.4 Blob Detectors — 12
     - 2.3.5 Feature Descriptors — 13
     - 2.3.6 Segmentation — 14
   - 2.4 Local Binary Pattern — 20
     - 2.4.1 LBP — Variants — 21
   - 2.5 Structure from Motion (SFM) — 23
     - 2.5.1 Constraints of FM — 25
     - 2.5.2 Improvements of FM — 27
   - 2.6 Other Issues — 34
     - 2.6.1 Intensity Normalization — 34
     - 2.6.2 Image Matching and Correspondence Problem — 35
     - 2.6.3 Camera Calibration — 36
   - 2.7 Think Ahead! — 36

3. **Action Representation Approaches** — 39
   - 3.1 Action Representation Approaches — 39

3.2	Classification of Various Dimensions of Representations	39
	3.2.1 Bag-of-Features (BoF) or Bag-of-Visual-Words (BoVW)	40
	3.2.2 Product Manifold Approaches	44
3.3	Action Recognition Approaches	49
	3.3.1 Interest-point-based Approaches	49
	3.3.2 Hidden Markov Model-based Approaches	53
	3.3.3 Eigenspace-based Approach	55
	3.3.4 Approaches to Manage Occlusion	56
	3.3.5 Other Approaches	56
3.4	View-invariant Methods	61
3.5	Gesture Recognition and Analysis	62
3.6	Action Segmentation and Other Areas	63
3.7	Affective Computing and Expression Analysis	63
	3.7.1 Games with Emotional Involvement	64
	3.7.2 Interactive Arts	66
	3.7.3 Anatomically-based Talking Head	66
3.8	Action Segmentation	67
	3.8.1 Gestures	67
	3.8.2 Basic Motion	67
	3.8.3 Fundamental Gesture	68
	3.8.4 Motion Alphabet	68
	3.8.5 Atomic Movement	68
	3.8.6 Direction-based Basic Motion	68
	3.8.7 Distinct Behaviors	69
	3.8.8 Motion Patterns based on Symbols	69
	3.8.9 Basic Movement Transition Graph	69
3.9	Gait Analysis	69
3.10	Action Recognition in Low-resolution	71
	3.10.1 Application Areas	71
	3.10.2 Related Works on Low-Resolution Video Processing	72
3.11	Discussion	73
	3.11.1 Salient Region and Its Associated Salient Region Construction	74
	3.11.2 Biologically-inspired Visual Representations	75
3.12	Conclusion	75
3.13	Think Ahead!	75

4. MHI – A Global-based Generic Approach — 77

4.1	Motion History Image (MHI)	77
4.2	Why MHI?	78
4.3	Various Aspects of the MHI — A Tutorial	79
	4.3.1 Formation of an MHI Image	79
	4.3.2 Motion Energy Image (MEI)	80
	4.3.3 Parameter — τ	82
	4.3.4 Parameter — δ	82
	4.3.5 Temporal Duration vs. Decay Parameter	82
	4.3.6 Update Function $\psi(x, y, t)$	83
	4.3.7 Feature Vector for the MHI	85
4.4	Constraints of the MHI Method	86
	4.4.1 Self-occlusion Problem	86
	4.4.2 Failure in Dynamic Background	87

		4.4.3	Improper Implementation of the Update Function	87
		4.4.4	Label-based Recognition	87
		4.4.5	Failure with Motion Irregularities	87
		4.4.6	Failure to Differentiate Similar Motions	87
		4.4.7	Not View-invariant Method	87
		4.4.8	Problem with Varied Motion Duration	88
		4.4.9	Non-trajectory Nature	88
	4.5	Developments on the MHI		88
		4.5.1	Direct Implementation of the MHI	88
		4.5.2	Modified MHI	91
	4.6	Solutions to Some Constraints of the Basic MHI		95
		4.6.1	Solutions to Motion Self-occlusion Problem	95
		4.6.2	Solving Variable-length Movements	100
		4.6.3	*timed*-Motion History Image	101
		4.6.4	Hierarchical-MHI	101
		4.6.5	Pixel Signal Energy	102
		4.6.6	Pixel Change History	102
		4.6.7	Motion Flow History	102
		4.6.8	Contour-based STV	102
		4.6.9	Solving View-Invariant Issue	103
	4.7	Motion Analysis		105
	4.8	Implementations of the MHI		105
		4.8.1	The MHI and its Variants in Recognition	106
		4.8.2	The MHI and its Variants in Analysis	106
		4.8.3	The MHI and its Variants in Interactions	107
	4.9	MHI and its Future		111
	4.10	Conclusion		112
	4.11	Think Ahead!		113
5.	**Shape Representation and Feature Vector Analysis**			**115**
	5.1	Feature Points Tracking		115
		5.1.1	Two-frame-based Approaches	115
		5.1.2	Long-sequence-based Approaches	116
		5.1.3	Discussions	116
	5.2	Shape Representation Schemes		119
		5.2.1	Contour-based Methods	121
		5.2.2	Region-based Methods	122
	5.3	Moment Invariants		122
		5.3.1	Hu Moments for Feature Sets	122
		5.3.2	Zernike Moments for Feature Sets	126
	5.4	Component Analysis Methods		128
		5.4.1	Appropriate Feature Selection	128
		5.4.2	Dimension Reduction	129
	5.5	Pattern Classifications		133
		5.5.1	Supervised Learning	134
		5.5.2	Unsupervised Learning	137
		5.5.3	Nearest Neighbor	138
		5.5.4	Cross-validation — Partitioning Scheme	142
	5.6	Evaluation Matrices		143
	5.7	Think Ahead!		145

6. Action Datasets — 147

- 6.1 Action Datasets — 147
- 6.2 Necessity for Standard Datasets — 147
  - 6.2.1 Motion Capture System — 148
- 6.3 Datasets on Single-person in the View — 149
  - 6.3.1 KTH Dataset — 149
  - 6.3.2 Weizmann Dataset — 150
  - 6.3.3 IXMAS Dataset — 151
  - 6.3.4 CASIA Action Database — 152
  - 6.3.5 UMD Dataset — 152
  - 6.3.6 ICS Action Database — 152
  - 6.3.7 Korea University Gesture Database — 152
  - 6.3.8 Wearable Action Recognition Database (WARD) — 153
  - 6.3.9 Biological Motion Library (BML) — 153
  - 6.3.10 HDM05 (Hochschule der Medien) Motion Capture Database — 153
- 6.4 Gesture Datasets — 153
  - 6.4.1 Cambridge Gesture Dataset — 153
  - 6.4.2 NATOPS Dataset — 153
  - 6.4.3 Keck Gesture Dataset — 154
- 6.5 Datasets on Social Interactions — 154
  - 6.5.1 Youtube Dataset — 154
  - 6.5.2 Youtube Video Dataset — 155
  - 6.5.3 Hollywood2 Human Action (HOHA) Datasets — 155
  - 6.5.4 UCF Sports Dataset — 155
  - 6.5.5 Soccer Dataset — 156
  - 6.5.6 Figure-skating Dataset — Caltech Dataset — 156
  - 6.5.7 ADL — Assisted Daily Living Dataset — 156
  - 6.5.8 Kisses/Slaps Dataset — 156
  - 6.5.9 UIUC Action Dataset — 157
- 6.6 Datasets on Other Arenas — 157
  - 6.6.1 Actions in Still Images — 158
  - 6.6.2 Nursing-home Dataset — 158
  - 6.6.3 Collective Activity Dataset — 158
  - 6.6.4 Coffee and Cigarettes Dataset — 161
  - 6.6.5 People Playing Musical Instrument (PPMI) — 161
  - 6.6.6 DARPA's Mind's Eye Program — 162
  - 6.6.7 VIRAT Video Dataset — 162
  - 6.6.8 UMN Dataset: Unusual Crowd Activity — 162
  - 6.6.9 Web Dataset — 162
  - 6.6.10 HumanEva Dataset — 162
  - 6.6.11 University of Texas Dataset — 164
  - 6.6.12 Other Datasets — 164
- 6.7 Challenges Ahead on Datasets — 165
- 6.8 Think Ahead! — 168

7. Challenges Ahead — 173

- 7.1 Challenges Ahead — 173
- 7.2 Key Challenges Ahead in Action Recognition — 173
- 7.3 Few Points for New Researchers — 177

	7.3.1 Intelligent Transport System	180
7.4	Conclusion	182
7.5	Think Ahead!	182

Bibliography   **183**

List of Figures

1.1 Various applications of action understanding. 4
1.2 Concept of *moveme* and action hierarchy. 5
1.3 Hierarchy according to [48, 91]. 6

2.1 Example of naive background subtraction method. 15
2.2 Example of frame subtraction method. 17
2.3 Optical flow vectors in an action frame. 18
2.4 Streaklines for crowd segmentation. 19
2.5 Streaklines in a video. 20
2.6 Streaklines vs. optical flow. 21

3.1 A typical concept of Bag-of-Words. 40
3.2 Some examples of pose-based body part segmentation. 41
3.3 A concept of learning from the Bag-of-Words as per [110]. 41
3.4 A flow-diagram for spatio-temporal interest points to classify. 42
3.5 An example for mixed approach with large-scale and small features. 46
3.6 A typical ML approaches for video-based human motion analysis. 47
3.7 Concept of localization and recognition based on prior model and training data. 59
3.8 Detecting group of people to understand their activities. 60
3.9 Understanding the actions of a group of people — talk 60
3.10 Examples for the concept of joint action recognition and localization. 64
3.11 An approach for action localization and understanding. 65
3.12 An approach for crowd segmentation by exploiting optical flow and streaklines. 65
3.13 An approach for abnormal behavior detection by exploiting streaklines. . . . 66

4.1 Template-based recognition. 77

4.2	Applications of the MHI and its variants. Related to activity analysis.	78
4.3	Applications of the MHI and its variants. Related to interactive applications.	81
4.4	Different *tau* values and the corresponding MHI images for an action.	83
4.5	Delta dependency.	84
4.6	Optic flow into four channels.	97
4.7	A flow diagram for the DMHI method for action recognition.	98
4.8	HMHH images for for patterns for six actions.	100
5.1	Shape representation — various approaches.	120
5.2	Classifier black-box.	134
5.3	Example of an unsupervised learning	138
5.4	Choice of k: an example.	141
6.1	A typical motion capture system layout.	149
6.2	Few frames for KTH action dataset.	150
6.3	Sample frames for Weizmann action dataset.	151
6.4	Few action samples for HOHA2 actions dataset.	155
6.5	Nursing-home dataset: Samples with some results.	159
6.6	Nursing-home dataset: Samples with some results of *fall* detection.	160
6.7	Sample images from the collective activity dataset.	161
6.8	UMN dataset: Unusual Crowd Activity — example with detection	169
6.9	Abnormal crowd dataset — few sample images.	170
6.10	Sample frames from HumanEva dataset.	171
6.11	Human interaction dataset.	171
6.12	Aerial-view activity dataset — person extraction from each class.	172
6.13	Wide-area activity dataset.	172
7.1	Choose the best-*pose* based on some *score*.	179

List of Tables

2.1 Background subtraction methods and their properties. 17

4.1 Recognition and related areas. 107
4.2 On motion analysis. 109
4.3 On motion analysis. 110

Chapter 1

Introduction

1.1 Introduction

This book deals with action and activity recognition. In seven chapters, this book covers nomenclature of actions, application realms, low-level processing issues for action representations, various approaches for action recognition, motion history image method, shape representations and feature vector analysis, action datasets, and some future issues. In this Chapter, we define action and its nomenclature, and applications of action recognition.

1.2 What is Action?

What constitutes an action — is difficult to define! Even though there is a great demand for a specific and established action/activity hierarchy, there is not any recognized action hierarchy in computer vision till now. In this chapter, various definitions are provided to define action or activity. Lan *et al.* [112] define action and activity as,

- *Action* to denote a simple, atomic movement performed by a single person.
- *Activity* to refer to a more complex scenario that involves a group of people.

A well-known action hierarchy can be defined as:

- Action primitives,
- Actions, and
- Activities

- though actions, activities, simple actions, complex actions, behaviors, movements, etc., are often used interchangeably by different researchers [500].

However, this distinction between action and activity is not approved and used by many others. It is usually difficult to distinguish actions of each individual person alone in a scene from a group of people. However, if one looks at a whole scene, he/she can easily recognize the activity of the group and the action of each individual. Lan *et al.* [111, 112] introduce a model for recognizing group activities by jointly considering the group activity, the action of each individual, and the interaction among certain pairs of individual actions.

On the other hand, Gaidon *et al.* [91] decompose actions into sequences of key atomic action units, each called an *actom*. These *action atoms* are key components of short duration, whose sequence is the characteristic of an action. An *actom* is a short *atomic action*, identified by its central temporal location around what discriminative visual information is present [91]. Obtaining this decomposition of actions in atomic units is challenging, especially in realistic videos, due to viewpoint, pose, appearance and style variations [91].

Furthermore, these atomic action units are action dependent and can be motions, poses or other visual patterns [90]. Very short sequences of 1 to 10 frames are mentioned as *action snippets* [90], which echo the concept of atomic actions. Most of the methods usually analyze an entire video and assign it a single action label, or use relatively large lookahead to classify each frame [90]. Contrary to these strategies, human vision proves that simple actions can be recognized almost instantaneously [90], even though till-to-date, it seems very difficult. However, it is important to understand how actions can be decomposed into the right basic units [90, 91, 120].

Reference [320] terms the smallest action unit as *basic motion*. Reference [462, 463] refers to their segmented smaller actions as *gesture*. *Fundamental gesture* is the term for the bottom-level action unit by [318]. So as we have seen, there is no clearly defined and well-taken classification so far.

1.3 Action Recognition in Computer Vision

Recognition is defined by the trial to determine whether or not an input data contains or resembles some specific object, feature, or activity. In computer vision, action recognition is to decipher an action/activity component from a video or image scenes. The problem of understanding human actions is complicated by many issues, including the fact that actions are dynamic and may not typically be recognized by simple attention to single moments in time [573]. Action recognition is further complicated by the variation between people and even between instances of a single person [573]. Finally, successful action recognition demands either explicit or implicit background removal; motions in the background are distracting and should be ignored [573]. There are various approaches for action or activity recognition and analysis. These will be covered more in the chapters ahead.

1.4 Application Realms of Action Recognition

Understanding motions or activities from video sequences is a very important but difficult task. The field of action and activity representation and recognition is relatively old, yet still not much mature for many real-life applications. Recognizing the identity of individuals as well as the actions, activities and behaviors performed by one or more persons in video sequences is very important for various applications. Diverse applications are already undertaken on this goal for proper video understanding, e.g., in —

- Human-robot interaction,
- Human-computer interaction,
- Intelligent video surveillance,
- Mixed reality,
- Face analysis,
- Object tracking,
- Video-processing and video-indexing,
- Video-conferencing,
- Obstacle avoidance,
- Smart aware-house and rehabilitation center,
- Robotics,
- The fields of biomechanics, medicine, and sports analysis,
- Film, games, etc.,

- to name a few. Figure 1.1 shows some application areas.
Several survey papers illustrated various applications related to action analysis and recognition (e.g., [436, 447, 448, 452, 481, 488–507, 641]).

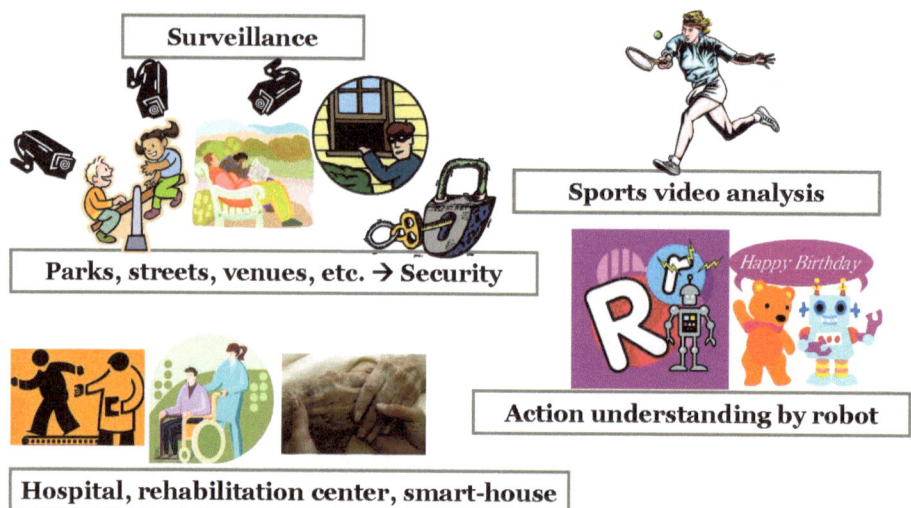

Fig. 1.1: Various applications of action understanding.

1.5 Categorization

There is no standard and well-accepted nomenclature or categorization for action or activity or human motion or gesture — for analysis and recognition. However, few proposals are available in literature. As per [89], "There exists an inherent ambiguity for actions — when does an action begin and end? Unlike object boundaries in static images, where one can often delineate the boundary between an object and its background, determining the temporal extent of an action is often subjective." Human activity should be decomposed into its building blocks, which belong to an *alphabet* of elementary actions that the machine knows [120]. Vecchio *et al.* [120] refer to these primitives of motion as *movemes*. The moveme is introduced earlier by [121]. Reference [122] also propose to divide human motion into elementary trajectories called *movemes*. The approach by [121] does not include an input and therefore is only applicable to periodic or stereotypical motions (e.g., walking or running) where the motion is always the same.

Reference [122] deal with the problem in a phenomenological and non-causal way: each moveme was parameterized by goal and style parameters. Later, [120] attempt to define movemes in terms of causal dynamical systems, where a moveme could be parameterized by a small set of dynamical parameters and by an input, which drives the overall dynamics. They [120] try to build an 'alphabet of movemes', so that it can compose to represent and describe human motion similar to the way phonemes are used in speech. They [120] analyze the concept through mouse trajectories generated by computer users as they 'point-and-click' (i.e., reach moveme) and trace straight lines (call this the draw moveme).

Fanti [119] explore the moveme in more details in his PhD work. He interprets various human motion in 3-level hierarchy (i.e., moveme, action, activity). At the highest layer, a single word is sufficient to provide a compact description of an 'activity'. The term 'action' is for shorter events that, joined together probabilistically, yields an activity. At the bottom layer, the movemes or atomic motions are presented, which are learnt without supervision from data, and do not necessarily pose a verbal description [119]. However, the concept of *moveme* remains mainly dormant in the community. Figure 1.2 shows the concept of action hierarchy based on *moveme*.

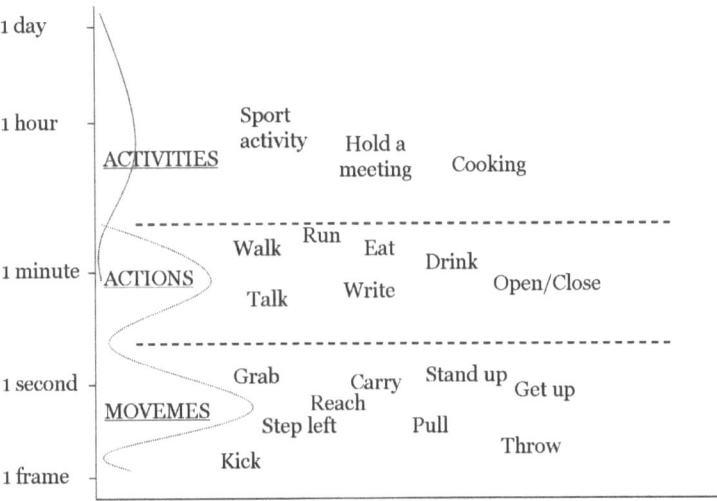

Fig. 1.2: Concept of *moveme* and action hierarchy.

Figure 1.3 shows another taxonomy, where interactions are also considered. Note that still action and activity are covered in one block and level [48, 91].

Human motion analysis can be typified into three broad areas [447], namely,

- Human motion and activity recognition,

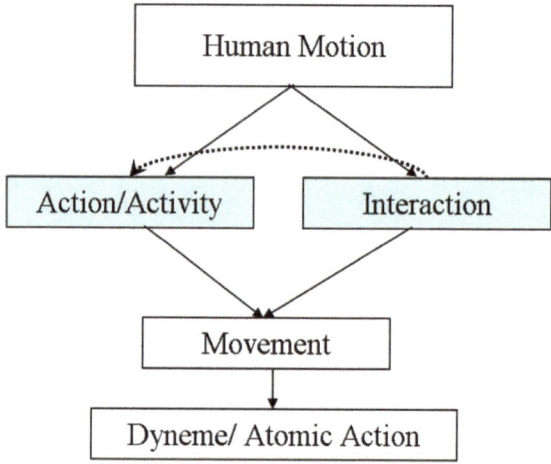

Fig. 1.3: Hierarchy according to [48, 91].

- Human tracking, and
- Human body structure analysis.

Two different types of techniques can be considered to recognize human posture [508]:

- Intrusive, and
- Non-intrusive techniques.

Intrusive techniques usually track body markers to recognize the posture of a person, whereas non-intrusive techniques observe a person with one or several cameras and use sophisticated vision algorithms.

Recognition approaches can be divided into [434]:

- Generic human model recovery,
- Appearance-based approaches, and
- Direct motion-based recognition approaches.

In another nomenclature, action recognition approaches can be categorized into one of the three groups [447, 509]:

- Template matching,
- State-space approaches, and
- Semantic description of human behaviors.

In another nomenclature, recognition methods can be divided into two main paradigms [503]:

- Static recognition, and
- Dynamic recognition.

The video sequence can be analyzed either by using static representation of individual frames or by using dynamic representation of the entire sequence. An approach using static representation analyzes the individual frames first and then combines the results into the sequence, whereas an approach using dynamic representation treats the entire sequence (or a fixed length of it) as its basic analysis unit; i.e., the analysis unit is the trajectory information across the sequence [503]. Most of static approaches have applied the method of template matching in recognition. Usually, dynamic recognition approaches employ Dynamic Time Warping (DTW), Hidden Markov Model (HMM), hierarchical Bayesian Network (BN), Dynamic Bayesian Network (DBN), etc.

Another useful distinction among recognition approaches is [503]:

- Direct recognition,
- Recognition by reconstruction, and
- Hybrid of the former two approaches.

The paradigm of direct recognition recognizes human actions directly from image data without the reconstruction of body parts' poses, whereas the other one requires constructing the object poses from image and then recognize human actions accordingly. A few methods combined both for recognition.

Recently, expressions are incorporating with action analysis (a good number of related papers are published in *IEEE Conference on Automatic Face and Gesture Recognition*). Nowadays, computers are more than ever regarded as partners and users tend to apply social norms to their computers [624]. Pittermann *et al.* [624] provide an overview on the definition of emotions, different aspects of emotion theories, annotation of emotions and emotional speech corpora. Emotion can be expressed in the face, voice, posture, and gesture [627]. There have been a lot of research on emotions and their non-verbal expressions in face, voice and body movements [625].

Expressions typically convey the emotional state of the individual, although they may be feigned, forced, or suppressed [566]. Expressions can be subdivided into [566],

- Macro-expressions, which usually occur over multiple regions of the face and are easily observed, and
- Micro-expressions, which are rapid and occur in small regions of the face.

Macro-expressions [566]:

A macro-expression typically lasts 3/4th of a second to 2 seconds. There are 6 universal expressions: happy, sad, fear, surprise, anger, and disgust. Spatially, macro-expressions can occur over multiple or single regions of the face, depending on the expressions. For instance, the surprise expressions generally causes motion around the eyes, forehead, cheeks, and mouth, whereas the expression for sadness typically generates motion only near the mouth and cheek region.

Micro-expressions [566]:

In general, a micro-expression is described as an involuntary pattern of the human body that is significant enough to be observable, but is too brief to convey an emotion [567]. Micro-expressions occurring on the face are rapid and are often missed during casual observation, or even sometimes extremely hard to observe. Lasting between 1/25th to 1/5th of a second [568], micro-expressions can be classified, based on how an expression is modified, into three types [567]:

- *Simulated expressions*: When a micro expressions is not accompanied by a genuine expression.
- *Neutralized expressions*: When a genuine expression is suppressed and the face remains neutral.
- *Masked expressions*: When a genuine expression is completely masked by a falsified expression.

1.6 Think Ahead!

(1) Make your own hierarchy covering various dimensions of action/activity/interaction/expression.
(2) Make a list of the *smallest possible elements* of human action/activity from the literature. Justify your list.
(3) Enlist application areas of action recognition apart from what is covered in this book.
(4) What are the future challenges of action recognition in computer vision?

Chapter 2

Low-level Image Processing for Action Representations

2.1 Low-level Image Processing for Action Representations

In this book, readers are assumed to have basic knowledge of various low-level image processing. Therefore, this chapter will not cover everything that is related to action representations and understanding. However, we cite some issues, which we consider more relevant and important for action analysis.

2.2 Pre-processing Steps

Haar-like features:

Haar-like features are well-known image features, which are used in real-time face detector. The name of these rectangular Haar-like features [28] arises from their intuitive similarity with Haar wavelets. Later, others introduce the concept of tilted (45 degree) Haar-like features and generic rotated Haar-like features. Various wavelets are also exploited for image analysis.

Image pyramids:

Image pyramids are used for multi-resolution and multi-scale representation, especially in computing optical flow. By splitting an image into various levels of lower resolution and doing analysis in lower levels make it faster. Geometric transformations of an image is another important area.

Structure from motion:

Structure from motion (SFM) is the process of recovering or finding 3D structure from 2D images and it is a very important research area in computer vision. This chapter presents more on the SFM and key approaches.

Filtering:

Different filtering approaches are available for image processing, e.g., in spatial domain — low-pass filters for smoothing/ blurring (demonstrates smooth areas by removing *fine* details), high-pass filters for sharpening (demonstrate edges, noises, details — by highlighting *fine* details), averaging filter, median filters, max filter, min filter, box filter, etc.; and in frequency domain — Butterworth low-pass filter, Gaussian low-pass filter, high-pass filter, Laplacian in the frequency domain, etc. Edge detections are mentioned above. In many cases, initially, images are smoothed by employing Gaussian or other low-pass filtering schemes.

Median filtering:

Median filter is a well-known and widely used filtering scheme. We can exploit the non-linear median filter to filter out noise. Median filtering reduces noise without blurring edges and other sharp details. Median filtering is particularly effective when the noise pattern consists of strong, spike-like components (e.g., *salt-and-pepper* noise). The median filter considers each pixel in the image and looks at its nearby neighbors to decide whether or not it is representative of its surroundings. Instead of simply replacing the pixel value with the mean of neighboring pixel values, it replaces it with the median of those values. The median is calculated by first sorting all pixel values from the surrounding neighborhood into numerical order. Then replace the pixel being considered by the middle/median pixel of that block. An image is passed into a median filter to smooth noisy patterns and hence we can achieve a smoothed image.

2.3 Segmentation and Extraction

This section concentrates on various feature detection and extraction approaches, which are widely employed in various methods for action representation for understanding and recognition.

2.3.1 Feature Detection from an Image

What is a *feature*?

What constitutes a *feature*?

It can not be clearly defined and hence, what constitutes a feature varies depending on the application. However, edges, corners, interest points, blobs, regions of interest, etc. are typically considered as image features and therefore, in image processing context, we try to extract one or more of these image features and analyze them for further processing. Note that in the presence of occlusion, shadows and image-noise, features may not find proper correspondence to the edge locations and the corresponding features.

2.3.2 Edge Detection

An edge can be defined as the points — where there is a sharp change in pixel values or gradient. Edge detection is important in many applications, and there are some edge-based representations for action analysis. Edge detection can be achieved in an image by various approaches employing,

- Gradient operators,
- Canny edge detectors,
- Sobel operators,
- Prewitt operators,
- Smallest Univalue Segment Assimilating Nucleus (SUSAN),
- Harris and Stephens / Plessey operators,
- Roberts operators,
- Laplacian operators,
- Krish operators,
- Isotropic edge operators, etc.

2.3.3 Corner Points

Corner points in an image are sometimes referred to as *interest points*. These corner points or interest points are very important cues for recent various methods related to action representation and image registration. Based on interest points, several smart local spatio-temporal interest point-based approaches are proposed with significantly good performances. These are covered in later chapters. Among various corner feature detectors,

- Features from Accelerated Segment Test (FAST) [3],
- Laplacian of Gaussian (LoG) [38, 419],
- Difference of Gaussians (DoG — DoG is an approximation of LoG) [559],
- Smallest Univalue Segment Assimilating Nucleus (SUSAN) [41],
- Trajkovic and Hedley corner detector (similar approach to SUSAN) [40],
- Accelerated Segment Test (AST)-based feature detectors,
- Harris and Stephens [39] / Plessey,
- Shi and Tomasi [145],
- Wang and Brady corner detector [37],
- Level curve curvature,
- Determinant of Hessian [419],

— etc. and some of their variants are mostly exploited in different applications.
Code:
FAST in http://mi.eng.cam.ac.uk/ er258/work/fast.html

2.3.4 *Blob Detectors*

Blob detectors are sometimes interrelated with corner detectors in some literatures and used the terms interchangeably. *Blob* or *regions* of interest cover the detection of those images, which are too smooth to be traced by a corner detectors. Instead of having point-like detection, a blob detector detects a region as a blob of circle or ellipse. Some important blob detectors are,

- Laplacian of Gaussian (LoG),
- Difference of Gaussians (DoG) [559],
- Determinant of Hessian,
- Maximally Stable Extremal Regions (MSER) [26],
- Principal Curvature-based Region Detector (PCBR) [36],
- Harris-affine [336],
- Hessian-affine [336],
- Edge-based regions (EBR) [336],
- Intensity Extrema-based Region (IBR) [336],
- Salient regions [336],
- Grey-level blobs.

2.3.5 Feature Descriptors

Various feature descriptors are proposed in order to detect and describe local features in images. Among various approaches, few of them achieved enormous attention in the community and are very widely used, e.g.,

- Scale-Invariant Feature Transform (SIFT) [35, 559],
- Speeded Up Robust Features (SURF) [341],
- Histogram of Oriented Gradients (HOG) [224],
- Local Energy-based Shape Histogram (LESH) [32],
- PCA-SIFT [340],
- Gradient Location-Orientation Histogram (GLOH) [367]

Speeded-Up Robust Features:
The SURF (Speeded-Up Robust Features) is a *scale-* and *rotation-*invariant interest point detector and descriptor. It has been employed for pedestrian navigation [418]. It approximates or even outperforms previously proposed schemes with respect to repeatability, distinctiveness, and robustness, yet it can be computed and compared much faster [417]. This is achieved by relying on integral images for image convolutions, by building on the strengths of the existing leading detectors and descriptors (by using a Hessian matrix-based measure [419] for the detector, and a distribution-based descriptor), but uses a very basic approximation, just like DoG [559], which is a very basic Laplacian-based detector. In this case, instead of using a different measure for selecting the location and the scale, the determinant of the Hessian is employed for both cases. Here, the Hessian matrix is roughly approximated by using a set of box-type filters. Given a point $\mathbf{x} = (x, y)$ in an image I, the Hessian matrix $H(\mathbf{x}, \sigma)$ at position $\mathbf{x}$ with scale σ is defined as follows,

$$H(\mathbf{x},\sigma) = \begin{bmatrix} L_{xx}(\mathbf{x},\sigma) & L_{xy}(\mathbf{x},\sigma) \\ L_{xy}(\mathbf{x},\sigma) & L_{yy}(\mathbf{x},\sigma) \end{bmatrix} \quad (2.1)$$

where, $L_{xx}(\mathbf{x}, \sigma)$ is the convolution of the Gaussian second order derivative,

$$\frac{d^2}{dx^2}(G(\mathbf{x};\sigma)). \quad (2.2)$$

— with the image I at point $\mathbf{x}$ and similarly for $L_{xy}(\mathbf{x},\sigma)$ and $L_{yy}(\mathbf{x},\sigma)$. These Gaussian derivatives are approximated (lets denote these by $G_{xx}(\mathbf{x},\sigma)$, $G_{xy}(\mathbf{x},\sigma)$ and $G_{yy}(\mathbf{x},\sigma)$) by considering box-type filters. Box filters can sufficiently approximate the Gaussian derivatives. The weights applied to the rectangular regions are kept simple for computational efficiency. Finally we get,

$$\det(H_{\text{approximate}}) = G_{xx}G_{yy} - (\omega G_{xy})^2. \qquad (2.3)$$

Here, ω is the relative weight of the filter responses and it is used to balance the expression for the Hessian's determinant. The approximated determinant of the Hessian represents the blob response in the image at location **x**. A few modifications are proposed by Ehsan and McDonald-Maier [420] on reduction of the integral image length, and by Schweiger *et al.* [421].

Even though the HOG is similar to the Edge Orientation Histograms (EOH), shape contexts [27] and the SIFT descriptors, it differs in that it is computed on a dense grid of uniformly spaced cells and to enhance accuracy, it exploits overlapping local contrast normalization. The EOH contains various difference features, e.g., dominant orientation features and symmetry features; and these features have become popular recently for a wide variety of applications.

The RIFT [34] is a rotation-invariant generalization of SIFT. The PCA-SIFT [340] and Gradient Location-Orientation Histogram (GLOH) [367] are proposed at the top of the SIFT. Generalized Robust Invariant Feature (G-RIF) [33] is another feature descriptor that encodes edge orientation, edge density and hue information in a unified form.

2.3.6 *Segmentation*

Segmentation of an object *or* an area of interest *or* interesting features in an image, is done in many applications. Human detection aims at segmenting regions of interest corresponding to people from the rest of an image. It is a significant issue in a human motion analysis system since the subsequent processes such as tracking and action recognition are greatly dependent on the performance and the proper segmentation of the region of interest [641]. The changes in weather, illumination variation, repetitive motion, and presence of camera motion or cluttered environment hinder the performance of motion segmentation approaches. Active contour, normalized cuts, graph cuts are some widely employed methods for region segmentation.

Various clustering methods (K-means clustering, spectral clustering [392]) are employed to cluster various regions for better segmentation. Moving object detection or pixel-change detection is the key to find the regions of interest from a scene. Possibilities for selecting *regions of interest* (ROI) are,

- Background subtraction,
- Image/frame/temporal differencing,
- Optical flow,
- Steaklines,
- Three-frame difference,
- Skin color,
- Edges, etc.

2.3.6.1 *Background Subtraction*

In the simplest level, background subtraction is a method to detect moving objects by calculating the differences between the current frame and the background image for each pixel and applying threshold to detect the areas of interest or foreground of the scene. Background subtraction is very important initial step for many vision-based problems, in order to extract the moving regions from a video. A naive approach for background subtraction is shown below and in Figure 2.1.

Background subtracted image = Input image − Background image.

Foreground image   Input Image   Background image

Fig. 2.1: Example of naive background subtraction method.

However, in the case of having no prior background information or image, it is a challenging task to create a background model on-the-fly. There are various methods for dynamic background modeling, e.g., by employing

- Average [13],
- Median [14],

- Gaussian Mixture Model (GMM) or Mixture of Gaussians (MoG) [12, 282],
- Parametric model,
- Non-parametric model,
- Running Gaussian average [281],
- Kernel Density Estimators (KDE) [286],
- Sequential Kernel Density Approximation (SKDA) [15],
- Mean-shift-based estimation [15],
- Combined estimation and propagation,
- Eigen-backgrounds [16], etc.

Various background subtraction techniques are reviewed by [29–31].

The background images are not fixed in moving scenes (not static background but dynamic) due to various factors, like — changes in illumination (various parts of the day have different sunlight, whereas illumination is usually static in indoor scene. Also, gradual or sudden variation of sun-light due to the presence of cloud or not); camera motion due to not having fixed camera (e.g., in ITS); movement in the background objects (e.g., movement of leaves and tree branches, sea waves, movement of objects of non-interest, etc.); changes in the background geometry (in outdoor scenes - shopping center, car-parking, road with moving cars, etc.). Therefore, based on the situation, the selection of an appropriate background subtraction model is important.

Among various methods of background subtraction, a comparative report based on some works is shown in Table 2.1.

2.3.6.2 Frame Subtraction

Frame to frame subtraction methods are well-known too, e.g., [287–292]. Image or, frame or, temporal differencing is defined by the differences between consecutive frames in time. Instead of subtracting a predefined or estimated background on-the-fly, a frame subtraction method considers every pair of frames of time t and $t-1$, and extract any motion change in it — in order to find the regions of interest. Figure 2.2 shows a simple approach for frame subtraction.

Table 2.1: Background subtraction methods and their properties.

Background Subtraction Method	Speed	Memory Requirement	Accuracy *
Average [13]	Fast	High	Acceptable
Running Average [281]	Fast	Low	Acceptable
Median [14]	Fast	High	Acceptable
Mixture of Gaussians [282]	Medium	Medium	Medium
Kernel Density Estimators (KDE) [286]	Medium	High	Better
Eigen-Background [16]	Medium	Medium	Medium
Sequential Kernel Density Approximation (SKDA) [15]	Medium	Medium	Better
Standard Mean-shift [15]	Slow	High	Better
Optimized Mean-shift [15]	Medium	Medium	Better

* Regarding *accuracy* — it is difficult to analyze due to the unavailability of all methods under a benchmark and unbiased comparison of their performances. Therefore, by *acceptable*, *medium* and *better* — we rank them with lower to higher accuracy based on the existing literatures.

Frame at time (t)   Frame at time (t-1)   Extracted info

Fig. 2.2: Example of frame subtraction method.

2.3.6.3 *Dense Motion Estimation*

Based on Lagrangian Framework of fluid dynamics, there are 3 representations of flow [109]:

- Optical Flow or Vector Field,
- Dense Particle Trajectories or Pathlines,
- Streaklines.

Usually optical flow [293–300, 560] is used with other features, due to the fact that optical flow is noisy and it is not even consistent between frames. Therefore, optical flow offers noise and motion confusions (Figure 2.3). Even though it provides noisy patterns, many researchers have employed optical flow. Several approaches exploit the human action recognition task from optical flow (e.g., [397, 401]). In [397], for every two consecutive frames, a local motion descriptor is calculated from the optical flow [560] orientation histograms collected inside the actor's bounding box. An action descriptor is built by weighting and aggregating the estimated histograms along the temporal axis. Few good methods for optical flow computations are — [398, 399, 560].

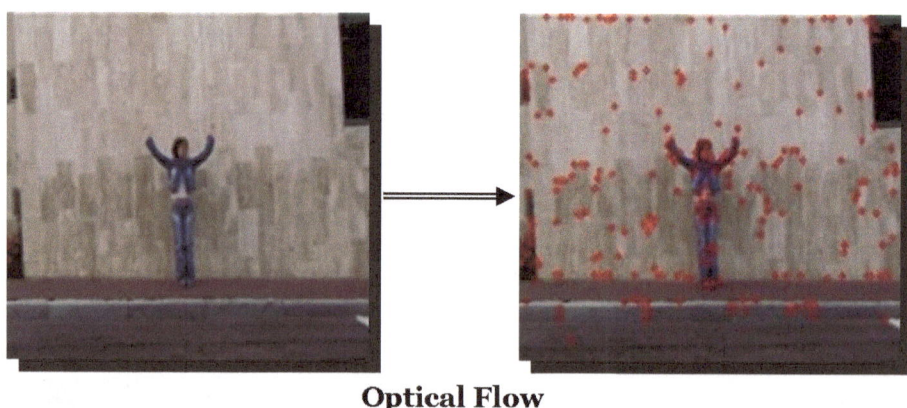

Optical Flow

Fig. 2.3: Optical flow vectors in an action frame.

Usually, optical flow produces good results even in the presence of a small camera motion. However, it is computationally complex and very sensitive to the presence of noise and texture. For real-time processing, optical flow methods may not compute fast. Beauchemin and Barron [293] and McCane *et al.* [294] have presented various methods for optical flow. Seven different methods are tested for benchmarking optical flow methods [294]. Several real-time optical flow methods [298–300] are developed for various motion segmentation and computations. These papers can help one to choose a better optical flow method to use for a specific application.

However, in scenes with dynamic motion, where the flow changes continuously,

- Optical Flow is instantaneous, ignores the continuity of motion;
- Trajectories represent the continuity of motion, not imminent to the capture of behavior transitions.

Therefore, *streaklines* are proposed, which are instantaneous and capture the continuity of motion [108, 109]. A recent approach called streakline is proposed by Mehran *et al.* [108] based on the Lagrangian framework for fluid dynamics. The streaklines are more effective in dynamic scenes in representing the changes in motion and behavior transitions, and it can be used to solve computer vision problems involving crowd and traffic flow. As per them, streaklines are traced in a fluid flow by injecting color material, such as smoke or dye, which is transported with the flow and used for visualization [108].

In the context of computer vision, streakline may be used in a similar way to transport information about a scene, and they are obtained by repeatedly initializing a fixed grid of particles at each frame, then moving both current and past particles using optical flow. Streaklines are the locus of points that connect particles, which originate from the same initial position [108]. Streak flows encapsulate motion information of the flow for a period of time [108]. This resembles the notion of particle flow (equivalent to average optical flow), where advection of a grid of particles over a window of time provides information for segmenting the crowd motion (Figure 2.4) [108].

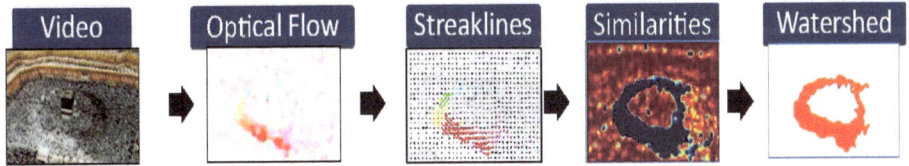

Fig. 2.4: Streaklines for crowd segmentation. (Courtesy: R. Mehran, UCF).

Streaklines are new to computer vision research. In this context, streaklines may be obtained by repeatedly initializing a grid of particles and moving all particles according to the optical flow, in the spirit of a Lagrangian fluid flow. In other words, place a particle at a point x and move the particle one time step with the flow. In the next time step, the point x is initialized with a new particle, then both particles are moved with the flow. Repeating this process on some time interval t produces particle positions from which streaklines are obtained.

Figure 2.5 gives an example of streaklines in a video. Two colors (in whitish and gray) represent the different directions of motion.

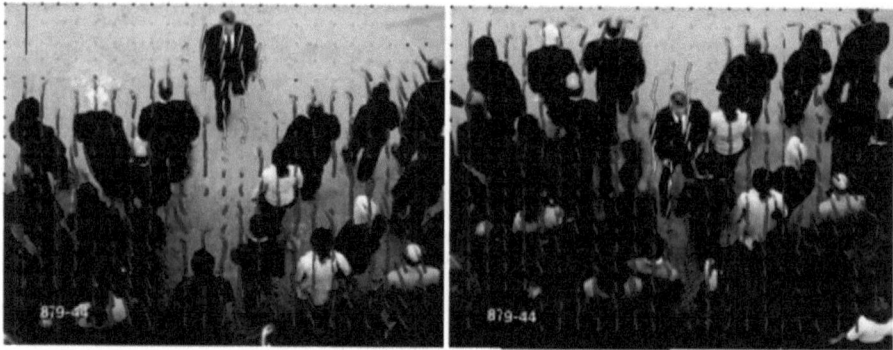

Fig. 2.5: Streaklines in a video. Two colors represent the different directions of motion. (Courtesy: R. Mehran, UCF).

Streak flow is an instantaneous vector field, which represents the accumulative motion of the scene. It resembles the temporal average of optical flow but it is more imminent. This vector field has following properties [109]:

- It averages the velocities in the direction of motion (does not average blindly) therefore, it relates to the group motion;
- Imminently reactive to changes in the scene (less lag than temporal average optical flow);
- Less noisy than optical flow (helpful in behavior recognition);

A comparison of Streak flow, optical flow, and average optical flow is given in Figure 2.6 (the Streak flow stands in the middle of average optical flow and instantaneous optical flow in capturing changes in the scene).

2.4 Local Binary Pattern

Local visual descriptors have become part of state-of-the-art systems in many areas of computer vision [366, 367]. The Local Binary Pattern (LBP) is widely exploited as an effective feature representation for various areas of face and gesture recognition and analysis. By combining the sign of the difference of central pixel intensity from those of its neighboring pixels, the Local Binary Pattern (LBP) [571, 572] implicitly encodes the micro-patterns of the input image such as flat areas, spots, lines and edges. Since the sign is invariant to monotonic photometric change, LBP is robust to lighting variation

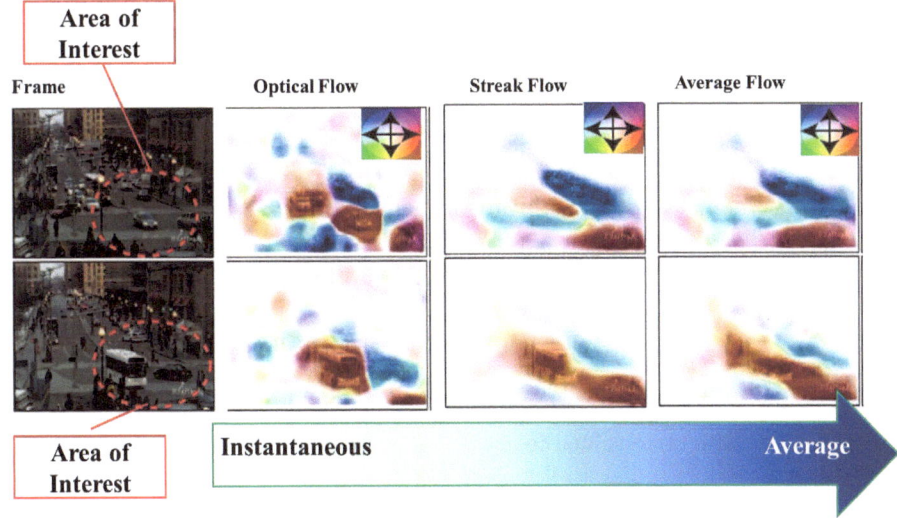

Fig. 2.6: Streaklines vs. optical flow. (Courtesy: R. Mehran, UCF).

to some extent.

Code:
LBP in http://www.cse.oulu.fi/MVG/Downloads/LBPMatlab

2.4.1 *LBP — Variants*

Several variations of the LBP have been proposed: e.g.,

- Local Ternary Patterns (LTP) [570],
- Elongated Local Binary Patterns,
- Uniform Local Ternary Pattern (ULTP) [569],
- Multi-scale LBPs [369],
- Patch-based LBPs [370],
- Center symmetric LBPs [371],
- LBPs on Gabor-filtered images [608],
- V-LGBP [372],
- LBPs on histograms of gradients [373],
- Discriminative Local Binary Patterns (DLBP) [366], etc.

Zhao and Pietikainen [606] extended LBP to the spatial-temporal domain. In order to make LBP robust to random and quantization noise in near-uniform face regions, Local Ternary Patterns (LTP) [570] have also been proposed. Tan *et al.* [570] introduce the Local Ternary Patterns (LTP) to improve the results in their Face Recognition system. It is enhanced from LBP [571] that is efficient in classifying given classes of texture with very high discrimination due to its invariant characteristics to the lighting effects. Given an image I, its LTP map is computed as follows,

$$LTP(x_c, y_c) = \sum_{t=0}^{P-1} 2^t s_{LTP}(p_t - p_c), \qquad (2.4)$$

where, t is the $P-1$ neighbors of the central pixel c, p_t and p_c are the pixel values. s_{LTP} is the indicator with three-valued codes:

$$s_{LTP}(p_t i p_c) = \begin{cases} 1 & p_t \geq p_c + r \\ 0 & |p_t - p_c| < r \\ -1 & p_t \leq p_c - r \end{cases} \qquad (2.5)$$

where, pixels around the central one p_c with radius r are set to zero, the ones below this are set to -1 and the ones above this are set to $+1$. The threshold r is selected manually. For simplicity, each ternary pattern is split into positive and negative maps. These two maps are then processed as two distinguished components of descriptors containing values of either 0 or 1. Thus, their histograms and similarity metrics are computed separately. They are then combined in the final step.

Although LTP can deal with illumination variations, it is still affected when rotating the image. Luu *et al.* [569] propose an advanced feature extraction method named Uniform Local Ternary Patterns (ULTP) that is the extension of LTP. Uniform Local Ternary Patterns (ULTP) are used as the local features in [569]. Compared with LTP, ULTP has the ability of both gray-scale and rotation invariance to give more stable local feature sets [569]. Sparsely Encoded Local Descriptor (SELD) is proposed for face recognition in [605].

By combining Gabor filtering (the phase and magnitude of a multi-scale and multi-orientation Gabor wavelet are used) with LBP, Local Gabor Phase Patterns (LGPP) [608] is proposed to extend LBP to multiple resolution and orientation. Reference [321] use a framework that involves convolving the normalized face image with 40 Gabor filters that is generated by using 5 scales and 8 orientations. 40 Gabor phase maps and magnitude maps with the same size as the image are obtained from the convolution. Uniform LBP is applied to these phase and magnitude maps by subdividing each image map spatially into blocks and histograms are computed from each block in the image map. The LBP feature vector is finally obtained by concatenating the histogram bin values [321]. This Local Gabor Binary Pattern (LGBP) is used for face representation [321].

The LBP operator in conjunction with the Gabor wavelets is used for effective feature representation [321, 323, 608]. Various methods based on *Gabor Wavelets* are:

- Elastic Bunch Graph Matching (EBGM) method [325],
- Gabor Fisher Classifier (GFC) [326],
- Local Gabor Binary Pattern Histogram Sequence (LGBPHS) [608],
- Histogram of Gabor Phase Patterns (HGPP) [607],
- Local Gabor Textons (LGT) [327],
- Learned Local Gabor Pattern (LLGP) [328],
- Local Gabor Binary Pattern Whitening PCA (LGBPWP) [329],
- Local Gabor XOR Pattern [609],
- Gabor Energy Filters,
- Local Matching Gabor method (LMG) [324, 330].

Reference [324] propose two improvements to the Local Matching Gabor (LMG) method [330]. The first one is based on weighting Gabor jets by an entropy measure between a given face and the faces in the gallery. The second improvement is in the Borda count classification stage where they propose to use a threshold to eliminate low score jets that act as noisy inputs to the classifier.

In addition, some local descriptors originally proposed for other object recognition tasks are also introduced for recognition, such as Histogram of Oriented Gradients (HOG) [611] or SIFT [559, 610].

2.5 Structure from Motion (SFM)

In this sub-section, we cover the well-known *structure from motion* (SFM) and the classical *Factorization Method* (FM) — as these are very much relevant for action understanding [185]. The reconstruction of shape and motion of a rigid object from an image sequence, usually known as the *structure from motion* (SFM) problem, is one of the most studied problems within computer vision community. It has wide applications such as scene modeling, robot navigation, object recognition, image-based rendering, man-machine interface, virtual reality and so on. In robotics, the video camera is an increasingly popular sensor for autonomous vehicles that need to construct a 3D model of the environment for navigation and recognition purposes.

Early approaches to the SFM used a single pair of frames and have shown to be very sensitive to image noise. The key to the robustness of the SFM methods is on exploiting the rigidity of the scene across a larger set of frames. Unfortunately, although using multiple frames leads to a more constrained problem, the multi-frame formulation is also more complex — the number of unknowns grows due to the larger number of camera poses to estimate. Among the approaches to multi-frame SFM, the *factorization method* (FM) [185], introduced in the early nineties, has become popular. It is further extended by [182] to weak and para-perspective views; and is later extended in several directions, e.g., from point features [182, 185] to line features, geometric projection model, 3D shape description, recursive formulation [180] and for the perspective projection model.

Given an image sequence, suppose that there are a set of P tracked feature points over F frames. For example, a rank 4 measurement matrix **W** [185] of dimension 30×45, which means that 45 feature points are tracked through 15 frames. In the factorization method, an image sequence is represented as a $2F \times P$ measurement matrix **W**. The **W** is made up of the horizontal and vertical coordinates of the tracked feature points (P) through F frames in an image stream. This measurement matrix can be factorized into the product of two matrices **R** and **S** — *where*,
R represents camera rotation matrix of size of $2F \times 3$; and
S represents shape matrix in a coordinate system attached to the object centroid, of size of $3 \times P$.

When there is occlusion or failure in proper feature tracking, the **W** is filled partially. The factorization method [185] is based on the *singular value decomposition* (SVD) technique of **W** for scene reconstruction with an orthographic camera — where the SVD factors the measurement matrix **W** into two matrices — **R** and **S**, the rotation matrix and the shape matrix respectively. The method is tested on a variety of real and synthetic images, and is shown to perform well even for distant objects, where traditional triangulation-based approaches tend to perform poorly [182]. In real situations, feature points are visible for a limited time since they go into and out of the field of view as the camera moves (imagine a camera going around one object).

Previous approaches for computing the 3-D shape and motion from a long sequence of images usually consider,

- Whether the camera is calibrated or not, and
- Whether a projective or an affine model is used.

The factorization method has been believed to be possible under linear approximations of imaging system and without camera calibration. Lately, the original factorization method has been extended to scaled orthographic, paraperspective and perspective projection.

2.5.1 Constraints of FM

Both shape and motion can be factorized directly from the measurement matrix constructed from feature points trajectories under orthographic camera model. In practical applications, the measurement matrix might be contaminated by noises and contains outliers and missing values. A direct SVD to the measurement matrix with outliers would yield erroneous result.

An orthographic formulation limits the range of motions the method can accommodate [182]. The applicability of the method is therefore limited to image sequences created from certain types of camera motions. The orthographic model contains no notion of the distance from the camera to the object. As a result, shape reconstruction from image sequences containing large translations toward or away from the camera often produces deformed object shapes, as the method tries to explain the size differences in the images by creating size differences in the object. The method also supplies no estimation of translation along the camera's optical axis, which limits its applicability in certain tasks.

The factorization algorithms assume that the problem of finding correspondence between frames has been solved. But the *correspondence problem* itself is one of the most difficult fundamental problems within computer vision. In practical applications, the tracked feature points trajectories are inevitably, not always correct. Moreover, in this approach, the nonlinear perspective projection is linearized by approximating it using orthographic projection, weak perspective projection, and paraperspective projection, which limits the range of motions that the approach can be accommodated [174]. The approximations lose some effects of perspective projection so that the accuracy of results is not always guaranteed and the range of motion is limited.

It is well-known it starts with the three largest singular values acquired by the SVD technique to factor the measurement matrix into two matrices. Then, by identifying the two matrices, shape and motion matrices can be obtained. Unfortunately, when the image noise is larger enough so that the fourth largest singular value can not be ignored, the traditional factorization method might fail to reach the accurate solution [173].

Although the factorization method is a useful technique, its applicability is, so far, limited to off-line computations for the following reasons [176]:

(1) The method is based on a batch-type computation; that is, it recovers shape and motion after all the input images are given;
(2) The singular value decomposition (SVD), which is the most important procedure in the method, requires $O(FP^2)$ operations for P features in F frames;
(3) Finally, it needs to store a large measurement matrix whose size increases with the number of frames.

These drawbacks make it difficult to apply the factorization method to real-time applications. The algorithm is not practical if one intends to process data in real-time since all measurements must be available in order to compute the decomposition [176]. In this case, storage requirements grow indefinitely (the number of rows in the measurement matrix increases with the number of frames) and the estimate is produced only at the last time instant.

To recover a dense representation of the 3D shape, the factorization approach of [182, 185] may not solve the problem satisfactorily because of two drawbacks,

- Being feature-based, it would be necessary to track a huge number of features to obtain a dense description of the 3D shape. This is usually impossible because only distinguished points, as brightness corners, can be accurately tracked.

- Even if it is possible to track a large number of features, the computational cost of the SVD involved in the factorization of the measurement matrix would be very high.

2.5.2 Improvements of FM

Some advancements are proposed by Tan and Ishikawa [179, 183, 184] for recovering 3-D motions of individuals at work employing an extended measurement matrix and for separating the motions into respective motions employing k-means clustering method. This method uses at least three fixed cameras and need non-rigid points to recover though it can also recover rigid points. Another recent work [181] uses two or more moving cameras and it requires rigid and non-rigid objects for recovery of non-rigid objects. It incorporates image transfer systems efficiently.

Xi [175] presents a new algorithm for computing the SVD by linear l_1-norm regression and applies it to structure from motion problem. It is robust to outliers and can handle missing data naturally. The linear regression problem is solved using weighted-median algorithm and is simple to implement. This robust factorization method with outliers can improve the reconstruction result remarkably. Quantitative and qualitative experiments illustrate the good performance of their approach. They review the original factorization method as defined in [174], presenting it in a slightly different manner to make its relation to the paraperspective method more apparent. They then present their paraperspective factorization method, followed by a description of a perspective refinement step. In [172], the authors propose a robust method for computing the SVD, which is based on the weighted-median algorithm. But when the rank of the input matrix is more than one, the algorithm can not give correct result. In [171], the authors propose a similar algorithm for computing subspaces, which is also based on the l_1-norm. They optimized the l_1-norm optimization problem using weighted-median algorithm too. But their method did not give the orthogonal left and right singular matrices explicitly. Also, since they compute the bases one by one, their method is prone to be trapped into some bad local minimum.

More recent works on the treatment of outlier trajectories include those by [169, 170] and [168]. In [170], a novel robust method for outlier detection in structure and motion recovery for affine cameras is presented. It can also be seen as an importation of the Least Median of Squares (LMedS) technique or RANSAC into the factorization framework. In [168], the authors extend the above method to multiple moving objects; they fit an appropriate subspace to the detected trajectories and remove those that have large residuals. Huynh *et al.* [169] present an outlier correction scheme that iteratively updates the elements of the image measurement matrix. The magnitude and sign of the update to each element is dependent upon the residual estimated in each iteration.

Costeria and Kanade [167] propose the multi-body factorization method for reconstructing the motions and shapes of independently moving objects. They use the shape interaction matrix to separate those objects. The shape interaction matrix is also derived from the SVD of the measurement matrix. The factorization algorithm achieves its robustness and accuracy by applying the SVD to a large number of frames and feature points. The 3D motion of the camera and 3D positions of feature points are recovered by first computing the SVD of the measurement matrix. Then the metric constraints are imposed. These factorization algorithms work by linearizing the camera observation model and give good results without an initial guess for the solution. The whole procedure is linear.

Nakamura *et al.* [166] divide the image sequence into a number of blocks and the factorization method is applied to each block for obtaining a part of the 3D shape of the object. The 3D shapes reconstructed from the block of the sequence are merged into one integrated 3D Model. For the merging, position and pose of each 3D shape is adjusted based on the surface normal of the overlapped area.

Yu *et al.* [174] present a new approach based on a higher-order approximation of perspective projection based on Taylor series expansion of depth to expand the projection equations around the origin of the object coordinate system, to recover 3D shape and motion from image sequences. The accuracy of this approximation is higher than orthographic projection, weak perspective projection and paraperspective projection, so it can be used in wider circumstances in the real world in wider range of motion.

The factorization method is also extended to more general geometric projection models [182] and to more general parametric descriptions of the 3D shape [165]. These methods assume that the projections of the features are available in all frames, i.e., that they are seen during the entire video frames, which is not correct in the real-world application as very often important regions that are seen in some frames are not seen in others, broadly due to the scene self-occlusion and the limited field of view [178]. Guerreiro *et al.* [164, 178] extend the factorization method to the more challenging scenario of observing incomplete trajectories of the feature points. In this way, they accommodate not only the features that disappear, but also features that, though not visible in the 1st image, become available later. Under this scenario, the observation matrix has missing entries. They introduce suboptimal algorithms to factor out matrices with missing data, and can compute approximation of any rank, though particularize for rank 4 matrices. It requires much smaller number of the SVD computations than the 'filling-in' method of [185].

Surface-based factorization [165] is simultaneously an extension and a simplification of [185]. The main ingredients of this approach are that they describe the unknown shape of the 3D rigid object by polynomial patches. Projections of these patches in the image plane move according to parametric 2D motion models. They recover the parameters describing 3D shape and 3D motion from the 2D motion parameters by factorizing a matrix that is rank 1 in a noiseless situation, not rank 3 as in [185].

The algorithm in [177] is able to maintain shape representation in a recursive way even when parts of the objects are occluded or leave the field of view. Since [177] use a recursive approach at each frame, it only has available one row of data. They show that if a point is not visible in subsequent frames, its future position can be estimated from visible points by exploiting linear dependence relations. However, this mechanism does not work backwards, that is, if a new point is selected it will not be able to reconstruct the past trajectory. The algorithm is recursive, therefore, past measurements are lost and the backward estimation process lacks data.

3D shape computation is of paramount importance in mobile robotic systems. Furthermore, real-time operation imposes particular constraints, namely recursivity. In real situations, shape computation algorithms must be able to deal with the possibility of a continuously moving camera viewpoint. This means that objects that are being viewed now will disappear in the future and new objects will come into the field of view. The ability to dynamically update 3D shape, as the scene changes without recurring to past stored measurements, is of fundamental importance. Reference [177] describe a method that adds this capability to the well known (recursive) factorization method for shape and motion determination. This method allows the buildup of 3D image mosaics of the viewed environment. Moreover, Morita and Kanade [176] modify the method so that storing old data is no longer required to estimate motion and shape.

As stated above, the fourth largest singular value of the measurement matrix is ignored. But when noise is larger enough so that the fourth largest singular value can not be ignored, it would be difficult to get reliable results by using the traditional factorization method. In order to acquire reliable results, Hwang *et al.* [173] start with adopting an orthogonalization method to find a matrix, which is composed of three mutually orthogonal vectors. By using this matrix, another matrix can be obtained. Then, the two expected matrices, which represent shape of object and motion of camera/object, can be obtained through normalization. They concentrate on factorization method from the Rank-Theorem perspective, and improve the step of factoring by the SVD technique. According to the Rank-Theorem, it would be possible to get three mutually orthogonal vectors from a measurement matrix. Once the three mutually orthogonal vectors are identified as one matrix, it would be easy to take a form of 3D linear combination equation for obtaining another matrix. Then the identification of the two matrices can help this study to recover object shape and camera motion easily. Hwang *et al.* [173] present a form of factorization under orthographic projection, although the form of factorization also can be easily extended to other projective models. This study also provides the field of structure-from-motion with advantages, such as:

- It can robustly recover object shape and camera motion even if the emergence of image noise;
- Its computation is very fast due to a simple algorithm.

Being feature-based method [185], it would be necessary to track a huge number of features to obtain a dense description of the 3D shape and thereby computationally costly. These drawbacks motivate the extension of the factorization approach to recover a parametric description of the 3D shape [163]. Instead of tracking point-wise features, they track regions for which the motion induced on the image plane is described by a single set of parameters. This algorithm is easily extended to the scaled-orthography and the paraperspective projections by proceeding as [182] does for the original factorization method. Reference [162] further improve the algorithm and has gained two relevant advantages over the algorithms of [163, 185]. Instead of imposing a common origin for the parametric representation of the 3D surface patches, as in [163], they allow the specification of different origins for different patches. This improves the numerical stability of the image motion estimation algorithm and the accuracy of the 3D structure recovery algorithm. Furthermore, [161] show how to compute the 3D shape and 3D motion by a simple factorization of a modified matrix that is rank 1 in a noiseless situation, instead of a rank 3 matrix as in [163, 185]. This allows the use of very fast algorithms even when using a large number of features (or regions) and large number of frames.

Computing the projective depth iteratively via iterative estimation of Euclidean shape [160] is equivalent to iterative estimation of the image coordinates by the paraperspective projection from those by the perspective projection. This method achieves accurate reconstruction of motion and shape, but is useful only in calibrated camera as Euclidean shapes are required in iterative computations. Reference [159] compute the projective depth in advance via epipolar geometry without performing iterative computation. However, the projective depth estimated via epipolar geometry is sensitive to measurement errors for feature points. Reference [158] estimate the measurement matrix containing projective depths as its elements using an evaluation function that treats all images as uniformly as possible. In this method, however, convergence of the iterative computation to estimate the measurement matrix containing projective depths takes a long time.

Recursive factorization methods can provide an updated 3D structure at each frame and at the small and fixed computational cost. Instead of one step factorization for points, a multi-step factorization method [157] is developed for lines based on the decomposition of the whole shape and motion into three separate substructures. Each of these substructures can then be linearly solved by factorizing the appropriate measurement matrices. It is also established that affine shape and motion recovery with uncalibrated affine cameras can be achieved with at least seven lines over three views.

Kurata *et al.* [180] focus on robustness against outliers, which include false matches and other objects, and the computational cost at each frame in order to apply the factorization method using point correspondences under affine projection to the real environment in real-time. Using the Least Median of Squares criterion, the method estimates the dominant 3D affine motion and can discard feature points that are regarded as outliers. The computational cost of the overall procedure is reduced by combining this robust-statistics-based method with a recursive factorization method that can at each frame provide the updated 3D structure of an object at a fixed computational cost by using the Principal Component Analysis (PCA). Although previous work [177] also use robust statistics for recovering the epipolar geometry and the multiple projective view relation, they do not describe how to cope with the increasing computational cost as the number of frames increases.

The recursive factorization method by Fujiki *et al.* [156] compress the motion matrix, the metric constraints, and the measurement matrix by using the principal component analysis (PCA) to reduce and to fix the computational cost at each frame. To fix the world coordinates through every image, they compute the orthogonal transformation between shape matrices of two frames instead of the one between motion matrices of two frames. However, they do not evaluate the breakdown points rigorously nor consider adding new feature points. Future research will have to address these issues. For online use, they will have to improve the performance of feature tracker by speeding it up and by using the updated structure and motion.

A real-time approach is developed by [176] that develops the factorization method by regarding the feature positions as a vector time series. This method produces estimates of shape and motion at each frame. A covariance-like matrix is stored, instead of feature positions, and its size remains constant as the number of frames increases. The singular value decomposition is replaced with an updating computation of only three dominant eigenvectors. Also, the method is able to handle infinite sequences, since it does not store any increasingly large matrices, so its implementation in VLSI or DSP is feasible. Experiments using synthetic and real images illustrate that the method has nearly the same accuracy and robustness as the original method [185], except that some extra frames are required to converge. However, faster convergence in the shape space computation could be achieved using more sophisticated algorithms, such as the orthogonal iteration with Ritz acceleration instead of the basic orthogonal iteration. Also, it is possible to use scaled orthographic projection or paraperspective projection [182] to improve the accuracy of the sequential factorization method.

Factorization method based on the affine projection has a limitation in reconstruction accuracy, and to achieve accurate reconstruction, the motion should be restricted. To overcome this problem, [155] present a recursive factorization method for the paraperspective model based on the perspective projection. This method is far superior to other ones in that it not only achieves accurate Euclidean reconstruction in a short time but also provides high stability in numerical computations. Moreover, the method produces stable reconstruction in almost all cases even if some images contain errors, because all images are treated as uniformly as possible and suitable for real-time. However, this method uses a calibrated camera.

Li and Brooks [154] propose a recursive method as a natural extension of both [185] and [176]. It estimates the shape space within a mean square errors (MSE) minimization framework. A recursive least squares (RLS) algorithm is developed for the MSE minimization, which uses as input the coordinates of feature points at each image frame. If P points are tracked through F frames, the recursive least squares method proposed by them updates the shape space with complexity $O(P)$ per frame. In contrast, [176] enables shape and motion to be updated at every frame. The cost of computing the critical shape space is $O(P^2)$ per frame. Additionally, a $P \times P$ covariance matrix is updated as part of the processing of each frame. The key SVD procedure of [185] has complexity $O(FP^2)$. Moreover, the method requires storage of a $2F \times P$ measurement matrix (its size therefore increasing with the number of frames) prior to computation of structure from motion. Hence, low computational complexity and good performance of [154] makes it suitable for real-time applications.

It is evident that the accuracy of the reconstruction will improve with better estimates of the 2D motion parameters. In turn, these estimates depend on the spatial variability of the brightness intensity pattern and on the size of the image region being tracked. The original factorization method [185] and the surface-based factorization method [165] provide equal weight to the contribution of each feature or region to the final 3D shape and 3D motion estimates. Intuitively, however, we should expect that weighting more the trajectories corresponding to 'sharp' features than the trajectories corresponding to features with smooth textures should lead to better overall estimates.

Aguiar and Moura [153] develop such an approach, which leads to the factorization of a modified measurement matrix rather than their original matrix in [162]. Besides better performance, it computes the weighted estimates with no additional cost. Reference [182] consider reliability weights to address occlusion when a feature is lost, and it gives the weight to zero and uses an iterative method to recover the 3D structure. As reported in [182], the iterative method may fail to converge. Aguiar and Moura [153] show that when the weights are time-invariant, the problem can be reformulated as the non-weighted factorization of a modified matrix. Then, any method can be used to factorize this matrix. This extension is called as the weighted factorization method.

So far, in this sub-section, crucial aspects of FM for SFM are presented. More research is required for the degenerate cases including the cases where the motions are degenerate. To achieve robustness under the presence of noise and occlusion, we need to relate its level with the thresholds necessary in some of the decision making processes. Real-time applications need to be considered carefully with less computational cost in future.

2.6 Other Issues

2.6.1 *Intensity Normalization*

In this last part, we present intensity normalization of an image. There are other normalizations for size management or other purposes. In calculating the templates for various actions or activities, we get different number of frames for different actions; even the same action which is done by different subjects may have different number of frames. For example, for the Motion History Image (MHI) [434] or the Directional Motion History Image (DMHI) method [484] (details will be in later chapters), the choice of parameter τ in calculating these images is crucial. Because, if an action takes 100 frames (i.e., $\tau = 100$) by one subject, then the maximum value in the produced DMHIs will be 100 (because $\tau = 100$); whereas, if the same action is slowly accomplished by another subject (e.g., taking longer period and hence 180 frames (i.e., $\tau = 180$) for the action), then the maximum value for the developed DMHIs will be 180. This intensity variation might produce slightly different feature vectors. Therefore, incorporation of intensity normalization in computing the MHI/DMHI templates can mitigate the constraint of different number of frames to employ. Hence, we can employ a developed refined method for recognition of different actions, done by different subjects with different frame numbers with robustness. Here, the pixel intensity values of the developed templates lie in the range of $[d^{\max}, d^{\min}]$, and we wish to transform it into the range of $[0, 1]$.

Let us denote d to the original dissimilarity, and ϱ to the normalized dissimilarity. Normalization can be achieved in different ways [511, 512], e.g., the following simple formulation can be used to normalize the templates into the range of [0, 1]. The intensity normalization transformation can be done as follows [511, 512]:

$$\varrho = \frac{d - d^{\min}}{d^{\max} - d^{\min}} \tag{2.6}$$

For the MHI or DMHI-based methods, by default, $[d^{\max}] = \tau$. It changes the intensity of templates into range of [0, 1]. If $[d] = [d^{\min}]$, then $\varrho = 0$. And if $[d] = [d^{\max}]$, then $\varrho = 1$. It is evident that the relationship of the parameters of $[d] - \varrho$ is linear and it depends on $[d^{\max}]$.

2.6.2 *Image Matching and Correspondence Problem*

Image matching has been a central research topic in computer vision over the last few decades. Correspondence or matching images having geometric and other variations is a challenging task. Various methods are proposed to solve this problem. Basically, there are two main approaches to solve the correspondence problem in images [331]:

- Model-based matching and
- Feature-based matching.

2.6.2.1 *Model-based Image Matching*

Model-based methods are able to solve the correspondence in difficult situations because the model encodes prior knowledge of the expected shape and appearance of an object class [331]. Active Shape Model (ASM) [342] is effective method to model the shape and appearance of objects. Several versions of Active Shape Model are,

- 3D Morphable Models (3DMM) [344],
- Active Appearance Model (AAM) [343],
- Kernel generalizations [345, 346],
- Active Conditional Model (ACM) [331], etc.

2.6.2.2 *Feature-based Image Matching*

Typical approaches to correspondence involve matching feature points between images. Lowe's SIFT descriptor [559], as mentioned above, is one of the state-of-the-art methods to construct geometric invariant features to match rigid objects. SIFT and its extensions [336, 339–341] have been successfully applied to many problems.

Alternatively, the correspondence problem can be formulated into a graph matching problem considering each feature point in the image as a node in a graph [332–335, 337, 338, 348].

2.6.3 *Camera Calibration*

In many cases, prior camera calibration is an important part, especially in applications where we require to reconstruct a world model, when a robot system interacts with the real world, and in stereo camera system. Usually, calibrations are done by using checkerboard patterns (Tsai grid). The most commonly used camera calibration method is the DLT (direct linear transformation) method [22].

In camera calibration, we need to estimate various camera parameters (internal and external parameters) in terms of rotation R and translation t with respect to the world coordinate system — to relate the camera's image plane's coordinate and the corresponding location of the scene plane. Some internal parameters are finding the position of image center in the image, skew factor, lens distortion (pin-cushion effect), focal length, different scaling factors for row pixels and column pixels.

For an in-depth analysis, we refer to the book by [23] and a tutorial on Tsai's camera calibration method by [21].

2.7 Think Ahead!

(1) Write a survey on segmentation methods for action recognition.
(2) List major background subtraction approaches and using a benchmark, compare their performances.
(3) What are the different approaches for optical flow, used in action recognition? List up their pros and cons for various applications.
(4) List up optical flow methods that are suitable for real-time applications.
(5) Make a judgmental research based on the existing feature point detectors — covering *which* one is the most suitable for *what* kind of images and applications.

(6) Study and evaluate the variants of Local Binary Pattern and find the most suitable approach that can be suitable for action representation.

Chapter 3

Action Representation Approaches

3.1 Action Representation Approaches

This chapter concentrates on various action or activity recognition approaches. The field of action and activity representation and recognition is relatively old, yet still immature [500]. However, various excellent surveys on human activity analysis and related issues have illustrated different methods and approaches for motion analysis [436, 447, 448, 452, 481, 488–507, 641]. This chapter concisely covers most of the recent advancements on human motion recognition. Among the various motion analysis related surveys, [436, 447, 448, 481, 489, 500–502, 641] cover the issues related to human motion recognition extensively.

Many approaches have been proposed to attack the action recognition problem. In this chapter, we attempt to cover mainly the later papers from the same issue from the same research group, so that we can get the essence of the latest developments from as much researchers as possible.

3.2 Classification of Various Dimensions of Representations

One prominent sub-division of the approaches of action recognition can be,

- Statistical approach (e.g., *Bag-of-Words* [110], *Bag-of-Vocabularies*).
- Structural approach (e.g., pose-based, body part-based, figure-centric).

In the Bag-of-Words or Bag-of-Vocabularies, the spatial arrangements of features are lost. Also, any sort of explicit modeling of the human figure can not be accomplished. So it fails to give localized information. Figure 3.1 shows a concept for the Bag-of-Words.

Approaches with Bag-of-Features [5] are discussed later in this chapter. Figure 3.2 shows some examples of pose-based body part segmentation.

The structural approaches suffer from the constraints related to pose estimation and analysis, and hence, to have a reliable human detection from this approach seems difficult in many cases. Note that human detection is usually very difficult through very crucial task to do. However, it can vividly provide localized information of an action.

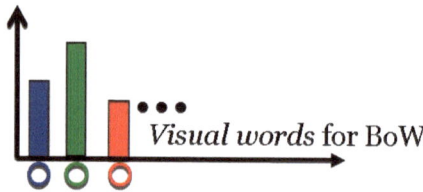

Fig. 3.1: A typical concept of Bag-of-Words. (Courtesy: G. Mori, SFU).

Different Approaches to Behavior Recognition:

The contemporary action and behavior recognition methods can be split into [381],

- Bag-of-Features (BoF) or, Bag-of-Visual-Words (BoVW) and
- Product Manifolds (PM).

3.2.1 *Bag-of-Features (BoF) or Bag-of-Visual-Words (BoVW)*

The Bag-of-Features approach [5] has become one of the most popular methods for human action recognition. Among recent action classification efforts, Bag-of-Features frameworks are those of most popular methods wherein visual vocabularies are learnt from descriptors. Several state-of-the-art action recognition approaches (e.g., [89, 110, 382, 383, 388, 390, 391, 440, 542, 578, 579, 584, 587, 592, 593, 598]) use the BoF/BoVW to exploit local spatio-temporal features. Figure 3.3 shows a concept of learning from Bag-of-Words. Usually, these approaches firstly generate a vocabulary of visual words and then characterize videos with the histograms of visual word counts. Li *et al.* [638] introduce another related term — *Bag-of-Points* for action recognition based on 3D points from the depth maps. Therefore, the related terms that are used interchangeably by the community to cover more or less similar concept are —

- Bag-of-Points [638]

Action Representation Approaches

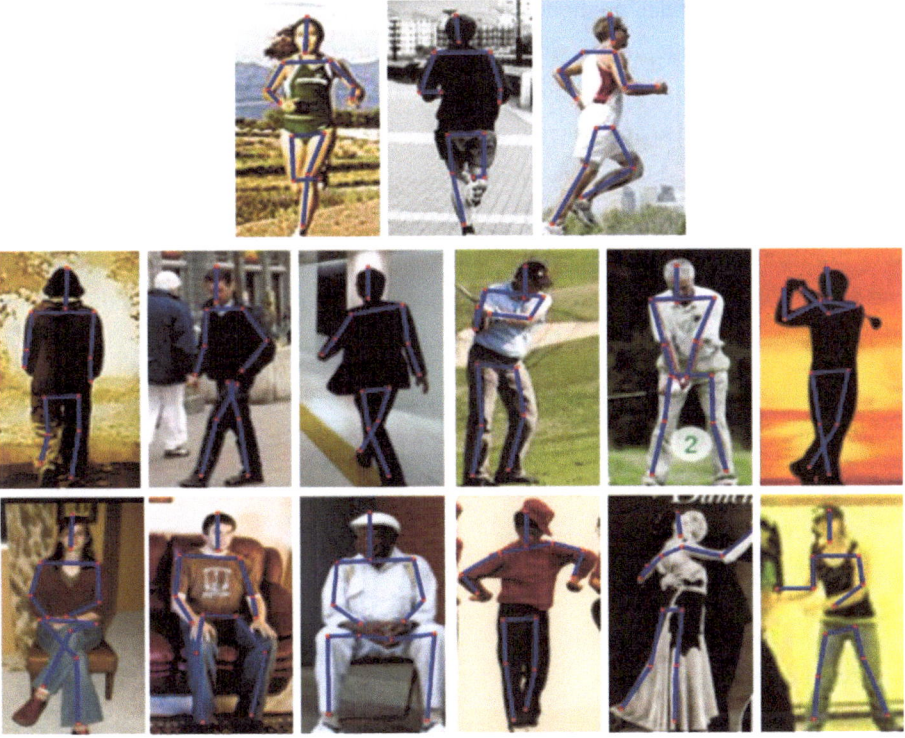

Fig. 3.2: Some examples of pose-based body part segmentation. (Courtesy: G. Mori, SFU).

- Bag-of-Features [5, 110, 579, 593]
- Bag-of-Words [110]
- Bag-of-Visual-Words [110]
- Bag-of-Video-Words [110]
- Bag-of-Vocabularies [381]

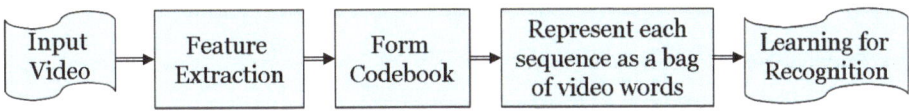

Fig. 3.3: A concept of learning from the Bag-of-Words as per [110].

As adapted from similar methods of image classification and retrieval, the Bag-of-Features approaches represent video clips as unordered sets of local space-time features. Features are quantized into discrete vocabularies, or codebooks. These space-time features in a video are assigned to their nearest neighbors in the codebook. The Bag-of-Features representation is typically a normalized histogram, where each bin in the histogram is the number of features assigned to a particular code divided by the total number of features in the video clip. Activity classification is often done by applying Support Vector Machines with appropriate kernels (χ^2 is common) to the Bag-of-Features representations.

There are many choices involved while implementing a Bag-of-Features approach. One must decide *how to sample the video to extract localized features*. Possible sampling strategies include [381],

- Space-time interest point operators,
- Grids/pyramids, or
- Random sampling.

Figure 3.4 demonstrates a flow-diagram for spatio-temporal interest points to classify.

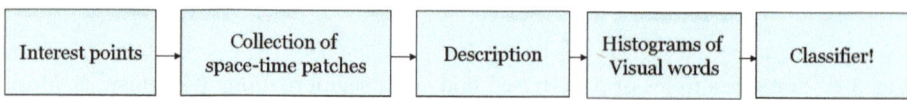

Fig. 3.4: A flow-diagram for spatio-temporal interest points to classify.

Each strategy comes with parameters including space and temporal scales, overlap, and other settings. From the sampled regions, an appropriate descriptor must be chosen to provide a balance between discrimination, robustness to small photometric and geometric perturbations, and compactness of representation [381].

Beyond feature detection and extraction, other design choices include [381],

- Codebook size,
- Quantization method (e.g., K-means), and
- Distance function to be used in nearest-neighbor assignments.

Advantages of the Bag-of-Features approach include [381],

- The relative simplicity of the representation compared to graphical or constellation models,
- The lack of any requirement to pre-process the videos to localize salient parts, perform segmentation, track moving objects, or any other image processing task beyond feature detection.

As such, they are attractive for use in unsupervised systems, which are designed to sample their environment and learn patterns without prior knowledge.

3.2.1.1 Constraints of BoF

The disadvantages of BoF/BoVW include,

- The difficulty in knowing precisely why two videos are considered similar, as there is little semantic meaning in the representation. For example, it is possible to correctly classify videos due to co-varying, but semantically irrelevant, background artifacts in the data set [381].
- These models discard the temporal information inherent to actions and are, thus, not well adapted to distinguish actions with several motion or posture changes (e.g., opening a door) and symmetric actions (e.g., sitting down vs. standing up) [91].
- Large size of vocabulary may introduce a sparse histogram for each video, yield more noise and reduce the discriminability of vocabulary.
- Moreover, if the vocabulary size is small, it may cause over-clustering and high intra-class distortion.
- Another problem with Bag-of-Features action recognition algorithms is credit assignment. As pointed out by others in the context of object/face recognition [384, 385], it is difficult to know what a Bag-of-Features approach is responding to.
- While encouraging results are achieved, Bag-of-Features methods have heavy training loads prior to classification [573].
- In particular, feature detection and codebook generation could consume tremendous amounts of time if the number of training samples is large.
- In addition, the descriptors and parameters are often *ad hoc* and rooted in specific applications.

Kovashka and Grauman [578] propose a Bag-of-Features method for learning discriminative features on space-time neighborhoods. The descriptors are modeled hierarchically and multiple kernel learning is exploited to characterize each action. Although

Bag-of-Features methods have shown encouraging results in action classification, the number of parameters is large and their selection typically is *ad hoc* [573]. In the case of Bag-of-Features, the number of visual features, the size of vocabularies, the level of hierarchies, and the number of kernels are required to be determined in advance.

In order to overcome some constraints of BoF, Yuan *et al.* [388] propose the *pyramid vocabulary tree*, which combines the vocabularies of different sizes and exploits a larger and more discriminative vocabulary efficiently. They cluster the interest points in the spatio-temporal space, which forms several cluster centers. At each cluster center they compute the histogram of the local features. Based on the spatio-temporal cluster centers, they propose a *sparse spatio-temporal pyramid matching kernel* (SST-PMK) to measure the similarities between video sequences [388].

3.2.2 Product Manifold Approaches

Geometric methods present an alternative approach to those based upon localized sampling. Geometric approaches attempt to map the high-dimensional video data into a lower dimensional space with some regular structure, such as a differentiable manifold. If a video can be represented as a point on a manifold, then the distance between two videos is the geodesic distance between these points [583].

The advantages of the Product Manifold approach include [381],

- The relatively small number of design choices,
- The lack of any training or lengthy codebook generation process, and
- The computational speed.

The disadvantages of Product Manifold are,

- The requirement to use fixed-size cubes in the representation. The video clips from the data sets must be cropped or scaled to a uniform-sized cube.
- As Product Manifold approaches process pixels, therefore, it is difficult to know whether the performance is due to motion or appearance or lighting or something else.

Unlike the Bag-of-Features frameworks, which require extensive efforts for model setup, geometric-based methods consider the geometry of space and characterize actions based on the intrinsic nature of the data [573]. The method of [583] — Product Manifold — factorizes action data and maps them to a Product Manifold. Lui and Beveridge [573] investigate an approach based on geometric method. Geometric methods explore the characteristics of space, and perform classification based on the intrinsic geometry inherent in action manifolds.

The work of Lui and Beveridge [573] is motivated by the use of tangent spaces [582, 586] and high order factorization to Grassmann manifolds [583]. Veeraraghavan *et al.* [586] capture shape changes on tangent spaces. The projections on tangent spaces of special manifolds are also noted for face recognition [582]. This implies that discriminating information can be obtained from the tangent space. Lui *et al.* [573, 583] factorize video to a set of factor manifolds for action classification. This indicates that spatio-temporal features are embedded in the factor manifolds.

Based on their prior works, Lui and Beveridge [573] propose an alternative and better geometric method to overcome some of the drawbacks from these previous approaches including,

- Silhouette images must be extracted and dynamics need to be learnt explicitly in [586];
- The geodesic distance (chordal distance) defined on Product Manifolds may not be precise enough when data are too far apart. This is because the chordal distance approximates the geodesic distance via a projective embedding on a sphere [575] and views the line segment between points as geodesic.

They [573] express the raw pixel videos as third order tensors and factorize the data tensor to a set of tangent spaces on a Grassmann manifold. A Grassmann manifold is a set of all p-dimensional linear subspaces of $\mathbb{R}^n$ [588]. The set of tangent spaces essentially represents the tangent bundle. The logarithmic mapping is exploited to map the factorized data from the manifold to the tangent space. Action classification is then performed on the collection of tangent spaces. As a result, the discriminating features on tangent spaces and the spatio-temporal information are utilized effectively while no silhouettes are extracted and no dynamics are explicitly learnt.

The use of *tangent bundles* in computer vision is relatively new. Ben-Yosef and Ben-Shahar [574] introduce the unit tangent bundle for curve completion. This method views the tangent space of an image as $\mathbb{R}^2 \times \mathscr{S}^1$ and the curve completion process is performed within this space.

Veeraraghavan *et al.* [586] model human shapes based on Kendall's theory of shape [589], where shapes are expressed on a shape manifold. The changes of shapes can then be captured on the tangent space, which is a linearization of the spherical shape space; i.e., it is Euclidean. A sequence of shape changes is then extracted from the tangent space and an autoregressive model is exploited to learn the dynamics of the human movement.

Silva *et al.* [585] exploit tangent bundles for motion tracking. To address the nonlinearity of a manifold, they partition the training data into a set of local patches and find the local coordinates by computing normal subspaces defined by the subspace with the smallest eigenvectors. The manifold charts are then estimated using PCA. Generally, this method can be characterized as local PCA.

Action Recognition — More Areas:

Approaches of action recognition can be divided into another set,

- Based on large-scale features (e.g., optical flow-based approaches, [435])
- Based on local patches (e.g., collection of local parts, block-histogram features [554, 600])

Individually, both approaches can perform well in different situations. However, if we could combine these two approaches in a smart manner, then the possibility hikes for better recognition. One recent mixed approach of these two can be formulated as in Figure 3.5, where large-scale and small features are combined for better representations.

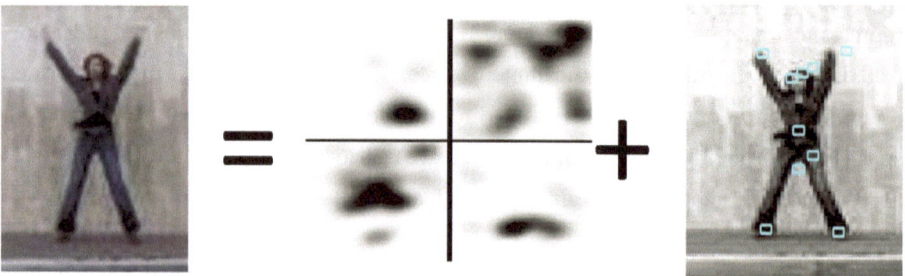

Fig. 3.5: An example for mixed approach with large-scale and small features. (Image Courtesy: Greg Mori, SFU).

Action Representation Approaches

For the template-based approaches, there exist two sorts of templates [388]:

- The first sort of templates directly use several key frames or segmented patches of the input videos [386, 387].
- The second sort of templates are obtained by linear or nonlinear transformation of the input videos [387].

Recognition methods are carried out in,

- Non-parametric models [402–404, 434, 435, 440, 592, 593]
- Parametric models by HMM, CRF, etc. [405–412, 519].

Machine learning (ML) approaches for video-based human motion analysis can be split mainly into [105],

- Discriminative approaches and
- Generative approaches.

Figure 3.6 shows the approaches based on [105].

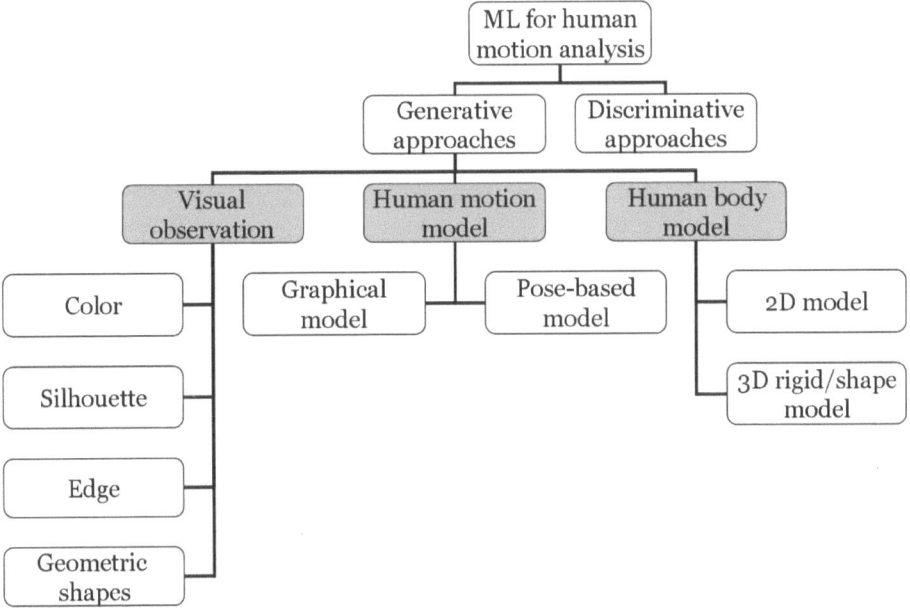

Fig. 3.6: A typical machine learning (ML) approaches for video-based human motion analysis.

Discriminative approaches tend to directly learn a mapping function from visual observations to body configurations based on training data, where the key is to handle the ambiguity and uncertainty of visual data due to the pose/view variability [105]. Few approaches under its belt are Relevance Vector Machine (RVM), probabilistic regression, nearest neighbor, temporal chaining and neural networks [105].

On the other hand, *generative approaches* can be split into few areas. These involve explicit models to explain the underlying visual/kinematic data via a few latent variables by which the motion/pose can be inferred. Discriminative approaches are more efficient and require less strict training, while generative approaches are more effective to incorporate prior knowledge in the inference process [105]. Visual observations cover various image descriptors, e.g.,

- Edges,
- Colors,
- Silhouettes [425, 429, 431, 432, 434, 543, 549, 553, 586, 615, 621],
- Histogram of Oriented Gradients (HOG) features [4, 224, 258, 579, 639],
- Pyramidal HOG (PHOG) [7],
- Shape contexts,
- Texture,
- Local Binary Pattern and its variants.

Models:

There are different models for human motion and human shape both in 2D and 3D. These are significantly based on pose estimations and figure-centric measurements. In 3D domain, the models are available based on either shape or rigid body. It is difficult to decipher, which approaches or strategies are dominating in human motion analysis. Some of the model types are,

- Patches
- Cylinders
- Mesh
- Stick-figures
- Ellipsoids
- Rectangles
- Super-quadratic ellipsoids

- Rectangular-elliptical cones
- Quadrangular
- Clay pattern [538, 539]
- Joint center
- Triangulated graph [530, 531]

3.3 Action Recognition Approaches

Recent approaches to action recognition in natural video argue that both shape and motion information are necessary for recognition. They often combine static image features and spatio-temporal features to capture appearance and motion. It has, however, been shown in psychology experiments on Point Light Displays [591] that it is possible to recognize human actions based entirely on the dynamics of body movement. The appearance of subjects or background is less important to the description of actions than dynamics [590].

3.3.1 *Interest-point-based Approaches*

Spatio-temporal features are considered by various researchers. *Interest point detection* in static images is a well-studied topic in computer vision. At the top of the Harris-Laplace detector, Laptev [382] proposes a spatio-temporal extension. Later, several *spatiotemporal interest/feature point* (STIP) detectors are exploited in video analysis for action recognition. Feature points are detected using a number of measures, namely —

- Global texture [415],
- Corner [382],
- Periodicity [416],
- Volumetric optical flow [440].

In the spatiotemporal domain, however, it is unclear which features represent useful interest points [416].

As mentioned earlier, the SURF (Speeded-Up Robust Features [341, 417]) is developed for interest point detection. In the arena of the local invariant feature detectors: Harris detector, SUSAN detector, Harris-Laplace/Affine detector, Hessian detector [419], Hessian-Laplace detector, Maximally Stable Extremal Region detector, Difference-of-

Gaussians [559], SURF (Speeded-Up Robust Features), FAST (Features from Accelerated Segment Test), etc. become prominent in different perspectives. These are based on whether regions of the image or the blob or corner should be detected as key interest points.

Analyzing actions directly using the spatio-temporal features can avoid some limitations of traditional approaches that involve —

- Computation of optical flow [540] (e.g., aperture problems, smooth surfaces, singularities, etc.),
- Feature tracking (e.g., self-occlusions, re-initialization, change of appearance),
- Key frames [541] (e.g., lack of information about the motion),
- Eigen-shapes of foreground silhouettes [428, 542].

Hence various approaches [390, 393, 413, 414, 440, 540–546, 590, 597] are proposed by looking at a video sequence as a space-time volume (of intensities, gradients, optical flow, or other local features).

Oshin *et al.* [590] investigate the sole use of body dynamics for automatic action recognition in complex videos. They propose a novel representation of actions in video, which captures the relative distribution of motion-based interest points by encoding their local spatio-temporal configuration in an efficient manner. This results in an action descriptor, which, in vectorized form, can be learnt using SVMs.

Oikonomopoulos *et al.* [546] extend the concept of saliency from the spatial to the spatio-temporal domain, to represent human motion by using a sparse set of spatio-temporal features that correspond to activity peaks, by measuring changes in the information content of neighboring pixels. However, space-time descriptors may strongly depend on the relative motion between the object and the camera and in [547], a Harris corner detector is extended in the temporal dimension, leading to a number of corner points in time, called space-time interest points to automatically adapt the features to the local velocity of the image pattern. But these space-time points are often found on highlights and shadows and sensitive to lighting conditions and reduce recognition accuracy [440]. Ke *et al.* [440] generalize the notion of 2D box features to 3D spatio-temporal volumetric features for real-time video analysis. It extends the rectangle features (cascaded AdaBoost) [545] into the spatio-temporal domain for video analysis.

Rittscher *et al.* [548] propose to classify the type of motion directly from the spatio-temporal features of the image sequence. In [549], another representation for actions using spatio-temporal volumes (called *action sketch*) is defined by computing point correspondences between consecutive contours (for each time slice) using a graph theoretical approach. In another approach, [542, 543] utilize the properties of the solution to the Poisson equation to extract space-time features (e.g., local space-time saliency, action dynamics, shape structure and orientation) for action recognition. It is robust to noise at the bounding contour of the extracted silhouettes as opposed to the local surface features in [548]. Yilmaz and Shah [549] use spatio-temporal action volumes for action recognition.

Several other approaches use information that could be derived from the space-time shape of an action, i.e., in XYT-space. Bobick and Davis [434] propose a spatio-temporal motion models for representation and recognition of action by motion history image (MHI) and motion energy images (MEI). In this appearance-based method, the MHI is a scalar-valued image where more recently moving pixels are brighter, and vice versa. The MEI is a cumulative binary motion image that describes where a motion is in the video sequence. Several variants are proposed on the top of the MHI method for various applications. Details of the MHI method and its variants are analyzed in latter parts of the book.

Many of the approaches make use of a sparse set of local interest points generated by the action [579, 584, 592, 594, 595], and demonstrate remarkable performance. Interest points are highlighted as salient regions based on response functions applied to the video, and eliminate the need for motion tracking and background subtraction, which are costly preprocessing steps. Examples include,

- Laptev and Lindeberg's [596] temporal extension of Harris 2D corners,
- Willems's [597] use of the determinant of the generalized 3D Hessian matrix,
- Dollar *et al.*'s [593] separable linear filters.

Several descriptors are proposed to encode the spatio-temporal support region of these interest points. These include,

- Local jet descriptors [592],

- Vector of concatenated pixel gradients [593],
- Generalization of the SIFT and SURF descriptors [534, 576, 597–599],
- Histograms of Oriented Gradient (HOG) descriptor [4, 7, 89, 224, 579, 639],
- Histograms of Optic Flow (HOF) descriptor [4, 89, 579],
- Point-trajectory features (Trajectons) [6, 89]
- Volumetric features [89, 473].

The Histograms of Oriented Gradient (HOG) descriptor is proposed for human detection by [224]. Apart from various human detection, the HOG is also employed in action recognition by [4, 89, 579, 639], because its performance is robust. The HOG descriptor provides detail of human poses. The essence of HOG is to describe local edge structure or appearance of object by local distribution of gradients [224].

The Histograms of Optic Flow (HOF) descriptors [4, 89, 579] are computed in a similar descriptor arrangement of the HOG and it is computed from the optical flow.

Kim and Cipolla [576] advocate a method combining Discriminant CCA with spatio-temporal SIFT features for gesture classification. This method partitions a video into XY-planes, YT-planes, and XT-planes. Each plane is then divided into blocks, where the orientation histogram is built. The SIFT descriptors are concatenated and learnt by the Discriminant CCA.

Detected interest points are typically used in —

- Discriminative model [592, 593], or
- Generative model [584].

A number of recent approaches show good recognition performance by capturing the *local spatio-temporal* configuration of interest points. Gilbert *et al.* [595] build compound hierarchical features based on relationships of detected interest points, and use data mining to discover reoccurring patterns. Ryoo and Aggarwal [602] use a set of pair-wise predicates to describe relationships between interest points, while Matikainen *et al.* [603] build relative location probability maps of interest points. Kovashka *et al.* [578] construct a hierarchy of vocabularies from spatio-temporal neighborhoods of interest points, encoding the points and a configuration of their neighbors. Savarese *et al.* [604] also capture pair-wise correlation of interest point labels based on their proximity. While these methods encode configurations based on the *appearance* and *location* of interest points, the approach of Oshin *et al.* [590] make use of their *locations and strengths only*, discarding appearance information.

3.3.2 Hidden Markov Model-based Approaches

Hidden Markov Model (HMM)-based approaches and related probabilistic models are well-known to analyze motion for understanding and recognition. In several cases, prior tracking is required. The HMMs have been frequently used for modeling human motions as it efficiently abstract time series data, and can be used for both subsequent motion recognition and generation. Davis and Tyagi [513] present a probabilistic reliable-inference framework to address the issue of rapid detection of human actions with low error rates. They incorporate the HMM temporal models (instead of hierarchical motion history images [453]) for the probabilistic evaluations.

3.3.2.1 *Star Skeleton*

Chen *et al.* [514] use *star skeleton* as a representative descriptor of human posture with the HMM. The star skeleton is a fast skeletonization technique by connecting from centroid of target object to contour extremes. An action is composed of a series of star skeletons over time and is transformed into a feature vector sequence for the HMM model. A posture codebook is designed to contain star skeletons of each action type and define a star distance to measure the similarity between feature vectors. They recognize both simple actions and activities.

3.3.2.2 *Non-parametric HMM Approach*

However, in the traditional HMM framework, the hidden states are typically coupled with the training data, which will bring many undesired problems to the learning procedure. Hence, [515] introduce a non-parametric HMM approach that uses continuous output HMMs with arbitrary states to learn the shape dynamics directly from large amounts of training data for view-dependent motion recognition.

3.3.2.3 *Factorial Hidden Markov Models*

Kulic *et al.* [516] apply Factorial Hidden Markov Models for recognition. Peursum *et al.* [517] integrate missing observation data with the HMMs to create a framework that is able to segment and classify action primitives from motion. Based on this framework, a model is trained to automatically segment and classify an activity sequence into its constituent sub-actions during inference. This is achieved by introducing action labels into the observation vector and assigning these labels as missing data during inference, thus forcing the system to infer the probability of each action label.

3.3.2.4 Dynamically Multi-Linked HMM

A Dynamically Multi-Linked HMM [518] is developed to interpret group activities involving multiple objects captured in an outdoor scene. The model is based on the discovery of salient dynamic interlinks among multiple temporal events using Dynamic Probabilistic Networks. Its performance on modeling group activities in a noisy outdoor scene is superior compared to that of a Multi-Observation HMM, a Parallel-HMM and a Coupled-HMM.

3.3.2.5 CRF and MEMM-based

Sminchisescu *et al.* [519] present algorithms for recognizing human motion, based on discriminative Conditional Random Field (CRF) and Maximum Entropy Markov Models (MEMM). Apart from simple actions, it can discriminate between *normal walk* and *wander walk*.

3.3.2.6 Hierarchical HMM

Nguyen *et al.* [520] use shared-structure hierarchical HMMs (HHHMM) to recognize two levels of actions. They also propose a Rao-Blackwellised particle filter for real-time recognition. Their result is superior to flat HMM and tree-HHMM for complex actions. Another different hierarchical approach is proposed in [521] where Bayesian networks are employed to understand two-person interactions.

3.3.2.7 Others

Ryoo and Aggarwal [522] propose to recognize complex human activities using context-free grammar (CFG)-based representation scheme to represent composite actions and interactions. They construct a HMM to detect a gesture. Shi *et al.* [523] introduce Propagation Networks (a form of dynamic Bayesian Networks) and the associated Discrete Condensation algorithm to represent and recognize sequential activities that include parallel streams of action. A boosting framework is applied for both recognition and anomaly detection tasks [524].

Ahmad and Lee [525] propose a view-independent recognition method by using the Cartesian component of optical flow velocity and human body shape feature vector information. Each action is represented by a set of HMMs and is modeled for any viewing direction by using the combined $(Q + R)$-dimensional features. Complex activities are recognized in outdoor, first by estimating the human body posture frame by frame and statistically modeling the temporal sequences of the detected postures using HMMs [526].

3.3.3 Eigenspace-based Approach

Principal Component Analysis (PCA) or eigenspace is employed in several developments for the reduction of dimension, etc., for faster recognition [247, 313, 427, 429, 527, 585], in face recognition as *eigenface* [377]. Eigenfaces are a set of eigenvectors for face classification [377]. These eigenvectors are derived from the covariance matrix of the probability distribution of the high-dimensional vector space of possible faces. The concept of eigenface can be explored into other areas as *eigenimage* or *eigenfeatures*.

Rahman and Ishikawa *et al.* [428] develop a tuned eigenspace method for recognition that can overcome dress effect significantly. A simple but efficient gait recognition algorithm using spatial-temporal silhouette analysis is proposed in [429] by employing eigenspace.

Actions can be described as the changing body pose over time [527]. A 2-mode PCA framework is described in [528] to linearly classify biological motions of male and female walkers. Their analysis reveals that the dynamic part of the motion contains more information about gender than motion-mediated structural cues. Davis and Gao propose a 3-mode PCA (body pose and time are the first two modes; and the third mode may correspond to gender, effort, age, etc.) framework for recognizing gender from walking movements [529], and for analyzing the efforts of a person carrying bags with various weights [527]. Low level motion features, computed using an IIR filter at every frame, are compressed using PCA to form points in eigenspace for recognition [424]. It creates several feature images for an action so that it can handle complex or repetitive actions.

3.3.4 Approaches to Manage Occlusion

The management of occlusion or missing frames is a key concern in computer vision applications [641]. Very few methods can handle various occlusions in smart manner and robust to full or partial occlusion [530, 626, 636–639].

To address the problem of occlusions, Peursum *et al.* [626, 636] propose to shift the responsibility for dealing with missing pose data away from the pose estimator and onto the action classifier, with data missing during both training and classification. They carry out the pose estimation by using a modified version of the *star skeletonization* proposed by [637].

In different a perspective, Li *et al.* [638] propose a method for action recognition based on a *Bag-of-Points* (BoPs), $x = q_i$, $i = 1, 2, \ldots, m$, where point q_i can be a pixel belonging to a silhouette or a Spatio-Temporal Interest Point. In this approach, there is no requirement to have the same number of points for each posture, and there is no correspondence between the points of different postures too. They propose an *action graph* for Bag-of-Points from depth maps, by adopting bi-gram with maximum likelihood decoding (BMLD) scheme. Action graph is an effective method to explicitly model the dynamics of human motion based on a set of salient postures shared among the actions [638]. The Bag-of-Points posture model can deal with occlusions through simulation to some extent. In their experiment, they divide the depth map of an action into four quadrants. Occlusion is simulated by ignoring among the 80 sampled 3D points, those points that fell into the specified occluded quadrants.

On the other hand, Wang *et al.* [639] propose a human detection approach capable of handling partial occlusion, by combining Histograms of Oriented Gradients (HOG) and Local Binary Pattern (LBP) as the feature set. They construct an occlusion likelihood map by using the response of each block of the HOG feature to the global detector.

3.3.5 Other Approaches

3.3.5.1 Actom Sequence Model

Gaidon *et al.* [91] introduce a temporally structured representation of actions in videos, called *Actom Sequence Model* (ASM). This representation encodes the temporal ordering constraints between actoms in a flexible way [91]. As mentioned in Chapter 1, *actoms* are specific to each action class and they obtain these by manual annotation (at training time only). They observe that the annotation cost for actoms is comparable to specifying beginning and end of a training clip.

3.3.5.2 *Spatio-temporal Silhouettes*

Another traditional method of motion representation is spatio-temporal silhouettes [434, 543, 549, 553]. Human actions can be represented as a sequence of silhouettes. In [553], an associated sequence of human silhouettes is converted into two types of representations, Average Motion Energy (AME), and Mean Motion Shape (MMS). Veeraraghavan *et al.* [586] model the dynamics of human silhouettes using an autoregressive model on the tangent space. The sequences of human shapes are compared by computing the distance between the autoregressive models.

Lee and Grimson [425] present a simple representation of human gait appearance based on moments computed from the silhouette of a walking person for the purpose of person identification and gender classification. Another automatic gait-based person identification as well as gender classification system is proposed in [432] that uses masking functions to measure the area of a dynamic temporal signal from a sequence of silhouettes of a walking subject. This signal is used as a signature for automatic gait recognition.

In a different dimension, Weinland *et al.* [473] describe a 3D method, called Motion History Volumes (MHV). Here, pixels are replaced with voxels. The space occupancy function is estimated using silhouettes that correspond to the visual hull. They automatically segment action sequences into primitive actions, which can be represented by a single MHV. They cluster the resulting MHVs into a hierarchy of action classes, which allow recognizing multiple occurrences of repeating actions. In *timed* MHI (tMHI) method [311], new silhouette values are copied in with a floating-point timestamp to develop a motion segmentation method.

However, extracting silhouette images from cluttered backgrounds is not trivial and learning the dynamics of human actions may require lots of training videos. It is well understood that small sample size is a challenging problem for machine learning-based methods.

Zhong *et al.* [554] classify spatial histogram feature vectors into prototypes. They detect unusual activities by finding spatially isolated clusters, where some useful local motion information could be lost in their spatial histogram features. Boiman and Irani [555] propose a probabilistic graphical model using ensembles of spatio-temporal patches to detect irregular behaviors in videos.

Xiang and Gong [556] use 7-D feature vectors from a blob of a scene-event to perform behavior profiling and abnormality detection. These 7-D feature vectors can only appropriately describe the gross information of movements. Cuntoor and Chellappa [557] propose an epitomic representation for modeling human activities, using kinematics of objects within short-time interval. Optical flow is used as a spatio-temporal descriptor for action recognition in [435].

Ali *et al.* [537] introduce a framework to characterize the non-linear dynamics of human actions by using the theory of chaotic systems. Trajectories of reference joints are used as the representation of the non-linear dynamical system that is generating the action.

Lai and Liao [538] propose a trajectory-based recognition system that uses a clay pattern to represent extracted trajectories. They consider a trajectory as a force pushing a moving articulated part. They apply the forces to a clay-like material that can deform and this deformed material concept represents the trajectories. Based on the 3D clay model by Dewaele and Cani [539], they develop their 2D clay model for human motion recognition based on this clay-like representation of trajectories.

In a model-based approach, we can consider various models, e.g., human motion model can be represented as a triangulated graph [530, 531]. Fanti *et al.* [530] combines appearance with positions and velocities [531] into both the learning and detection phases. They introduce global variables in the model to represent global properties (e.g., translation, scale or view-point). It is robust to occlusions, and shows higher recognition rate.

While earlier action recognition methods are evaluated on simulated actions in simplified settings, more recent work has shifted focus to natural actions in unconstrained

Action Representation Approaches

scenarios, e.g., personal video collections and movies. As a result of the increase in complexity of these actions, some approaches [579, 600, 601] make use of a *combination of feature types*.

The use of prototype trees in a joint shape-motion space is presented for action classification in [581]. During the training phase, action prototypes are learned from the computed shape-motion descriptors. The recognition process is a two-stage process consisting of frame-to-prototype and prototype-video based matching. Interestingly, the prototype-video matching was performed on a frame-by-frame basis using the optimal alignment path.

Several methods are proposed for understanding various interactions in a group of people. A method for action localization and recognition in the contexts of group-person interaction and person-person interaction is proposed by [112]. Figure 3.7 shows a flow-diagram for the concept of localization and recognition based on prior model and training data. Detecting a group of people in a scene is important (Figure 3.8) and understanding them, i.e., what they are doing in the scene is a very difficult task (and not many research groups are working in this zone). For example, in Figure 3.9 shows that five people are standing and if we look carefully, we can find that there are two different groups of people and they are talking. Therefore, clustering different actions based on groups of people, are important to understand real-life activities.

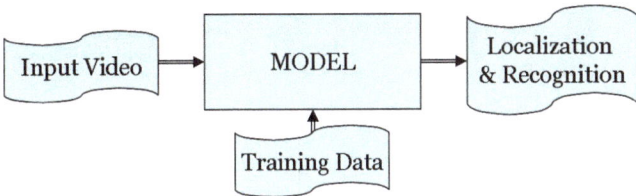

Fig. 3.7: A flow-diagram for the concept of localization and recognition based on prior model and training data.

Fig. 3.8: Detecting group of people to understand their activities.

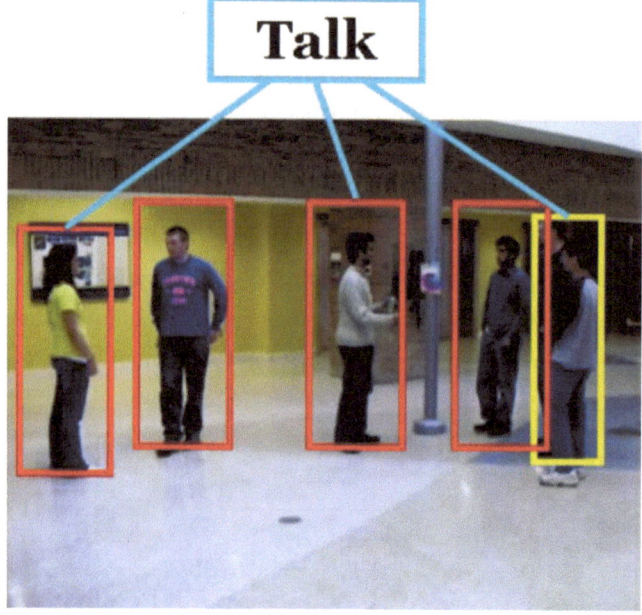

Fig. 3.9: Understanding the actions of a group of people — in this case, the action is — *talk*. (Courtesy: G. Mori, SFU).

3.3.5.3 *Robustness in Camera Movement*

Most of the methods for action and behavior analysis fail if the camera has significant movement in it. The main reasons is that when a camera has movement or vibration, one of the following concerns may hinder the performance of a method —

- Background changes intermittently,
- The correspondence of feature points from frame-to-frame fails significantly,
- Computation of optical flow provides noisy vectors,
- Variations in object sizes (e.g., in PTZ camera),
- Possible occlusion.

Few methods claim to be robust in the presence of camera motion, e.g., [427, 477, 533, 534]. Action recognition *in presence of camera motion* is possible by using epipolar geometry between two cameras [533]. With the rotational and translational camera motions, a new *temporal fundamental matrix* is developed. Uemura *et al.* [534] present an approach to human action recognition via local feature tracking and robust estimation of background motion, based on KLT tracker and SIFT as well as a method for estimating dominant planes in the scene. It shows robust motion compensation.

3.4 View-invariant Methods

It is very difficult to develop a system that is fully view-invariant. Actually, approaches that are proposed and claimed as view-invariant methods usually use multi-camera information and process them mostly in 3D. However, due to the —

- Presence of partial occlusion,
- Presence of self-occlusion due to body parts,
- Similarities of more than one actions — seen from different angles,
- Multi-camera coordination problem,
- Higher computing cost,
- Lack of datasets with much variability, etc.

— view-invariant methods become more challenging. Few methods that claim as view-invariant based on different datasets are presented by [218, 219, 221, 233, 250, 362, 363, 444, 451, 453, 473, 525, 532, 535, 536]. Among these methods, [250] employ PTZ camera system. Sugiura *et al.* [363] use omni-directional camera to capture multi-view images.

Bodor *et al.* [535] introduce a method for human motion recognition by employing image-based rendering. They employ image-based rendering to generate views orthogonal to the mean direction of motion. Rao *et al.* [536] present a view-invariant representation of human actions considering the dramatic changes in the speed and direction of the trajectory. This system automatically segments video into individual actions, and computes the view-invariant representation for each action.

Static and temporally varying 3D invariants (restricted-3D and full-3D version) are proposed for capturing the spatio-temporal dynamics of a general human action to enable its representation in a compact, view-invariant manner [532]. Ahmad and Lee [525] propose a view-independent recognition method.

3.5 Gesture Recognition and Analysis

In some cases, some of the gestures are considered as actions or *atomic* action elements by some researchers. For example, [462] analyze complex motion sequences (e.g., dances) and segment them into shorter motion sequences, which they called as *gestures!* There are some clearly-defined hand or body or head gesture datasets (details in Chapter 6), e.g., Cambridge gesture dataset [577], Naval Air Training and Operating Procedures Standardization (NATOPS) aircraft handling signals database [69], Keck gesture dataset [581] and Korea University Gesture (KUG) database [77]. Approaches for action segmentation into its basic elements or in some cases into gestures are covered in later part of this chapter. Moreover, while presenting various methods and algorithms for action recognition (as above), we cover most of the dominant methods for gesture recognitions. Therefore, in this section, instead of repeating, we mention the papers on gesture recognition as — [317, 318, 320, 434, 461, 462, 522, 550, 576, 577, 581, 627, 628].

A traditional method of motion representation is *motion trajectory* [550–552]. For example, a principal curve is computed to describe gestures in gesture recognition [550]. In [551], the central points of face and hands in a video sequence are fitted into several quadratic curves, and six invariants from each quadratic curve are computed to construct a feature vector. However, the motion trajectory only carries global motion information, i.e., the motion status of the whole foreground, and it does not contain shape or local motion information, i.e., the motion status of each local area (even each pixel) of the foreground, but these two pieces of information are also useful for behavior recognition.

By *gesture*, according to www.thefreeDictionary.com, we understand that a gesture is,

- A motion of the limbs or body made to express or help express thought or to emphasize speech; or
- The act of moving the limbs or body as an expression of thought or emphasis; or
- An act or a remark made as a formality or as a sign of intention or attitude; or
- A motion of hands or body to emphasize or help to express a thought or feeling; or
- A movement of the head, hand, etc. to express an idea, etc.

The vision community is still far from these definitions to achieve by various smart methods. Moreover, a recent phenomenon is the incorporation of sign language analysis and recognition. However, both sign language analysis and some gestures seem similar and methods are related. Gesture from facial expressions and head movements are more challenging than by hands. We present some discussions and approaches on these issues later in the section on affective computing and expression analysis.

3.6 Action Segmentation and Other Areas

Lan *et al.* [113] propose a method of joint action recognition and localization. Figure 3.10 shows a typical localized representation of an action. Figure 3.11 shows a person riding on a horse and localize this in the video and recognize the action is done by [113]. The streaklines concept is employed in few applications. For example, [109] use Streaklines for motion segmentation. As per the concept, regions of similar motion would have similar streakline. Therefore, if we can compute the frame by frame optical flow and then we compute streaklines, we can find a similarity map for the neighboring streakline. Through this manner, it is possible to concentrate the regions of coherent motion from a video. Figure 3.12 shows an example of motion segmentation of a crowded scene (Figure 3.12) [109].

In another example, streaklines are explored to detect lanes as parts of a segmented region that fall between two contours of the stream function by a simple intersection operation. Also, abnormal behaviors are detected (Figure 3.13). They [108] present an algorithm to detect abnormal behavior in crowds using potential functions for the flow.

3.7 Affective Computing and Expression Analysis

Ekman's six basic emotions (i.e., joy, anger, fear, sadness, disgust and surprise) [632] are well-known and well-studied material in affective computing and human emotion

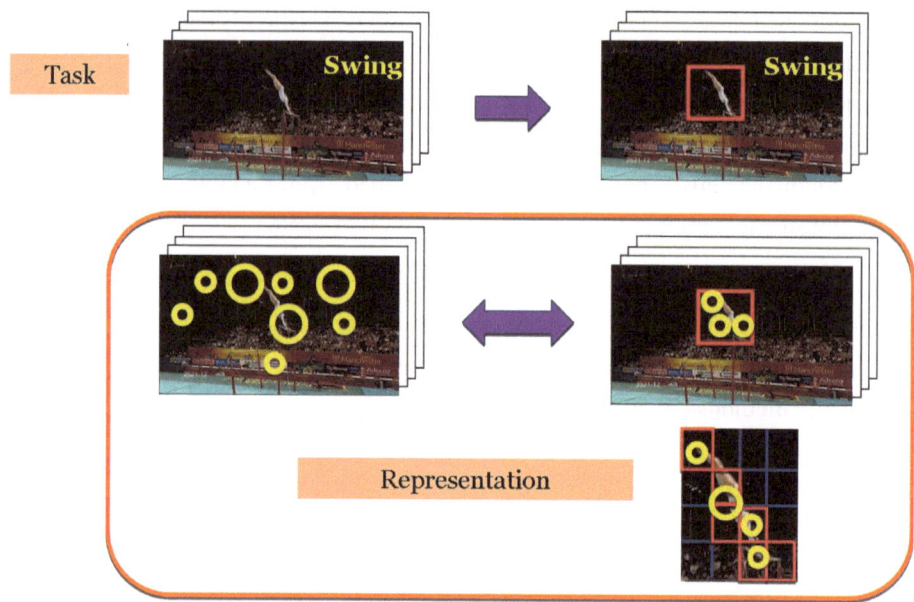

Fig. 3.10: Examples for the concept of joint action recognition and localization. (Image Courtesy: G. Mori, SFU).

and/or expression analysis. In the relatively new field of affective computing, it is a research aim to enable machines to read a person's emotions through various sensors or by understanding various gestures and actions [627, 628]. Though this is difficult to accomplish, some limited progresses have been made in application to PC-based video games and other interactive systems [2].

3.7.1 *Games with Emotional Involvement*

Location-based games offer opportunities for us to learn more about people's interactions and feelings towards the environment they are in as well as to understand more about the mental models and locations associated with known environments [628]. Baillie *et al.* [628, 630] manipulate the activities in a game to take advantage of certain locations in the hope of producing certain emotional reactions. They develop a methodology for location-based games that aims at capturing the players' emotional reactions to some normal activities in a game whilst in certain locations.

Wang *et al.* [633] conduct a series of studies on human emotions and facial expression

Action Representation Approaches

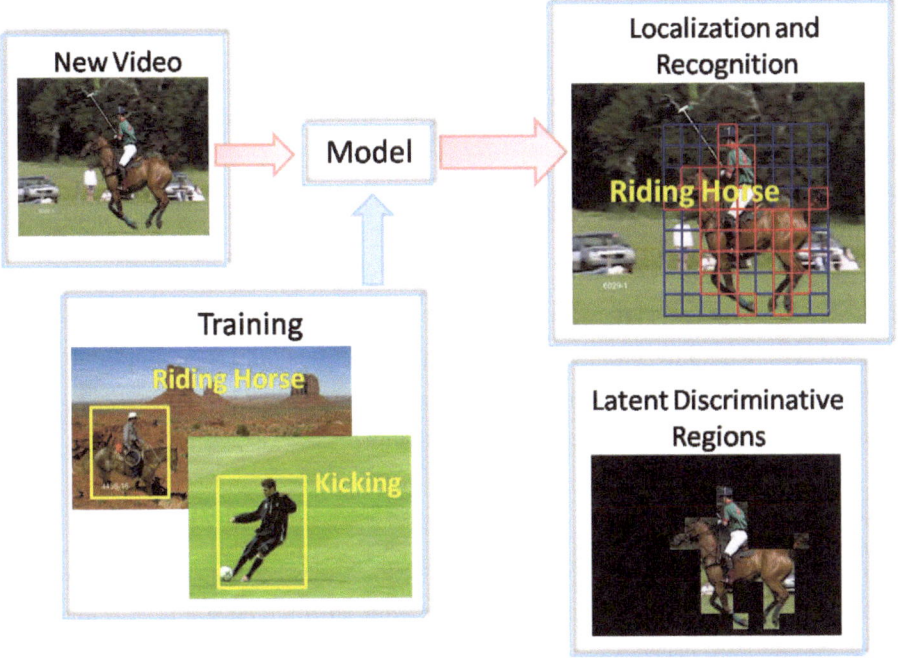

Fig. 3.11: An approach for action localization and understanding. (Image Courtesy: G. Mori, SFU [113]).

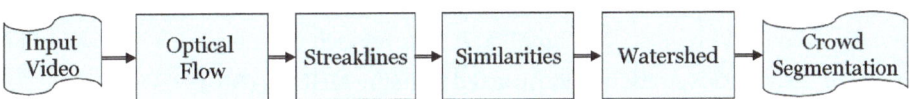

Fig. 3.12: An approach for crowd segmentation by exploiting optical flow and streaklines. (Image Courtesy: R. Mehran).

using the Emotion Evoking Game and a high-speed video camera. Wang and Marsella [629] introduce a dungeon role playing game intended to induce emotions such as boredom, surprise, joy, anger and disappointment. From their preliminary study, facial expressions indicating boredom and anger are observed. Individual differences are found on appraisal and facial expression of surprise, joy and disappointment.

In another work by [634], the role of emotions and expressive behavior in socially interactive characters are employed in educational games by using a social robot and us-

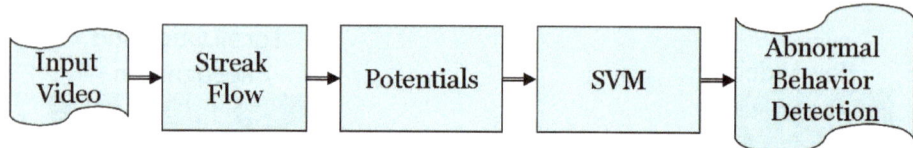

Fig. 3.13: An approach for abnormal behavior detection by exploiting streaklines. (Image Courtesy: R. Mehran).

ing chess as the game scenario. It is found that the emotional behavior embedded in the character helped the users to have a better perception of the game. Kim *et al.* [625] present a game-based simulation and tutoring-system to provide students with an environment to practice preparing for and conducting bilateral negotiations.

3.7.2 Interactive Arts

By using the motion history image (MHI), some interactive systems are developed [449, 454, 455, 635]. Bobick *et al.* [449] develop an interactive and narrative play space for children, called KidsRoom by using the MHI method. The KidsRoom is a perceptually-based environment in which children could interact with monsters while playing in a story-telling scenario. Davis *et al.* [455] develop a virtual aerobics trainer that watches and responds to the user as he/she performs the workout. Nguyen *et al.* [635] introduce the concept of a motion swarm, a swarm of particles that moves in response to the field representing an MHI. It is developed for interactive arts. Another interactive art demonstration is constructed from the MHI by [454].

3.7.3 Anatomically-based Talking Head

Albrecht *et al.* [631] present an algorithm for generating facial expressions for a continuum of pure and mixed emotions of varying intensity. Based on the observation that in natural interaction among humans, shades of emotion are much more frequently encountered than expressions of basic emotions, a method to generate more than Ekman's six basic emotions [632] is required. They present a flexible approach to generate non-basic, mixed emotional states in the facial expressions of an anatomically-based talking head.

3.8 Action Segmentation

An activity can be segmented into several action units or atomic actions by several methods. By these segmentation or separation into atomic actions, we can understand and analyze various continuous activities. Therefore, this kind of research areas are very important for various applications. Gesture analysis, understanding sign language and human behavior analysis from continuous action scenes are areas under the belt of this section. We present several important methods related to this action segmentation [305–310, 313–320, 461–463, 483, 484].

3.8.1 *Gestures*

For temporal motion segmentation approach, Kahol *et al.* [461, 462] focus on developing a gesture segmentation system based on HMM states. This hierarchical activity segmentation method analyzes complex motion sequences (e.g., dances) by segmenting them into shorter motion sequences, which they called *gestures*. This algorithm employs a dynamic hierarchical layered structure to represent the human anatomy, and uses low-level motion parameters to characterize motion in the various layers of this hierarchy, which correspond to different segments of the human body. Prior to their work, Adam Kendon shows that human beings initially segment a gesture, and then recognize or tag it — a process analogous to segmentation of spoken words from a continuous stream of audio, and then recognition of the segmented word by a neuro-audio system in humans [463].

Yuan *et al.* [477] present a method for detecting motion regions in video sequences observed by a moving camera, in the presence of strong parallax due to static 3D structures. In another approach, Peker *et al.* [315] segment video, based on the connections between (i) certain low-level and computationally simple features; and (ii) high-level, semantically meaningful features.

3.8.2 *Basic Motion*

Osaki *et al.* [320] propose a method to divide all the motion data into segmental motions *based on breaking points*. After segmentation, all the data is classified into clusters, called *basic motion* using nearest neighbor method. In some cases, gestures are considered as elementary action units and used for recognition and action analysis. However, it is very difficult to enumerate all possible gestures and hence it is difficult to consider it as elemental units [319]. However, application-specific systems can perform well with several combinations of action units or gesture units.

3.8.3 Fundamental Gesture

Ihara *et al.* [318] propose a gesture-description model based on synthesizing fundamental gestures. They develop a gesture semantics database based on *fundamental gestures*, which are defined on some set of meaningful actions.

3.8.4 Motion Alphabet

Wang *et al.* [317] present an approach for automatically segmenting sequences of natural activities into atomic sections and clustering them. Like words are extract from long sentences, they extracted primitive gestures from sequences of human motion and clustered using the HMM. The segmentation is overly fine and can be considered as finding the *alphabet of motion* [317]. However, this approach is suitable for structured human motion where every gesture is repeated many times.

3.8.5 Atomic Movement

Vitaladevuni *et al.* [316] present a Bayesian framework for action recognition based on psycho-kinesiological observations. The framework leads to an efficient and robust algorithm for temporally segmenting videos into atomic movements. Kadone and Nakamura [314] propose methods for motion patterns of humanoid robots observed as a continuous flow using pattern correlations and associative memory. Initially, patterns are segmented by pattern correlations and then stored into the associative memory.

3.8.6 Direction-based Basic Motion

Another motion segmentation approach is proposed based on motion history templates [434], by using gradient-based optical flow [483, 484]. It can parse continuous motion sequences (i.e., complex motion) into basic movements or shorter motion sequences, based on four directions (e.g., left, right, up and down motion) motion history images. This process is different and simpler than Labanotation or Benesh movement notation [312], though it requires some empirical parameters as threshold values.

3.8.7 Distinct Behaviors

Barbic *et al.* [313] propose three approaches for segmentation where they segment *behaviors* into *distinct behaviors* (e.g., running, walking, etc.). These approaches segment human motion automatically based on statistical properties of the motion. Their first approach chooses segments using an indication of intrinsic dimensionality from Principal Component Analysis (PCA), the second approach creates segments using a probabilistic model of motion obtained from Probabilistic PCA, and the third approach generates segments based on a Gaussian mixture model representation.

3.8.8 Motion Patterns based on Symbols

Mimesis models based on HMMs are proposed for humanoid robot [305]. This model abstracts the whole-body motions as symbols, generates motion patterns from the symbols, and distinguishes motion patterns based on the *symbols*. Takano and Nakamura [306, 307] exploit this Mimesis model in its automatic motion segmentation method.

3.8.9 Basic Movement Transition Graph

Kim *et al.* [308] propose a novel scheme based on the *basic movement transition graph* for extracting motion beats from given rhythmic motion data. Given a rhythmic sound signal, such as, music together with the direction and speed to move, this scheme can generate a new rhythmic motion on-the-fly. Based on this scheme, Shiratori *et al.* [309] develop a method that can automatically detect the musical rhythm and segment the original motion, and classify them to the primitive motions. Arikan *et al.* [310] present a framework that allows a user to synthesize human motion while retaining control of its qualitative properties, by using some chosen vocabulary and dynamic programming.

3.9 Gait Analysis

Gait recognition is very crucial due to various different applications in computer vision arena. The term gait recognition is typically used to signify the identification of individuals in image sequences *by the way they walk* [422]. Human gait or the bipedal locomotion (e.g., walking, running, limping, etc.) provides a great amount of information, which are useful for various applications, e.g., biomechanics, sports analysis, security surveillance, robotics, psychology, gender recognition, etc. to name a few [422, 423]. Marker-less gait analysis is more important to have less constraint environment for gait analysis.

Usually, running, jogging and walking motions; or running and walking motions only are considered in gait recognition (because jogging could be easily understood as slow running or very fast walking in most of the cases [424, 443]).

Various methods are presented on gait analysis in [642]. References [359–363, 422–427, 429–432, 529, 550–552] present different approaches for gait analysis. Fihl and Moeslund [423] present a good summary on recent gait analysis.

Ben-Arie et al. [427] present a motion-based, correspondence-free technique for human gait recognition in monocular video. The PCA is used to reduce the dimensionality of the plots, and then uses the k-nearest neighbor rule in this reduced space to classify an unknown person. This method is robust to tracking and segmentation errors, to variation in clothing and background, and also invariant to small changes in camera viewpoint and walking speed. The method is tested on outdoor sequences, and achieves a classification rate of 77%. It is also tested on indoor sequences of 7 people walking on a treadmill, taken from 8 different viewpoints. The classification rate of 78% is obtained for near-front-parallel views and 65% for over all views.

Wang et al. [429] recognize gait where for each image sequence, a background subtraction algorithm and a simple correspondence procedure are first used to segment and track the moving silhouettes of a walking figure. Then, eigenspace is applied. Liu and Sarkar [430] explore the possibility of using both face and gait in enhancing human recognition at a distance in outdoor conditions and achieve enhanced performance by the combination of face and gait. Another system for gait recognition is based on the matching of linearly time-normalized gait walking cycles [431]. They propose a novel feature extraction process for the transformation of human silhouettes into low-dimensional feature vectors consisting of average pixel distances from the center of the silhouette.

Lee and Grimson [425] present a simple representation of human gait appearance based on moments computed from the silhouette of the walking person for the purpose of person identification and gender classification. Another automatic gait-based person identification as well as gender classification system is proposed in [432] that uses masking functions to measure area a dynamic temporal signal from a sequence of silhouettes of a walking subject. This signal is used a signature for automatic gait recognition.

Currently, most of the modeling and analysis of gait recognition performance by observation conditions are focused on two key points [359],

- Observation view and
- Distance between the subjects and the camera (i.e., resolution).

Regarding the observation view, Yu *et al.* [360] model the relationship between the performance and the view angle on appearance-based gait recognition. Makihara *et al.* [361] analyze reference views' effect on the performance for View Transformation Model (VTM). Wang *et al.* [362] propose a multi-view fusion algorithm based on the Dempster-Shafer rule, and analyze the performance in terms of the pair of different observation views. Sugiura *et al.* [363] use an omni-directional camera to capture multi-view gait images form a single sequence, and report that the performance increased as the number of observation views increased. As for the distance between the subjects and the camera (resolution), the performance decreases as the resolution decreases [364, 365].

3.10 Action Recognition in Low-resolution

3.10.1 *Application Areas*

Video surveillance, activity analysis, motion recognition, etc., are very crucial applications in computer vision. The demand and usage of CCTV is increasing for surveillance and hence low-resolution video analysis is crucial. However, low-resolution image simply consists of a small amount of pixels, causing the image to be jaggy. However, low-resolution video processing, motion analysis and recognition are very difficult due to the loss of significant motion information due to the presence of less number of pixels. For example, various techniques are developed for recognition of objects in photographs, but they often fail when applied to recognition of the same objects in video. A critical example of such a situation is seen in face recognition, where many technologies are already intensively used for passport verification and where there is no technology that can reliably identify a person from a surveillance video. The reason for this is that video provides images of much lower quality and resolution than that of photographs [612].

For video surveillance and other related purposes, we need to analyze and recognize actions from poor-quality and low-resolution video. VIRAT dataset [66] and University of Texas's Aerial Dataset (http://cvrc.ece.utexas.edu/SDHA2010/Aerial_View_ Activity.html) have very low pixel height for the objects of interest (more details on these are in Chapter 6). Therefore, these are difficult to process.

3.10.2 *Related Works on Low-Resolution Video Processing*

Most of the works in human tracking and activity recognition are only appropriate for 'near field' with higher resolution frames. Even the MHI method [434] and its variants require reasonably high-resolution video. Usually, detection of pedestrians is very difficult in surveillance applications, where the resolution of the images is low (e.g., there may only be 100-200 pixels on the target) [545]. In various image and video processing, low-resolution processing is a demanding task in computer vision, and image processing arena (e.g., biometrics identification [613], range image sequence analysis in roads for safety [614], document analysis, face recognition [615], sports analysis [616], etc.). There is not much development in low-resolution video analysis and action recognitions, though some researches related to document analysis [617, 618], license plate recognition [619], automatic detection and tracking of human hands [620], etc. in low-resolution are available in the computer vision community.

A neuro-associative approach for recognition, which can both learn and identify an object from low-resolution low-quality video sequences is introduced by Gorodnichy [612]. This approach is derived from a mathematical model of biological visual memory, in which correlation-based projection learning is used to memorize a face from a video sequence and attractor-based association is performed to recognize a face over several video frames. In many sports, natural daily views or surveillance, the camera covers a large part of the sports arena or scene, so that the resolution of the person's region is low. This makes the determination of the player's gestures and actions a challenging task, especially if there is a large camera motion. To overcome these problems, Roh *et al.* [615, 621] propose a method based on curvature scale space (CSS) templates of the player's silhouette in low-resolution. Their proposed spotting method provides probabilistic similarity and is robust to noisy sequences of data [621].

Jun *et al.* [622] propose a new method of extracting four directional features for character recognition at low-resolution. The characteristic of their method is to use dynamic scenes. This is achieved by using images shifted by half a pixel in the low resolution. The recognition results show effectiveness at low resolution. Another approach employs a new laser-based camera that produces reliable low-resolution depth images at video rates, to decompose and recognize hand poses. For low-resolution face recognition, Lee *et al.* [616] propose a new method of extending the Support Vector Data Description learning methods for the one-class problem.

Efros *et al.* [435] recognize human actions at a distance, at resolutions where a whole person may be, say, 30 pixels tall. They introduce a motion descriptor based on optical flow measurements in a spatio-temporal volume for each stabilized human figure, and an associated similarity measure to be used in a nearest-neighbor framework. A pedestrian detection system that integrates image intensity information with motion information at very small scale is developed by [545]. They employ a detection style algorithm that scans a detector over two consecutive frames of a video sequence. The detector is trained using AdaBoost to take advantage of both motion and appearance information to detect a walking person. It detects pedestrians at very small scales (as small as 20 × 15 pixels). Cutler and Davis [623] develop a system that works directly on images, which can be of low resolution and poor quality.

3.11 Discussion

A crucial issue in motion representation is what features should be used to facilitate subsequent operations such as abnormality detection and behavior recognition. To this end, global motion information and shape information seem rather insufficient. In order to discriminate behaviors with local motion differences, local motion information should also be considered. In addition, motion duration, i.e., temporal information, is also quite helpful for discriminating similar behaviors with different speeds. Hence, a good representation should include —

- Global motion,
- Local motion,
- Motion duration,
- Shape information,

— from which more discriminative features could be extracted for further motion analysis. It seems possible to get such a representation by processing point-wise motion status of the foreground pixels, which are extracted by performing point-wise correspondences between consecutive frames. However in most cases, it is difficult to perform the point-wise correspondences due to the fact that non-rigid objects may be deformed and that the existing matching algorithms are mostly suitable for sparse corner points [558] or other key-points [559].

Although the classical optical flow methods including the Lucas-Kanade method [560] try to find the point-wise correspondences, they usually cannot deal with large motion (a rapid move across frames). In addition, when the point-wise correspondences of the foreground pixels are obtained, if they are used directly as a motion representation, such a representation could not have provided more representative information as shown in the experiments.

Dong *et al.* [561] propose a novel representation called point-wise motion image (PMI), which is a color image in the HSV color space, where the color components of each pixel represent the point-wise motion speed, point-wise motion orientation and point-wise motion duration respectively.

3.11.1 *Salient Region and Its Associated Salient Region Construction*

Kadir and Brady [226] apply an information-theoretic criterion to define salient regions for image registration and object recognition. In their works, salient regions centered at each foreground pixel are identified, and only a small number of them reveal some good discriminative ability, while the majority of them are not quite useful for extracting discriminative features. Dong *et al.* [561] define and detect both a new salient region for each foreground pixel in the current video frame and its associated salient region at the same position in the preceding video frame. The considered pixels are only from the foreground, so the motion information is contained in such constructed salient regions and associated regions.

3.11.2 Biologically-inspired Visual Representations

Cox and Pinto [562] use two basic classes of biologically-inspired visual representations. We know that area V1 is the first stage of cortical processing of visual information in the primate and is the gateway of subsequent processing stages [563].

- As a control, they use V1-like, a one-layer model characterized by a cascade of linear and nonlinear processing steps and designed to encapsulate some of the known properties of the first cortical processing stage in the primate brain. Their V1-like implementation is considered without any modification from their earlier works in [563, 564].
- They use two and three layer models following the basic multi-layer model scheme in [565]. These models consist of multiple stacked layers of linear/nonlinear processing stages, similar to those in the V1-like model.

3.12 Conclusion

Human motion analysis is a challenging problem due to large variations in human motion and appearance, camera viewpoint and environment settings [499]. The field of action and activity representation and recognition is relatively old, yet not well-understood [500]. Some important but common motion recognition problems are even now unsolved properly by the computer vision community. However, in the last decade, a number of good approaches are proposed and evaluated subsequently by many researchers. Among those methods, few methods show promising results with significant attentions by other researchers. We hope that more robust and smart methods will be developed and lead the computer vision field.

3.13 Think Ahead!

(1) Make a list of different approaches for action recognition that are suitable for outdoor applications.
(2) What are the key barriers for action recognition in real-life situations?
(3) What are the major challenges ahead in gait analysis?
(4) How can we solve occlusion problems?
(5) To start with, what kind of challenges of action recognition should we ponder about?

(6) What are the possible future application areas for action recognition? (consider 5 years goal and 10 years goal — separately and list up your points)
(7) How can we integrate multi-modal issues in action recognition field and what are the major challenges?
(8) Classify action recognition methods based on various parameters.
(9) What are challenges of pose-based body-parts segmentation in action recognition and analysis?
(10) Write a review on the existing *survey/review papers* on action recognition.

Chapter 4

MHI – A Global-based Generic Approach

4.1 Motion History Image (MHI)

The Motion History Image (MHI) approach is a view-based temporal template approach, which is simple but robust in representing movements and is widely employed by various research groups for action recognition, motion analysis and other related applications. In this paper, we overview the Motion History Image (MHI)-based human motion recognition techniques and applications. Since the inception of the Motion History Image template for motion representation, various approaches have been adopted to improve this basic MHI technique. Ahad *et al.* [641] survey the MHI and its variants.

As we have pointed in earlier chapters, action recognition approaches can be categorized into one of the three groups [447, 509],

- Template matching approaches (Figure 4.1)
- State-space approaches
- Semantic description of human behaviors

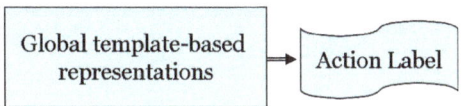

Fig. 4.1: Template-based recognition.

The MHI method is a template matching approach. Approaches based on template matching first converts an image sequence into a static shape pattern (e.g., the Motion

History Image (MHI), the Motion Energy Image (MEI) [434]), and then compares it to pre-stored action prototypes during recognition [509]. Template matching approaches are easy to implement and require less computational load, although they are more prone to noise and more susceptible to the variations of the time interval of the movements. The MHI is a view-based or appearance-based template-matching approach. Appearance-based motion recognition is one of the most practical recognition methods that can recognize the gesture without any incorporation of sensors on the human body or its neighborhoods.

This chapter points some areas for further research based on the MHI method and its variants. Figure 4.2 shows the system flow of the basic MHI approach for motion classification and recognition.

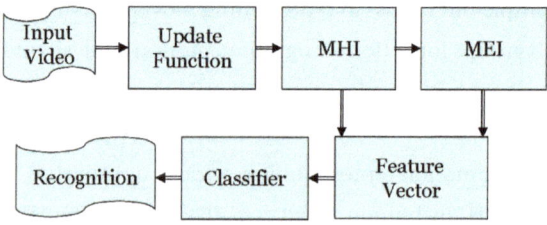

Fig. 4.2: Applications of the MHI and its variants. Related to activity analysis.

4.2 Why MHI?

There are excellent surveys on human motion recognition and analysis [436, 447, 448, 452, 481, 488–507, 641]. These papers cover many detailed approaches along with the Motion History Image (MHI) method [434] as one of the dominant approaches for action representation.

In the MHI, the silhouette sequence is condensed into gray scale images, while dominant motion information is preserved. Therefore, it can represent motion sequence in a compact manner. This MHI template is also not so sensitive to silhouette noises, like holes, shadows, and missing parts. These advantages make these templates as a suitable candidate for motion and gait analysis [272]. It keeps a history of temporal changes at each pixel location, which then decays over time [273]. The MHI expresses the motion flow or sequence by using the intensity of every pixel in temporal manner. The motion history recognizes general patterns of movement, thus it can be implemented with cheap cameras and CPUs having low specification [311]. It can also be implemented in low light areas where structure can not be easily detected.

One of the advantages of the MHI representation is that a range of times may be encoded in a single frame, and in this way, the MHI spans the time scale of human gestures [311]. Another benefit of using the gray-scale MHI is that it is sensitive to the direction of motion, unlike the MEIs; and hence the MHI is better-suited for discriminating between actions of opposite directions (e.g., sitting down versus standing up) [274].

4.3 Various Aspects of the MHI — A Tutorial

In this section, we present a tutorial of the Motion History Image method.

4.3.1 *Formation of an MHI Image*

The Motion *History* Image (MHI) is first proposed as a representation of a video action. Intensity of each pixel in the MHI is a function of motion density at that location. Usually, the MHI is generated from a binarized image, obtained from frame subtraction [474], using a threshold ξ:

$$\psi(x, y, t) = \begin{cases} 1 & \text{if } D(x, y, t) \geq \xi, \\ 0 & \text{otherwise}, \end{cases} \quad (4.1)$$

where, $D(x, y, t)$ is defined with difference distance Δ as:

$$D(x, y, t) = |I(x, y, t) - I(x, y, t \pm \Delta)|. \quad (4.2)$$

Here, $I(x, y, t)$ is the intensity value of pixel location with coordinate (x, y) at the tth frame of the image sequence. The MHI $H_\tau(x, y, t)$ can be computed from update function $\psi(x, y, t)$:

$$H_\tau(x, y, t) = \begin{cases} \tau & \text{if } \psi = 1, \\ \max(0, H_\tau(x, y, t-1) - \delta) & \text{otherwise}, \end{cases} \quad (4.3)$$

where,
x, y represent pixel position;

t is time;

$\psi(x, y, t)$ signals object presence (or motion) in the current video image $I(x, y, t)$;

τ decides the temporal duration of MHI;

δ is decay parameter.

This update function $\psi(x, y, t)$ is called for every new video frame analyzed in the sequence. The result of this computation is a scalar-valued image where more recently moving pixels are brighter and vice-versa [424, 434].

A final MHI image records the temporal history of motion in it. We can get the final MHI template as $H_\tau(x, y, t)$.

4.3.2 *Motion Energy Image (MEI)*

The Motion *Energy* Image (MEI) describes where there is motion (the spatial pattern) in a moving scene. References [274, 434] present the construction of a binary Motion Energy Image (MEI) or Binary Motion Region (BMR) [275] that represents *where motion has occurred* in an image sequence. The MEI describes the motion-shape and spatial distribution of a motion.

The cumulative binary MEI image can describe where a motion is in the video sequence, computed from the start frame to the final frame. The moving object's sequence sweeps out a particular region of the image and the shape of that region (where there is motion instead of *how* as in the MHI concept) can be used to suggest the movement occurring region [276]. As $\psi(x, y, t)$ represents binary image sequence indicating regions of motion, a binary MEI $E_\tau(x, y, t)$ is achieved by,

$$E_\tau(x, y, t) = \bigcup_{i=1}^{\tau-1} D(x, y, t-i). \tag{4.4}$$

The MEI can also be generated from the MHI. Therefore, when we need to have the MEI image, we just need to take the binarized version of the MEI of that moment. The MEI is achieved by thresholding an MHI image above zero, as per the following equation,

$$E_\tau(x, y, t) = \begin{cases} 1 & \text{if } H_\tau(x, y, t) \geq 1, \\ 0 & \text{otherwise.} \end{cases} \tag{4.5}$$

In many cases, we need both the MHI and the MEI images for representing motion. Both of them cover important motion information that can be exploited further for various purposes. The two images together provide better discrimination than each of them

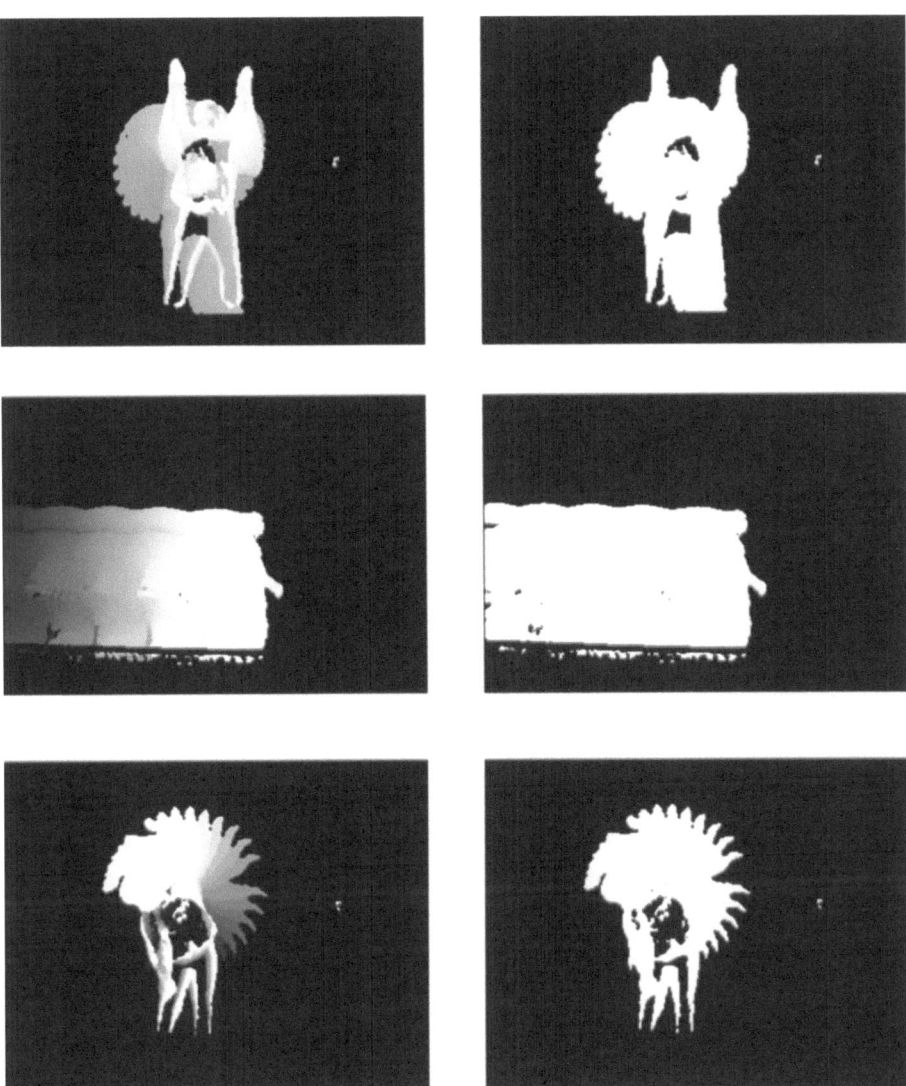

Fig. 4.3: Applications of the MHI and its variants. Related to interactive applications.

separately [434]. The MEI and the MHI templates are two components of temporal template, where each component of each pixel is a function of the motion at that pixel position [434]. Incorporation of both the MHI and the MEI templates constitute the basic MHI method. Figure 4.3 shows some MHI and MEI images.

4.3.3 Parameter — τ

In computing the MHI, the parameter τ decides the temporal duration of the MHI. It is a very important parameter and a proper usage of τ can produce better action representation. As per [641], Figure 4.4 shows the dependence on τ while producing the MHI. The τ is the maximum possible value that a pixel can have. Therefore, if δ is small and τ is small, then there is high chance to miss the initial movement of an action (especially, if the action has a long duration). Figure 4.4 shows an action of hand-waving in upper direction, and different MHIs with different values for τ. If the τ value is smaller than the number of frames, then we may lose prior information of the action in its MHI. On the other hand, if the temporal duration value is set at very high value compared to the number of frames (e.g., 250 in this case for an action with less number of frames), then the changes of pixel values in the MHI template is less significant. Usually, for a gray-scale MHI image, one can use 255 as a value for τ. In some cases, one may use the total no. of frames. However, sometimes normalization can be done after having the MHIs for different actions.

4.3.4 Parameter — δ

The decay parameter (δ) subtracts the pixel value from its prior value at time $t-1$, if there is no moving information at that time t on that specific pixel value. Actually, through this manner, the decay parameter consumes the *history* of motion information in the final MHI template. Therefore, this parameter can play an important role while forming an MHI image. Usually, $\delta = 1$ in the basic MHI method. Ahad *et al.* [641] introduce this parameter in more specific manner.

The value of this parameter can be chosen empirically, based on a dataset. Figure 4.5 shows the importance of the decay parameter. The Figure shows final MHI images for an action with different δ values (i.e., 1, 5 and 10). It is noticeable that for the higher values of δ, more missing information of prior motion sequence.

4.3.5 Temporal Duration vs. Decay Parameter

The values of τ and δ combine to determine how long it takes for a motion to decay to 0. Therefore, both of these parameters determine the temporal window size of the MHI. However, different settings can lead to the same temporal window (e.g., $\tau = 10$ and

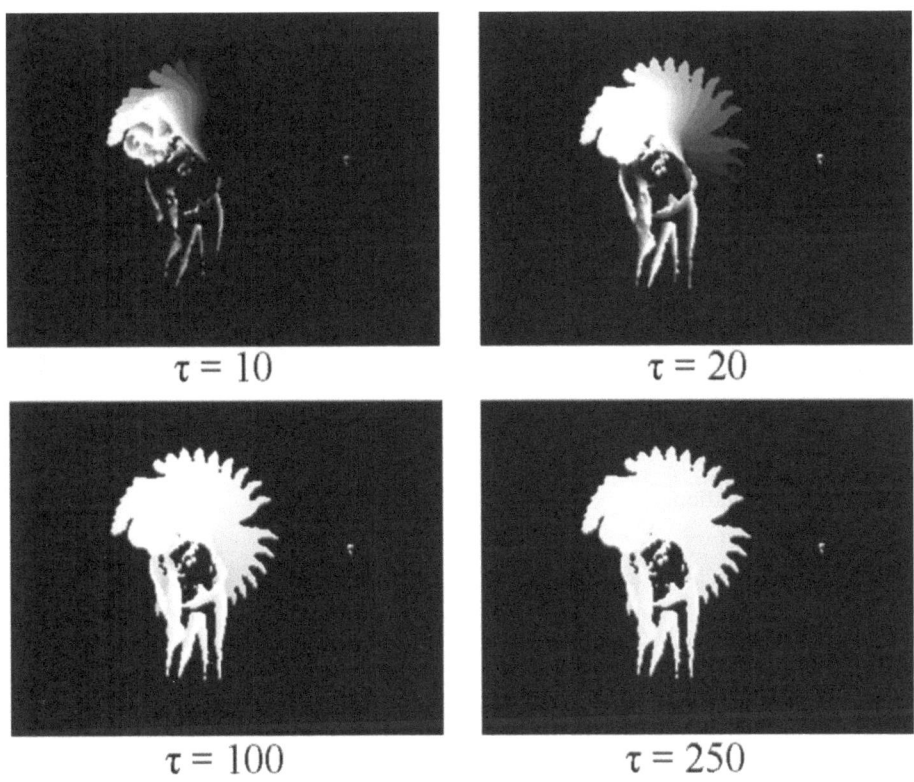

Fig. 4.4: Different *tau* values and the corresponding MHI images for an action.

$\delta = 1$ leads to the same temporal window as $\tau = 100$ and $\delta = 10$) [641]. The joint effect of τ and δ is to determine how many levels of quantization the MHI will have, thus the combination of a large τ and a small δ gives a slowly-changing continuous gradient, whereas a large τ and large δ provides a more step-like, discrete quantization of motion. This provides us an insight into not only what parameters and design choices one has, but what is the impact of choosing different parameters or designs [641].

4.3.6 Update Function $\psi(x, y, t)$

We know that many vision-based human motion analysis systems start with human detection [509]. This goes with the MHI as well. The computation of update function is the key for appropriate motion segmentation. Some possible image processing techniques for defining this update function $\psi(x, y, t)$ can be,

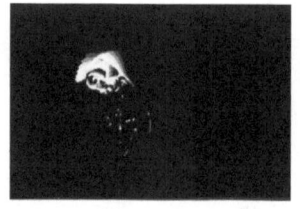

delta = 1 delta = 5 delta = 10

Fig. 4.5: Delta dependency.

- Background subtraction,
- Frame differencing,
- Optical flow,
- Edge accumulation,
- Intensity,
- Flesh color,

4.3.6.1 *Background Subtraction*

Based on the static or dynamic background, the performance and method for background subtraction vary. For static background (i.e., with no background motion), it is trivial to do background subtraction (as described in Chapter 2). Few dominant methods are enlisted in [277–286]. Some of these methods employ various statistical approaches, adaptive background models (e.g., [279, 282]) and incorporation of other features (e.g., color and gradient information in [283]) with adaptive model, in order to negotiate dynamic background or other complex issues related to background subtraction. For the MHI generation, background subtraction is employed initially by [274, 434].

4.3.6.2 *Frame to Frame Difference*

Frame to frame subtracting or differencing methods are widely used for motion segmentation too. Some well-known approaches are: [287–292]. These can be split into —

- Temporal differencing methods between two consecutive frames, e.g., [287–290];
- Temporal differencing methods between three consecutive frames, e.g., [291, 292].

One key concern is the usage of a smart threshold for differencing. Otherwise, there is a possibility to miss out important minor moving information or, it may generate holes or gaps inside the moving object.

4.3.6.3 Optic Flow

As mentioned in Chapter 2, optical flow methods [293–301, 560] are one of the very well-known methods for motion segmentation from a moving scene. Therefore, optical flow can be used for the generation of the MHI. Ahad *et al.* [484] employ optical flow for motion segmentation to extract the moving object.

4.3.6.4 Outlier Removal

Optical flows are noisy and outliers may hinder from better representations. Therefore, some approaches are proposed for outlier removal, e.g.,

- RANdom Sample Consensus (RANSAC) [92]
- Preemptive RANSAC [25]
- PROgressive SAmple Consensus (PROSAC) [24]

RANSAC (RANdom Sample Consensus) method [92] is the most well-known method for this purpose and it is useful in different applications. There are variants at the top of RANSAC to deal with cases when the number of measurements is quite large. When the number of measurements are very large, the Preemptive RANSAC [25] and PROgressive SAmple Consensus (PROSAC) [24] significantly speed up its performance compare to RANSAC. The Progressive Sample Consensus approach exploits the linear ordering defined on the set of correspondences by a similarity function used in establishing tentative correspondences. Therefore, a proper approach is crucial based on the dataset or environment, especially for outdoor environment.

4.3.7 Feature Vector for the MHI

From the MHI and the MEI templates, we compute feature vector for recognition purpose. There are various approaches for computing feature vector from the templates. The MHI method in its basic form [434] employs the seven Hu [438] invariants. Afterwards, different researchers exploit different methods, even though Hu moments are used by many groups. Hu moments are widely used for shape representation [275, 302–304, 311, 434, 454, 468, 484, 485]. Though Hu invariants are widely employed for the MHI or related methods, other approaches (e.g., Zernike moments [256, 304], global geometric shape descriptors [304], Fourier transform [316]) are also utilized for creating feature vectors. Several researchers [256–258, 304, 468] employ the PCA to reduce the dimensions of the feature vectors. Various approaches [255, 438, 464, 478] for feature vector analysis is covered in Chapter 5.

4.3.7.1 Classification

As per the system flow diagram of the MHI method, once we have the feature vectors for each action class, we can go for classification to recognize any unknown action. For classification, various approaches are explored in the MHI approaches, e.g.,

- Support Vector Machine (SVM) [256, 259–262, 304]
- K-nearest neighbor (KNN) [263–265, 468, 472, 480, 484]
- Multi-class nearest neighbor [256, 266]
- Mahalanobis distance [275, 311, 434]
- Maximum Likelihood (ML).

4.4 Constraints of the MHI Method

The MHI method is simple to implement and it performs well in constrained situations [641]. However, it has few basic constraints that hinder the MHI method to be implemented in different situations. We explain these here. Most of these problems are solved by some additional development and these developments are presented in later sections of this chapter.

4.4.1 Self-occlusion Problem

The MHI method usually fails to separate the motion information when there is motion *self-occlusion* or *overwriting* [259–262, 264, 269, 270, 472, 484]. A simple example can explain this problem. In this problem, if an action (e.g., sit and then stand) has opposite directions in its atomic actions, then the previous motion information (e.g., sitting down) is deleted or overwritten by the latter motion information (e.g., standing). Therefore, if a person sits down, and then stands up, the final MHI image should contain brighter pixels in the upper part of the image to represent the stand-up motion only. It can not vividly distinguish the direction of the motion. This *self*-occlusion of the moving object or person overwrites the prior information.

4.4.2 Failure in Dynamic Background

It can not produce good MHI template in scenes where the backgrounds are dynamic [268]. However, by employing approaches that can segment motion information from dynamic background, the MHI method can be useful in dynamic scenes as well.

4.4.3 Improper Implementation of the Update Function

In the presence of occlusions of the body, or improper implementation of the update function, the MHI fails to cover most of the motion regions. These cause recognition failures [434]. A more sophisticated motion detection algorithm would increase its robustness [434].

4.4.4 Label-based Recognition

The MHI method is limited to label-based (token) recognition. Hence, it can not produce any information other than specific identity matches (e.g., it could not report that *upward* motion was occurring at a particular image location) [265, 453, 455]. This is due to the fact that the holistic generation (and matching) of the moment features are computed from the entire template [453].

4.4.5 Failure with Motion Irregularities

The MHI representation fails to capture information about irregularities in motion [270].

4.4.6 Failure to Differentiate Similar Motions

This method requires to have stationary objects, and it can not significantly distinguish among similar actions [302] (e.g., running, jogging and walking are different actions, but the MHI may not isolate running between jogging; jogging between walking in many cases).

4.4.7 Not View-invariant Method

The MHI method is appearance-based and view-based method. Therefore, its multi-camera arrangements may be a question to have view-invariant performance from the MHI method without any modifications. However, there are possibilities that by employing several cameras from different directions and by combining moment features from these directions, action recognition can be achieved. One common problem of any multi-camera system that due to some similar representations for different actions (but from different camera-views), the MHI method may not produce good recognition for an action.

4.4.8 Problem with Varied Motion Duration

Similar to many other template matching approaches, the MHI method is sensitive to the variance of movement duration [501]. However, state space approaches may solve this problem by defining each static posture as a state, though it incorporates other problems.

4.4.9 Non-trajectory Nature

The MHI method has no information about the trajectory of the motion path, even though the intensity concentrated regions can direct some trajectory information [219]. Though this seems a good point — realistically, this non-trajectory nature of it can be a problem for cases where tracking could be necessary to analyze a moving car or a person. However, the MHI representation is being exploited with tracking information for some applications (e.g., by [302]).

4.5 Developments on the MHI

In this Section, the MHI-based approaches are presented.

4.5.1 Direct Implementation of the MHI

The MHI method is employed directly (without any modification from the basic MHI [434]) by different researchers.

Shan *et al.* [268] employ the MHI for hand gesture recognition considering the trajectories of the motion. They employ the Mean Shift Embedded Particle Filter, which enables a robot to robustly track natural hand motion in real-time. Then, an MHI for hand gesture is created based on the hand tracking results. In this manner, spatial trajectories are retained in a static image, and the trajectories are called Temporal Template-Based Trajectories (TTBT). Hand gestures are recognized based on statistical shape and orientation analysis of TTBT.

Meng *et al.* [235] develop a simple system based on the SVM classifier and the MHI representations, which is implemented on a reconfigurable embedded computer vision architecture for real-time gesture recognition. In another work by Vafadar and Behrad [236], the MHI is employed for gesture recognition for interaction with handicapped people. After constructing the MHI for each gesture, motion orientation histogram vector is extracted for hand gesture recognition.

A system is trained using different subjects performing a set of examples of every action to be recognized [302, 468]. Given these samples, k-nearest neighbor, Gaussian, and Gaussian mixture classifiers are used to recognize new actions. Experiments are conducted using instances of eight human actions performed by seven different subjects and good recognition results are achieved. Rosales and Sclaroff [302] propose a trajectory-guided recognition method. It tracks an action by employing Extended Kalman Filter and then uses the MHI for action recognition via a mixture of Gaussian classifier.

Action characteristics by MHIs for some hand gesture recognition and four different actions (i.e., jumping, squatting, limping and walking) are modeled by [234]. They introduce discriminative actions, which describe the usefulness of the fundamental units in distinguishing between events.

A suspicious person in a restricted parking-lot environment is analyzed by [271]. It displays erratic pattern in the walking trajectories, where the trajectory information is collected and its MHI (based on profiles of changes in velocity and in acceleration) is computed. T. Jan [271] profiles the highest, average and median MHI values for each individual on the scene.

The MHI is used in visual speech recognition experiments. [474, 475] decompose MHIs into wavelet sub-images using Stationary Wavelet Transform (SWT). The MHI demonstrate its ability to remove static elements from the sequence of images and preserve the short duration complex mouth movement. The MHI is also invariant to the skin color of the speakers due to the difference of frame and image subtraction process involved in the generation of the MHI. The Stationary Wavelet Transform is used to denoise and to minimize the variations between the different MHIs of the same consonant.

A silhouette-based action modeling for recognition by [266] is modeled by employing the MHI directly as the input feature of the actions. Then these 2D templates are projected into a new subspace by means of the Kohonen Self Organizing feature Map (SOM) and actions are recognized by a Maximum Likelihood (ML) classifier.

Tan and Ishikawa [238] employ the MHI method and their proposed method to compare six different actions. Their results produce poor recognition rate with the MHI method. After analyzing the datasets, it seems that actions inside the dataset have motion overwriting and hence, it is understandable that the MHI method may have poor recognition rate for this type of dataset. Also, [259–262] and [484] compare the recognition performances of the MHI method with their HMHH and DMHI methods respectively.

The MHI is used to produce input images for the line fitter, which is a system for fitting lines to a video sequence that describe its motion [237]. It uses the MHI method for summarizing the motion depicted in video clips. However, it fails with rotational motion. Rotations are not encoded in the MHIs because the moving objects occupy the same pixel locations from frame to frame, and new information overwrites old information. Another failure example is that of curved motion. Obviously, the straight line model is inadequate here. In order to improve performance, a more flexible model is needed.

An adaptive camera navigation model is constructed for video surveillance by automatically learning locations of activity region of interest by [250]. It measures activity from the MHI at each view across the full viewable field of a PTZ camera. For each MHI blob of the scene, it determines whether the blob is a potential candidate for human activity. Using this iterative candidacy-classification-reduction process, it produces an activity map. In this activity map, brighter areas correspond to locations with more activity.

Higher-order Local Autocorrelation (HLAC) features are extracted from the MHIs for motion recognition [252]. These features are tested by using image sequences of pitching in the baseball games. They achieve good recognition results for their action datasets.

A Bayesian framework for recognizing actions through ballistic dynamics is proposed by [316]. This method temporally segments videos into its atomic movements. It enhances the performance of the MHI feature. This ballistic segmentation with the MHI improves the recognition rate.

4.5.2 Modified MHI

Few methods and applications are developed with slight modification of the MHI. Some of these methods consider the concept of the MHI and then explore to develop for various applications, e.g., action recognition, gait analysis, etc.

4.5.2.1 Gait Energy Image (GEI)

Gait Energy Image (GEI) is proposed by [239, 240] for gait analysis. The GEI is developed based on the MEI. As compared to the MEI and the MHI, the GEI targets specific normal human walking representation [240]. Given the preprocessed binary gait silhouette images at time t in a video sequence, the gray-level $GEI(x, y)$ is defined as,

$$GEI(x, y) = \frac{1}{N} \sum_{t=1}^{N} B_t(x, y). \tag{4.6}$$

where,
N is the number of frames in the complete cycle(s) of a silhouette sequence,
t is the frame number in the sequence (moment of time) [240].

The $GEI(x, y)$ becomes a time-normalized accumulative energy image of a human walking in the complete cycle(s). Though it performs very well for gait recognition, it seems from the construction of the equation that for human's activity recognition, this approach might not perform as smartly as the MHI method does.

Similarly, Zou and Bhanu [303] employ the GEI and Co-evolutionary Genetic Programming (CGP) for human activity classification. They extract Hu moments and normalize histogram bins from the original GEIs as input features. The CGP is employed to reduce the feature dimensionality and learn the classifiers. Bashir *et al.* [241, 242] and Yang *et al.* [243] implement the GEI directly for human identification with different feature analyzes.

4.5.2.2 Action Energy Image (AEI)

Action Energy Image (AEI) is proposed for activity classification by Chandrashekhar et al. [257]. They use eigen decomposition of an AEI in eigen activity space obtained by PCA, which best represents the AEI data in least-square sense. The AEIs are computed by averaging silhouettes. The MEI captures only *where* the motion occurred, but the AEI captures *where* and *how* much the motion occurred. The MEI carries less structural information since they are computed by accumulating motion images obtained by image differencing. On the other hand, the AEI incorporates the information about both structure and motion. They experiment with the AEI concept for walking and running motions and achieve good result.

4.5.2.3 Gait History Image (GHI)

Liu and Zheng [272] propose a method called Gait History Image (GHI) for gait representation and recognition. The $GHI(x, y)$ inherits the idea of the MHI, where the temporal information and the spatial information can be recorded in both cases. The $GHI(x, y)$ preserves the temporal information besides the spatial information. It overcomes the shortcoming of no temporal variation in the $GEI(x, y)$. However, each cycle only obtains one $GEI(x, y)$ or $GHI(x, y)$ template, which easily leads to the problem of insufficient training cycles [244].

4.5.2.4 Gait Moment Energy (GMI)

Gait Moment Energy (GMI) method is developed by Ma et al. [245] based on the $GEI(x, y)$. The $GMI(x, y)$ is the gait probability image at each key moment of all gait cycles. In this approach, the corresponding gait images at a key moment are averaged as the $GEI(x, y)$ of this key moment. They introduce Moment Deviation Image (MDI) by using silhouette images and the GMIs. As a good complement of the $GEI(x, y)$, the MDI provides more motion features than the $GEI(x, y)$. Both MDI and $GEI(x, y)$ are utilized to present a subject.

4.5.2.5 Dominant Energy Image (DEI)

It is not easy for the GMI to select key moments from cycles with different periods. Therefore, to compensate this problem, Chen et al. [244] propose a clustered-based $GEI(x, y)$ approach. In this case, the GEIs are computed from several clusters and the Dominant Energy Image (DEI) is obtained by denoising the averaged image of each cluster. The frieze and wavelet features are adopted and HMM is employed for recognition. This approach performs better (due to its clustered concept) than the $GEI(x,y)$, the $GHI(x,y)$ and the $GMI(x,y)$ representations, as it is superior when the silhouette has incompleteness or noise.

4.5.2.6 Average Motion Energy (AME)

Wang and Suter [553] directly convert an associated sequence of human silhouettes derived from videos into two types of computationally efficient representations. These are called — Average Motion Energy (AME) and Mean Motion Shape (MMS) — to characterize actions. These representations are used for activity recognition. The MMS is proposed based on shapes, not silhouettes.

The process of generating the AME is computationally inexpensive and can be employed in real-time applications [246]. This AME is computed exactly the similar manner of the computation of the GEI. The AME is exploited for action recognition, whereas the GEI method is used for gait recognition.

4.5.2.7 Motion Energy Histogram (MEH)

In calculating the AME, Wang and Suter [553] employ the Sum of Absolute Difference (SAD) for action recognition to obtain good recognition results. However, for large image size or database, the computation of SAD is inefficient and computationally expensive. This constraint is addressed by Yu *et al.* [246] who propose a histogram-based approach to efficiently compute the similarity among patterns. As an initial approach, an AME image is converted to the Motion Energy Histogram (MEH).

From a histogram point of view, the AME is regarded as a two-dimensional histogram whose bin value represents the frequency on position during time interval. A multi-resolution structure is adopted to construct the Multi-Resolution Motion Energy Histogram (MRMEH).

4.5.2.8 Superposed Motion Image (SMI)

Another method based on a modified-MHI is proposed, called a Superposed Motion Image (SMI) [247]. Using a multi-valued differential image ($f_i(x, y, t)$) to extract information about human posture, they propose a modified-MHI. An SMI is the maximum value image that is generated from summing the past successive images with an equal weight. An eigenspace is employed where each SMI plays a role of a reference point. By calculating the correlation between reference SMIs and the MHI generated from an unknown motion sequence, a match is found with images described in the eigenspace to recognize an unknown motion [247].

4.5.2.9 Intra-MHI, Rear-MHI, Front-MHI

A moving object is segmented by employing adaptive threshold-based change detection by [248]. In this method, several MHI images, called *rear*-MHI and *front*-MHI, are developed to represent a motion. These MHIs are used to segment and measure a motion. After that, the motion vectors with orientation and magnitude are generated from chamfer distance [150]. This method generates an intra-MHI image inside a moving body.

4.5.2.10 Motion Color Image (MCI)

A Motion Color Image (MCI) is developed by [249] based on the usage of the MHI and the MEI. The MCI is a combination of motion and color information. The MCI is constructed by bit-wise OR of the MEI for four previous levels and color localization data.

4.5.2.11 Silhouette History Image (SHI)

Silhouette-based history and energy images are constructed by [251, 256, 304]. These are similar to the concept of the MHI and the MEI. The motion templates are called the Silhouette Energy Image (SEI) and the Silhouette History Image (SHI). The SEI and the SHI are constructed by using the silhouette image sequence of an action. They employ Korea University gesture database [204] and the KTH database [592] for recognition.

4.5.2.12 Edge-based MHI

An Edge-based Motion History Image (EMHI) [253, 258] is computed by combining edge detection and the MHI computation. The EMHI method by [253, 258] extracts a temporal-compressed feature vector from a short video sequence. Usually, background is not easy to be extracted in news and sports videos with complex background scenes. Therefore, instead of using the MHI directly, [253, 258] propose to use edge information detected in each frame to compute an EMHI.

On the other hand, [2] proposed an Edge-Accumulated History Image (EHI), which is computed by the accumulation of detected edges. Canny edge detector is employed for edge detection in the EHI method.

4.5.2.13 IIR-measured Feature Image

The method by Masoud and Papanikolopoulos [424] has similarity with the MHI method. At each frame, motion information is represented by a feature image, which is calculated efficiently using an *Infinite Impulse Response* filter. The response of the *Infinite Impulse Response* filter is employed as a measure of motion in the image. The idea is to represent motion by its *recentness*: recent motion is represented as brighter than older motion (similar to the concept of the MHI [434]). In this method, an action is represented by several feature images [424].

4.6 Solutions to Some Constraints of the Basic MHI

As mentioned above, the MHI method suffers from some limitations. To overcome some of these, various developments are proposed since its inception. In this section, we present these methods with the hope that a researcher will find the concept inherent in these developments for further progress.

4.6.1 *Solutions to Motion Self-occlusion Problem*

We start with the motion overwriting problem of the MHI method. This is one of the key limitations of the MHI method and it shows poor performance in the presence of motion overwriting due to self-occlusion. Several methods are directed to recognize multi-directional activities.

4.6.1.1 *Multiple-level MHI Method*

Multiple-level MHI (MMHI) method [264, 472] tries to overcome the problem of motion self-occlusion by recording motion history at multiple time intervals (i.e., multi-level MHIs). They believe that the MMHI data representation can offer many benefits in applications, where confusions caused by motion self-occlusion are common (e.g., in hand gesture recognition, waving the hand is often confused with moving the hand from left to right only) [472]. Initially, the input image sequences may have different numbers of frames. So, while the MHIs are temporally normalized, the number of history levels in them may still differ from one image sequence to the others. It creates all MHIs to have a fixed number of history levels n. So, each image sequence is sampled to $(n+1)$ frames. The MMHI ($MMHI_t(x, y, t)$) is computed according to,

$$MMHI_t(x, y, t) = \begin{cases} s * t & \text{if } \Psi(x, y, t) = 1, \\ MMHI_t(x, y, t-1) & \text{otherwise,} \end{cases} \quad (4.7)$$

where,

$s = (255/n)$ is the intensity step between two history levels; and $MMHI_t(x, y, t) = 0$ for $t \leq 0$.

The final template is found by iteratively computing the above equation for $t = 1, \ldots, n+1$. This method encodes motion occurrences at different time instances on the same pixel location in such a manner that it can be uniquely decodable afterwards. The number of history levels can be known experimentally. The MMHI approach is used in the detection of facial action units (AU) [472]. This method encodes motion occurring at different time instances on the same pixel location such that it is uniquely decodable afterwards. It uses a simple bit-wise coding scheme. If a motion occurs at time t at pixel location (x, y), it adds 2^{t-1} to the old motion value of the MMHI as follows,

$$MMHI(x, y, t) = MMHI(x, y, t-1) + \Psi(x, y, t) . 2^{t-1}. \quad (4.8)$$

Due to the bitwise coding scheme, it is possible to separate multiple actions occurring at the same position [472]. In action recognition study, the Multi-level Motion Energy Image (MMEI) template is used for more information to aid the recognition process to have higher recognition results [484].

4.6.1.2 Directional MHI Method

Directional Motion History Image (DMHI) is proposed to solve the motion overwriting or self-occlusion problem of the MHI method, and it has been found that the DMHI method performed well in solving the problem [485]. Optical flows are computed between frames. Then the flow vectors are split into four channels based on the concept of [435]. Figure 4.6 shows this division. Based on this strategy, one can get four-directional motion templates for left, right, up and down directions. Based on a threshold ξ on pixel values on the update function $\psi_x^+(x, y, t)$, four DMHI images are computed,

MHI – A Global-based Generic Approach

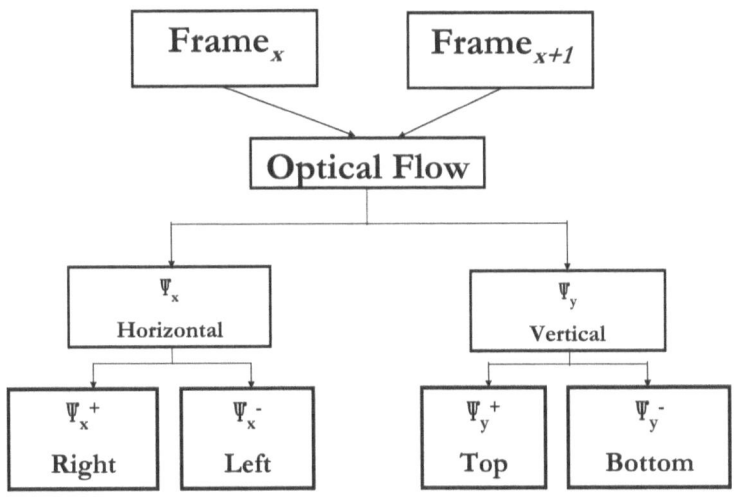

Fig. 4.6: Optic flow into four channels.

$$H_{\tau}^{r}(x, y, t) = \begin{cases} \tau & \text{if } \psi_x^+ > \xi, \\ \max(0, H_{\tau}^{r}(x, y, t-1) - \delta) & \text{otherwise,} \end{cases}$$

$$H_{\tau}^{l}(x, y, t) = \begin{cases} \tau & \text{if } \psi_x^- > \xi, \\ \max(0, H_{\tau}^{l}(x, y, t-1) - \delta) & \text{otherwise,} \end{cases}$$

$$H_{\tau}^{u}(x, y, t) = \begin{cases} \tau & \text{if } \psi_y^+ > \xi, \\ \max(0, H_{\tau}^{u}(x, y, t-1) - \delta) & \text{otherwise,} \end{cases}$$

$$H_{\tau}^{d}(x, y, t) = \begin{cases} \tau & \text{if } \psi_y^- > \xi, \\ \max(0, H_{\tau}^{d}(x, y, t-1) - \delta) & \text{otherwise.} \end{cases}$$

Here, r, l, u and d denotes *right*, *left*, *up* and *down* directions respectively. $H_{\tau}^{left}(x, y, t)$ and $H_{\tau}^{right}(x, y, t)$ components are for motion history images for positive and negative horizontal direction, whereas, $H_{\tau}^{top}(x, y, t)$ and $H_{\tau}^{down}(x, y, t)$ components are representing the positive and negative vertical directions respectively.

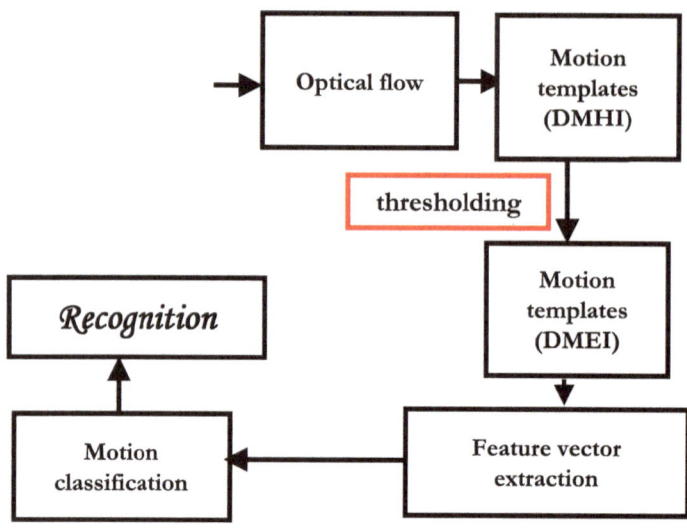

Fig. 4.7: A flow diagram for the DMHI method for action recognition.

Similar to the MEI concept, the corresponding four energy images are computed by thresholding these history images above zero,

$$E_\tau^r(x, y, t) = \begin{cases} 1 & \text{if } H_\tau^r(x, y, t) \geq 1, \\ 0 & \text{otherwise,} \end{cases}$$

$$E_\tau^l(x, y, t) = \begin{cases} 1 & \text{if } H_\tau^l(x, y, t) \geq 1, \\ 0 & \text{otherwise,} \end{cases}$$

$$E_\tau^u(x, y, t) = \begin{cases} 1 & \text{if } H_\tau^u(x, y, t) \geq 1 \\ 0 & \text{otherwise} \end{cases}$$

$$E_\tau^d(x, y, t) = \begin{cases} 1 & \text{if } H_\tau^d(x, y, t) \geq 1, \\ 0 & \text{otherwise.} \end{cases}$$

Figure 4.7 demonstrates a flow diagram for the DMHI method, starting from the computation of optical flow. Several complex actions and aerobics (which have more than one direction in these actions) are tested in indoor and outdoor scenes with good recognition results. The DMHI method requires four history templates and four energy templates for four directions; hence the size of the feature vector becomes large, and hence it becomes computationally a bit more expensive than the MHI.

The DMHI method works well in low-resolution actions, due to the fact that the DMHI templates can retain significant information of the motion in low resolution with a limit [479]. This method can work well in actions of different duration or pace [485].

4.6.1.3 Hierarchical Motion History Histogram Method

Meng et al. [259] propose a SVM-based system called Hierarchical Motion History Histogram (HMHH). In [235, 259–262], they compare other methods (i.e., the modified-MHI, the MHI) to demonstrate the robustness of the HMHH in recognizing several actions. This representation retains more motion information than the MHI, and also remains inexpensive to compute [235]. Due to the formation of the MHI, it keeps the later information of the presence of 1 (i.e., motion) in a specific pixel when there are some earlier movement in the same pixel. For example, for a pixel, the last 1 in the sequence are retained in the MHI at that pixel. The previous 1s in the sequence, when some action occurred, are not represented. And usually almost every pixel has more than one 1 in their sequence. In the HMHH, to solve the overwriting problem, they define some patterns P_i in the motion mask ($D(x,y,:)$) sequences, based on the number of connected 1, e.g.,

$$P_1 = 010, P_2 = 0110, P_3 = 01110, \ldots, P_M = 01\ldots10M1s \quad (4.9)$$

Lets define a subsequence $C_i = b_{n1}, b_{n2}, \ldots, b_{ni}$ and denote the set of all sub-sequences of $D(x,y,:)$ as $\Omega D(x,y,:)$. Then for each pixel, count the number of occurrences of each specific pattern P_i in the sequence of $D(x,y,:)$ as shown,

$$HMHH(x,y,P_i) = \sum_j \mathbf{1}_{C_j = P_i | C_j \in \Omega D(x,y,:)} \quad (4.10)$$

Here, **1** is the indicator function. From each pattern P_i, one can construct one gray-scale image, called Motion History Histogram (MHH), and all MHH images construct the Hierarchical-MHH (HMHH)). Figure 4.8 shows some HMHH images for several actions. It shows images for 1st four patterns.

These solutions are compared [485] to show their respective robustness in solving the overwriting problem of the MHI method [434]. The employed dataset has some activities that are complex in nature and have motion overwriting. For the HMHH method, four patterns are considered as more than four patterns do not provide significant information. For every activity, the DMHI representation outperforms the HMHH, the MMHI and the MHI methods.

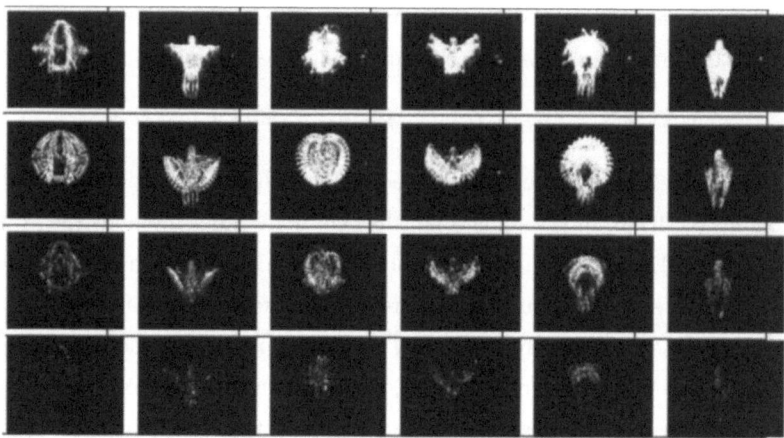

Fig. 4.8: HMHH images for for patterns for six actions (top-row shows for pattern-1 to bottom-row denotes for Pattern-4; and each column represents one action).

4.6.1.4 Local Binary Pattern Histogram-based Method

Vili *et al.* [269] extract spatially enhanced Local Binary Pattern (LBP) histograms from the MHI and the MEI temporal templates and model their temporal behavior with HMMs. They select a fixed frame number. The computed MHI is divided into four sub-regions through the centroid of the silhouette. All MHI and MEI LBP features are concatenated into one histogram and normalized to one. In this case, the temporal modeling is done by using HMMs. This texture-based description of movements can handle overwrite problem of the MHI. One key concern of this approach is the choice of the sub-regions division scheme for every action.

4.6.2 Solving Variable-length Movements

Davis [227] presents a method for recognizing movement that relies on localized regions of motion, which are derived from the MHI. He offers a real-time solution for recognizing some movements by gathering and matching multiple overlapping histograms of the motion orientations from the MHI. In this extension from the original work [434], Davis explains a method to handle variable-length movements and occlusion. The *directional histogram* for each body region has twelve bins (30 degree each), and the feature vector is a concatenation of the histograms of different body regions.

4.6.3 *timed-Motion History Image*

In another update, the MHI is generalized by directly encoding the actual time in a floating point format, which is called timed-Motion History Image (tMHI) [311]. In tMHI, a new silhouette values are copied in with a floating-point timestamp. This MHI representation is updated not by considering the frame numbers but time stamp of the video sequence [311].

This method makes the representation independent of the system speed or frame rate (within limits) so that a given gesture can cover the same MHI area at different capture rates. They also present a method of motion segmentation based on segmenting layered motion regions that are meaningfully connected to movements of the object of interest. This approach is employed for tracking objects in real-time applications by [228].

4.6.3.1 *Motion Gradient Orientation*

The Motion Gradient Orientation (MGO) is computed by Bradski and Davis [311] from the interior silhouette pixels of the tMHI. These orientation gradients are employed for recognition. Wong and Cipolla [229, 230] exploit the MGO images to form motion features for gesture recognition. Pixels in the MGO image encode the change in orientation between nearest moving edges shown on the MHI. The region of interest is defined as the largest rectangle covering all bright pixels in the MEI. The MGO contains information about *where* and *how* a motion has occurred [230].

4.6.4 *Hierarchical-MHI*

The MHI's limitation relating to the *global image* feature calculations can be overcome by computing dense local motion vector field directly from the MHI for describing the movement [453]. Davis [453] extends the original MHI representation into a hierarchical image pyramid format to provide with a means of addressing the gradient calculation of multiple image speeds — with faster speeds residing at higher levels. An image pyramid is constructed until reaching a desired size of spatial reduction. Based on the orientations of the motion flow, a Motion Orientation Histogram (MOH) is produced. The Hierarchical-MHI (HMHI) is computationally inexpensive [236].

4.6.5 *Pixel Signal Energy*

An advantage of the MHI is that although it is a representation of the history of pixel-level changes, only one previous frame needs to be stored. However, at each pixel location, explicit information about its past is also lost in the MHI when current changes are updated to the model with their corresponding MHI values 'jumping' to the maximal value [273]. To overcome this problem, Ng and Gong [231] propose a Pixel Signal Energy (PSE) in order to measure the mean magnitude of pixel-level temporal energy over a period of time. It is defined by a backward window, whose size is determined by the number of stored frames [232].

4.6.6 *Pixel Change History*

Pixel Change History (PCH) [273] measures the multi-scale temporal changes at each pixel. The MHI is a special case of the PCH. A PCH image is equivalent to an MHI image when the *accumulation factor* is set to 1. Similar to that of the PSE [231], a PCH can also capture a zero order pixel-level change, i.e., the mean magnitude of change over time [273].

4.6.7 *Motion Flow History*

The MHIs can be used to detect and interpret actions in compressed video data. Human motion in the compressed domain is recognized by the Motion Flow History (MFH) [263, 265]. The MFH quantifies the motion in compressed video domain. Motion vectors are extracted from the compressed MPEG stream by partial decoding. The MHI and the corresponding MFH are constructed at macro-block resolution instead at pixel resolution.

The MFH gives the information about the extent of the motion at each macro-block (*where* and *how* much the motion has occurred). Features are extracted from the MHI and the MFH for recognition. However, self-occlusion on the image plane remains as a problem.

4.6.8 *Contour-based STV*

Yilmaz and Shah [549] propose two modifications on the MHI representation. In their representations, motion regions are represented by contours, not by the entire silhouettes. Contours in multiple frames are not compressed into one image but directly represented as a spatial-temporal volume (STV) by computing the correspondences of contour points across frames.

4.6.9 Solving View-Invariant Issue

Above approaches are based on the 2D-based MHI and hence these are not view-invariant. Several 3D extensions of the basic MHI method are proposed for view-invariant 3D motion recognition [218, 233, 444, 451, 473]. The Motion History Volume is introduced in 3D. 3D moments are used for feature vector [220].

4.6.9.1 Motion History Volume

D. Weinland *et al.* [221, 473] develop a 3D extension of the MHI method, called Motion History Volume (MHV). The MHV is based on visual hull for viewpoint-independent action recognition. Here, pixels are replaced with voxels, and the standard image differencing function $D(x, y, t)$ is substituted with the space occupancy function $D(x, y, z, t)$, which is estimated using silhouettes and thus, corresponds to a visual hull. Voxel values in the MHV at time t are defined as:

$$MHV_\tau(x,y,z,t) = \begin{cases} \tau & \text{if } D(x,y,z,t)) = 1, \\ \max(0, MHV_\tau(x,y,z,t-1)-1) & \text{otherwise.} \end{cases} \quad (4.11)$$

They automatically segment action sequences into primitive actions, which can be represented by a single MHV. Later they cluster the resulting MHVs into a hierarchy of action classes, which allow recognizing multiple occurrences of repeating actions [221]. Though it offers an alternative to action recognition with multiple cameras, additional computational cost due to calibration, synchronization of multiple cameras, and parallel background subtraction are challenging areas for the method [270].

4.6.9.2 3D Motion History Model

Shin *et al.* [218] present a 3D Motion History Model (3D-MHM). The 3D-MHM approach with disparity information provide view-invariance property as well as more reliability in recognition. They also propose a Dynamic History Buffering (DHB) to solve the gesture duration problem. The DHB mitigates the problem by using the magnitude of motion.

4.6.9.3 Volume Motion Template

Another (similar to [218]) view-invariant 3D recognition method, called Volume Motion Template (VMT) is proposed [444]. It extracts silhouette images using background subtraction and disparity maps. Then it calculates volume object in 3D space to construct a VMT. With ten different gestures, it achieves good recognition result.

4.6.9.4 Multi-view MHIs

Davis [219, 453] develop a system by concentrating at the problem of combining MHIs from multiple views (e.g., eight different views [219]) to perform view-invariant recognition.

4.6.9.5 3D MHI by Canton-Ferrer

Similar to the MHV [473], Canton-Ferrer *et al.* [222, 451] propose another 3D version of the MHI by adding information regarding the position of the human body limbs. They employ multiple calibrated cameras. An ellipsoid body model is fit to the incoming 3D data to capture body part in which the gesture occurs. They first compute Motion Energy Volume (MEV) from binary dataset, which indicates the region of motion. This measure captures the 3D locations where there is a motion in last few frames.

To represent the temporal evolution of the motion, they define a Motion History Volume (MHV), where intensity of each voxel is a function of the temporal history of the motion at that 3D location. They exploit 3D invariant statistical moments [220] for shape analysis and classification. Petras *et al.* [223] use it to detect unusual behavior.

4.6.9.6 Volumetric MHI

Albu *et al.* [233, 270] present a 3D motion representation, called the Volumetric Motion History Image (VMHI), to analyze irregularities in human actions. It is invariant to motion self-occlusion, speed variability and variable-length motion sequences. The VMHI is computed by,

$$VMHI(x,y,\kappa) = \begin{cases} S(x,y,\kappa) \triangledown S(x,y,\kappa+1) & \text{if } \psi S(x,y,\kappa) \neq \psi S(x,y,\kappa+1), \\ 1 & \text{otherwise,} \end{cases} \quad (4.12)$$

where,
$\psi S(x,y,\kappa)$ is the one pixel thick contour of the binary silhouette in frame κ and Δ is the symmetric difference operator.

4.7 Motion Analysis

A temporal motion segmentation method is proposed by [484]. It can segment a complex motion into four labels (ℓ — which can be one of the four directions of left, right, up or down). It is based on the directional motion *history* images. For consecutive frames, pixel volumes (v_τ) are computed by summing up the DMHIs' brightness levels according to,

$$v_\tau^\ell = \sum_{x=1}^{M} \sum_{y=1}^{N} H_\tau^\ell(x, y, t) \tag{4.13}$$

This can decide the label (ℓ) of the segmented motion after some threshold values, where,

Θ_α — denotes the starting point for a motion;
Θ_β — denotes that the motion has stopped;
Δ_t^ℓ — denotes the difference between two volume of pixel values (v_τ) for two frames;
κ — denotes the frame number, where the value of κ might be 1 or more. For consecutive two frames, $\kappa = 1$.

The computations are done according to the following equations,

$$\Delta_{t+\kappa}^\ell = v_{t+\kappa}^\ell - v_t^\ell \tag{4.14}$$

$$\ell = \begin{cases} \ell & \text{if } \Delta_t^\ell > \Theta_\alpha, \\ \Phi & \text{if } \Delta_t^\ell < \Theta_\beta. \end{cases} \tag{4.15}$$

If the difference Δ_t^ℓ is more than a starting threshold value Θ_α, it decides the label of the segmented motion.

If the Δ_t^ℓ reduces to $\Theta_\beta > \Delta_t^\ell$ — it is assumed that there is no motion in the scene, or the motion is no longer present (Φ).

4.8 Implementations of the MHI

The MHI/MEI method/representations or their variants are used in different applications and systems, under various dimensions and environments. These are covered in details in [641]. These can be summed up into the following three main groups:

- The MHI and its variants in *Recognition*;
- The MHI and its variants in *Analysis*;

- The MHI and its variants in *Interactions*.

We present these in more details in Tables 4.1–4.3.

4.8.1 The MHI and its Variants in Recognition

The MHI method is employed mostly for action or gesture recognition by [211–213, 216, 218, 221, 227, 233, 234, 238, 240, 247, 249, 250, 259–263, 265, 268–273, 275, 302, 311, 434, 444, 449, 451, 453–455, 468, 472–476, 479, 480, 484, 485, 641].

Davis [227, 453] and Bradski and Davis [311, 454] recognize some actions by the MHI method. A PDA-based recognition system is developed by Leman *et al.* [216]. Eight human actions are recognized by Rosales [468]. With the MHI/MEI/MCI, a real-time recognition system is demonstrated by Singh *et al.* [249]. [263, 265] develop a method based on the MHI for some action recognition.

In the gesture recognition domain, [212, 213, 234, 268] employ the MHI representations. On the other hand, several gait recognition and person identification methods are proposed by [239–241, 243–246, 257, 272, 303, 553] based on the concept of the MHI and MEI.

Apart from the various approaches for motion representations, the development strategies of feature vectors and then the classification methods are varied for different methods. Even in some comparative analyzes (e.g., in [235, 246, 259, 485]) of some methods, they do not follow the same strategies of the other methods to compare.

4.8.2 The MHI and its Variants in Analysis

The MHI method is employed for various motion analyzes, e.g., to detection and localization [465, 476], to track [211, 302], for video surveillance system [250], to detect unusual behavior [223, 270] and other applications [233, 248, 270, 470, 484].

Son *et al.* [470] calculate the MHI and then combine with a background model to detect the candidate road image. A video surveillance system is developed by using PTZ cameras by [250]. Jin *et al.* [248] segment human body and measure its motion by employing the MHI. Another motion segmentation method is developed by [484]. Albu *et al.* [233, 270] develop the MHI method to use it for the analysis of irregularities in human actions. Petras *et al.* [223] and Albu and Beugeling [270] develop systems for unusual behavior detection by using the MHI. . The MHI is also used to produce input images for *line fitter* — a system for fitting lines to a video sequence that describe its motion [237].

4.8.3 The MHI and its Variants in Interactions

Some interactive systems are developed by exploiting the MHI representation (e.g., [215, 264, 449, 454, 455, 472, 474, 475, 635]). Some of these are:

- *Kidsroom* — an interactive and narrative play space for children is developed and demonstrated by [449].
- Davis *et al.* [455] develop a *virtual aerobics trainer* that watches and responds to the user as he/she performs the workout.
- For interactive arts, motion swarm is demonstrated by [635].
- Another interactive arts system is demonstrated by [454].
- Valstar *et al.* [215, 472] and Pantic *et al.* [264] detect few facial action units (AU).
- Yau *et al.* [474, 475] develop a method for visual speech recognition.

Table 4.1: Applications of the MHI and its variants.
Recognition and related areas.

[Ref.]	Approach/ Method	Experiment	Results
[244]	DEI, HMM, Wavelet	CASIA Gait Database — B [206]	93.9% recognition
[246]	MEH, Quad-tree	CASIA Gait Database — B[206]	96.4% recognition
[241, 242]	GEI	CASIA gait database [206]	90.5% recognition
[239, 240, 303]	PCA, MDA (Multiple Discriminant Analysis)	USF HumanID Gait Database [207]	71% recognition
[243]	GEI, Gabor	USF HumanID Gait Database [207]	More than 71% recognition
[245]	GMI, MDI, GEI, KNN	USF HumanID Gait Database [207]	66% recognition
[244]	DEI, HMM, Wavelet	CMU Mobo Gait Database	82% recognition

Continued on next page

Table 4.1 – continued from previous page

[Ref.]	Approach/ Method	Experiment	Results
[316]	MHI, Fourier, DTW	14 gestures, 5 subjects, with repetitions	92% recognition
[213]	MHI	10 gestures, stereo camera	90% recognition
[249]	MCI/MHI/MEI	11 gestures	90% recognition
[269]	MHI, MEI, LBP, HMM	15 gestures, 5 subjects [205]	95% recognition
[269]	MHI, MEI, LBP, HMM	10 actions, 9 subjects	97.8% recognition
[444]	VMT	10 gestures, 7 viewpoints, with repetitions	90% recognition
[212]	Hu moment, ANN	5 gestures, 5 subjects, with repetitions	96% recognition
[268]	Hu moment, Mean-shift tracker, PF, Mahalanobis distance	7 gestures by a robot	Good recognition
[218]	Global gradient orientation, Least square	4 gestures, stereo camera	90% recognition
[216]	MHI	PDA-based recognition	Normal
[434]	MHI, Hu moment, Mahalanobis distance	18 aerobics, 1 instructor, with repetitions, multi-camera	Good recognition
[219]	MHI, Hu moment, Likelihood, BIC	3 actions, 3 subjects, 8 different viewpoints	77% recognition
[468]	MHI, Hu moment, PCA, KNN	8 actions, 7 subjects	Good recognition
[265]	KNN, Neural network, SVM, Bayes Classifier	7 actions, 5 subjects, with repetitions	98% recognition
[247]	SMI, MMHI, Eigenspace	6 actions, 9 subjects, with repetitions	79.9% recognition
[222, 451]	3D-MHI model, 3D moment, PCA	8 actions, 5 calibrated wide-lens cameras	98% recognition
[221, 445, 473]	3D-MHI model, LDA, Mahalanobis distance	INRIA IXMAS action dataset [208]	93.3% recognition
[258]	EMHI, PCA, SVM	6 actions	63% recognition
[234]	MHI, FDA	15 videos, 4 gestures	92% recognition
[234]	MHI, FDA	4 actions, 20 subjects	90% recognition

Continued on next page

Table 4.1 – continued from previous page

[Ref.]	Approach/ Method	Experiment	Results
[257]	AEI, GMM, PCA	9 activities, 9 subjects [542]	93.8% recognition
[246]	MEH, Quad-tree	7 actions, 9 subjects [542], extra 10 subjects	98.5% recognition
[553]	AME, MSS, KNN, NN	10 activities, 9 subjects [542]	almost 100% recognition
[251]	SHI, SEI, Hu moment, Zernike moment	6 actions, 25 subjects [592]	87.5% recognition
[259]	MHI, HMHH, SVM	6 actions, 25 subjects [592]	80.3% recognition
[484, 485]	MHI, DMHI, Optic flow, Hu moment, KNN	10 aerobics, 8 subjects	94% recognition
[209]	MHI, DMHI, Optic flow, Hu moment, KNN	5 actions, 9 subjects, multi-camera	93% recognition
[238]	MHI	6 actions, 9 subjects, 4 cameras [247]	Poor recognition
[316]	MHI, Fourier, DTW	7 videos, 6 subjects	85.5% recognition
[266]	SOM, ML	INRIA IXMAS Action dataset [208]	77.27% recognition
[316]	MHI, Fourier, DTW	INRIA XMAS Action Dataset [208]	87% recognition
[256, 304]	SHI, SEI, Hu moment, Zernike moment	14 actions, 20 subjects [204]	89.4% recognition
[266]	SOM, ML	20 actions, 9 actors [61]	98.5% recognition
[252]	MHI, HLAC, PCA	Pitching of baseball	Recognition — 100% with 90×90 image resolution, 96.7% with 25×25 image resolution

Table 4.2: Applications of the MHI and its variants.
Related to activity analysis.

[Ref.]	Approach/ Method	Experiment	Results
[211]	MHI, Kalman Filter	3 sequences of PETS dataset-1 [50]	Good tracking
[228]	MHI, CAMSHIFT, Haar-like features, Neural network	3-DOF robotic manipulator	Average result

Continued on next page

Table 4.2 – continued from previous page

[Ref.]	Approach/ Method	Experiment	Results
[214]	MHI, Kalman Filter, Camera motion compensation	Tracking a robot in real-time	Good tracking
[302]	MHI, Kalman Filter	Outdoor activities	Good tracking
[271]	MHI, Neural network	Threat assessment for surveillance in car parking	Poor tracking
[465]	MHI	Moving object	Poor tracking
[250]	MHI, Adaptive camera models	PTZ cameras, outdoor scenes	Promising results for video surveillance
[273]	MHI, HMM	Some indoor and outdoor scenes	Good modeling for understanding behavior
[454]	MHI, Motion Gradients	Actions	Good analysis in real-time
[476]	MHI, RANSAC	Thermal imagery images	Moving object localization
[233, 270]	3D-MHI model	5 actions	Analysis of irregularities of human action, overcome motion self-occlusion problem
[203, 223]	3D-MHI model [451]	Unusual behavior, outdoor	Real-life abnormal beahvior detection and tracking
[484]	TMS, DMHI	Indoor and outdoor actions	Good results
[227]	MHI, Motion Orientation Histogram	Different actions	Good result
[237]	MHI	Line fitter	Average result
[470]	MHI, Fuzzy sets	Road area in traffic video	Good detection and localization of road area

Table 4.3: Applications of the MHI and its variants.
Related to interactive applications.

[Ref.]	Approach/ Method	Experiment	Results
[635]	MHI	Interactive art demonstration	Good results in complex environment

Continued on next page

Table 4.3 – continued from previous page

[Ref.]	Approach/ Method	Experiment	Results
[454]	MHI	Interactive art demonstration	Good results
[449]	MHI	Interactive playground for kids	Good results
[455]	MHI	Interactive virtual aerobics trainer	Good performance, it can respond to an user when the user performs an aerobics
[474, 475]	MHI, Hu moment, Zernike moment, Wavelet, ANN	3 consonants	Voiceless speech recognition, elementary result
[215, 264, 472]	MMHI, MHI	Facial Action Unit (AU), MMI-Face-DB, Cohn-Kanade Face Dataset	Poor result

4.9 MHI and its Future

The future of the MHI is detailed in [641]. Based on that discussion, we present some perspectives on the future of the MHI and its applications in the computer vision community. The MHI and MEI representations and its variants can be employed for action representations, understanding and recognition in various applications. Methods to solve the view-invariance problem of the MHI and several other constraints are presented earlier. Though these methods have shown good performance based on some datasets, these methods depend on multiple-camera systems, and subsequently contain extra computational overhead. Besides, similar to the basic MHI method, most of the other 2D variants are having the same problem of view-invariance. By using multiple cameras, the recognition improves but at the same time, for some actions, one camera mirrors another action from another angle. These issues are not easy to solve and more explorations are required. Incorporation of image depth analysis will be a cue to tackle this issue.

Some of the methods in 2D domain — for example, the MHI, the MMHI, the HMHH, etc. — show poor performance to recognition some situations, e.g.,

- In the presence of multiple moving persons in the scene;

- In the presence of multiple moving objects in different directions;
- In the presence of movement towards optical axis of the camera;
- In differentiating walking, jogging, and running;
- In the presence of camera movement;
- In the presence of occlusion.

Recognizing or distinguishing walking from running motion for video surveillance is very difficult with the present manifestation of the MHI [641]. Similar to the MHI method, other variants show almost similar motion templates for both walking and running, and hence demonstrate poor recognition results. The AEI method [257] present some results on very limited dataset that walking and running motion can be separated. To manage multiple moving persons/objects and their movements in the scene, one can explore the incorporation of image depth analysis or multi-camera systems, with a good dataset.

The MHI method at its basic format is very easy to understand and implement. From the MHI and MEI image, using Hu moment or other shape representation approaches, we can easily get the feature vectors for recognition. However, the MHI is a global-based approach, and hence, motions from objects that are not the target of interest will deter the performance (STIP-based methods are better in this context) [641]. The MHI is a representation of choice for action recognition when temporal segmentation is available; when actors are fully visible and can be separated from each other; and when they do not move along the z-axis of the camera.

4.10 Conclusion

This chapter analyzes the Motion History Image (MHI) method due to its importance and massive attention by computer vision community. It is one of the key methods, and a number of variants are developed from this concept. The MHI is simple to understand and implement; hence many researchers employ this method or its variants for various action/gesture recognition and motion analysis, with different datasets.

4.11 Think Ahead!

(1) Based on the discussions above, do you think that the MHI has a future in the computer vision community?
(2) What are the challenges ahead for the MHI method?
(3) How can you modify the MHI representation for groups of people in a video?
(4) How to differentiate moving objects and moving persons in the scene?
(5) Is the MHI representation illumination-invariant?
(6) How can you modify the MHI representations for the case of moving camera or in a dynamic background?

Chapter 5

Shape Representation and Feature Vector Analysis

5.1 Feature Points Tracking

In earlier chapters, we present various feature points for different perspectives. However, one key concern is to track these points from one frame to another or on image sequences. This section analyzes frame-to-frame feature point detection and tracking algorithms due to their importance in action understanding. In order to reconstruct a 3D structure from image sequences we have to track feature points on the sequence. Besides manual tracking algorithms, existing techniques for tracking a set of discrete features over a sequence of images generally fall into two categories [146, 147],

- Two-frame-based approaches; and
- Long-sequence-based approaches.

5.1.1 *Two-frame-based Approaches*

In this category, finding feature correspondences over a sequence of images is broken into successive, yet independent problems of two-view matching. For example, Weng *et al.* [141] use multiple attributes of each image point such as,

- Intensity
- Edgeness
- Cornerness

— which are invariant under rigid motion in the image plane along with a set of constraints to compute a dense displacement field and occlusion areas in two images. Cui *et al.* [140] then use an intensity-based cross-correlation method to refine the two-view matching results and obtain feature point correspondences over the sequence. Another approach is to first apply an image registration technique to compensate for the motion of the camera between two consecutive frames. The *feature point correspondence problem* is then solved by repeatedly identifying the corresponding points to sub-pixel accuracy using the correlation matching method.

5.1.2 *Long-sequence-based Approaches*

In this category, *smoothness constraints* are employed to exploit the temporal information existing in the sequence. For example, assuming that the motion of an object does not change abruptly, Sethi and Jain [139] formulate the correspondence problem as an optimization problem. The trajectories of a set of feature points are obtained by searching for a set of trajectories each of which has maximal smoothness. Blostein and Huang [646] use Multistage Hypothesis Testing (MHT) to detect small moving objects in each image; a feature trajectory is determined by repeatedly detecting the same feature point over the sequence.

Chang and Aggarwal [138] assume a 2-D kinematic motion model and apply the Joint Probabilistic Data Association Filter (JPDAF) to track line segments with the ability to initiate or terminate the trajectory of a line segment. Employing a 3-D kinematic motion model and a Mahalanobis distance-based matching criterion, Zhang and Faugeras [137] apply an Extended Kalman filter (EKF) to track a set of line segments. A fading memory type statistical test is suggested to take into account the occlusion and disappearance of line segments.

5.1.3 *Discussions*

In essence, when the motion of the camera is smooth such that the smoothness constraints hold, long-sequence-based approaches are likely to outperform two-frame-based methods. On the contrary, if the movements of the camera between two frames vary often in the sequence and results in a non-smooth image motion, two-frame-based schemes seem to capture the variations more promptly.

Yao and Chellappa [147] present a model-based algorithm for tracking feature points over a long sequence of monocular noisy images with the ability to include new feature points detected in successive frames. The trajectory for each feature point is modeled by a simple kinematic motion model.

A Probabilistic Data Association Filter (PDAF) – is originally proposed for tracking a moving object in a cluttered environment [146]) and it is first designed to estimate the motion between two consecutive frames. A matching algorithm then identifies the corresponding point to sub-pixel accuracy and an Extended Kalman Filter (EKF) is employed to continuously track the feature point. An efficient way to dynamically include new feature points from successive frames into a tracking list is also addressed by them.

In [146], the merits of both long-sequence and two frame-based methods are considered in designing a localized feature tracking algorithm for finding trajectories of a set of feature points over a sequence. However, their algorithm [146] is explicitly designed to establish feature point trajectories over an image sequence such that the full or partial knowledge regarding the ego-motion of the camera can be recovered later. Since a correlation-type matching method is employed to identify the corresponding points in subsequent frames, the algorithm is therefore unable to track points on the boundary of moving objects, which move independently from the camera.

No feature-based vision system can work smartly unless good features can be identified and tracked from frame to frame. Selecting features that can be tracked well and which correspond to physical points in the world is still hard. Shi and Tomasi [145] propose an affine model – a feature selection criterion that is optimal by construction because it is based on how the tracker works, and a feature monitoring method that can detect occlusions, dis-occlusions, and features that do not correspond to points in the world. This proves adequate for region matching over longer time spans [144]. These methods are based on a new tracking algorithm that extends previous Newton-Raphson style search methods to work under affine image transformations. They introduce a technique for monitoring features during tracking.

Shi and Tomasi [145] specifically maximizes the quality of tracking and is therefore optimal by construction, as opposed to more *ad hoc* measures of texturedness. Monitoring is computationally inexpensive and sound, and helps discriminating between good and bad features based on a measure of dissimilarity that uses affine motion as the underlying image change model.

Of course, monitoring feature dissimilarity does not solve all the problems of tracking. In some situations, a bright spot on a glossy surface is a bad (i.e., nonrigid) feature, but may change little over a long sequence: dissimilarity may not detect the problem. However, even in principle, not everything can be decided locally. Rigidity is not a local feature, so a local method cannot be expected to always detect its violation.

On the other hand, many problems can indeed be discovered locally and these are investigated in [145]. Their system classifies a tracked feature as good (reliable) or bad (unreliable) based on the residual of the match between the associated image region in the first and current frames; if the residual exceeds a user-defined threshold, the feature is rejected. Visual inspection of results demonstrate good discrimination between good and bad features, but the authors do not specify how to reject bad features automatically. And this is the problem that [144] solves. They [144] extend the Shi-Tomasi-Kanade tracker [142, 145] by introducing an automatic scheme for rejecting spurious features. They employ a simple, efficient, model-free outlier rejection rule, called X84, and prove that its assumptions are satisfied in the feature tracking scenario. Experiments with real and synthetic images confirm that the algorithm makes good features to track better, in the sense that outliers are located reliably. Moreover, it points out the pronounced sensitivity of the Shi-Tomasi-Kanade tracker to illumination changes.

There are some other methods to track feature points on image sequence. One is to track the feature points and remove outliers by the geometric constraints described with fundamental matrix between successive images, where the *fundamental matrix tracking*,

- First, selects candidates of correspondences using local correlation.
- Then, removes the incorrect matches using the geometric constraints on the corresponding points.

Another method is to track the feature points, and remove incorrect correspondences by using the geometry constraints of trifocal tensor, called *trifocal tensor tracking*. One is to track the feature points and remove outliers by the geometric constraints between successive images. Another approach considers a camera optical system, which is approximated by the affine camera model and tracks feature points (called *affine space tracking*). Naito *et al.* [148] take some image sequences and compare the results of experiments of the feature point tracking. They obtain correct correspondences with higher probability by using geometric constraint-based approaches. However, the number of correspondences is small. On the other hand, they obtain many correct correspondences and some incorrect correspondences in this method by using the affine space constraint.

Wang et al. [149] develop a method of feature point tracking based on a α-β filter and a genetic algorithm. The outliers and occlusion points can be solved by this method. However, the feature points are attached on the cloth beforehand and therefore, in some cases, because of the movement of cloth, robustness of the estimation suffers. Hager and Belhumeur [143] report a modification of the Shi-Tomasi-Kanade tracker based on explicit photometric models.

As pointed out above, it is evident that none of these approaches are robust in overall sense and can't work efficiently in the presence of outliers and occlusions. And therefore, research should be directed to unearth a robust tracking algorithm ('robust' tracking means detecting automatically unreliable matches, or outliers, and occlusion over an image sequence) suitable for frame to frame feature point tracking automatically so that it can be cost effective and computationally less expensive. False feature point tracking is another problem that needs to be managed.

5.2 Shape Representation Schemes

In the earlier chapters, we discuss various representations and methods by which we can get a replica of the action in a format (e.g., template). From these, we need to compute feature vectors by different means (e.g., by computing moment invariants, Fourier) — so that we can go for classification by different methods (e.g., SVM, KNN). There are various approaches for shape representation in the literature, e.g., in [478, 641, 644, 645]. These are divided into broadly two categories [478], namely (Figure 5.1) —

- Boundary/Contour-based shape representations
- Region-based shape representations

Both of them can be sub-divided into,

- Morphological/Structural approach
- Global approach

Another categorization for shape description techniques can be [643] —

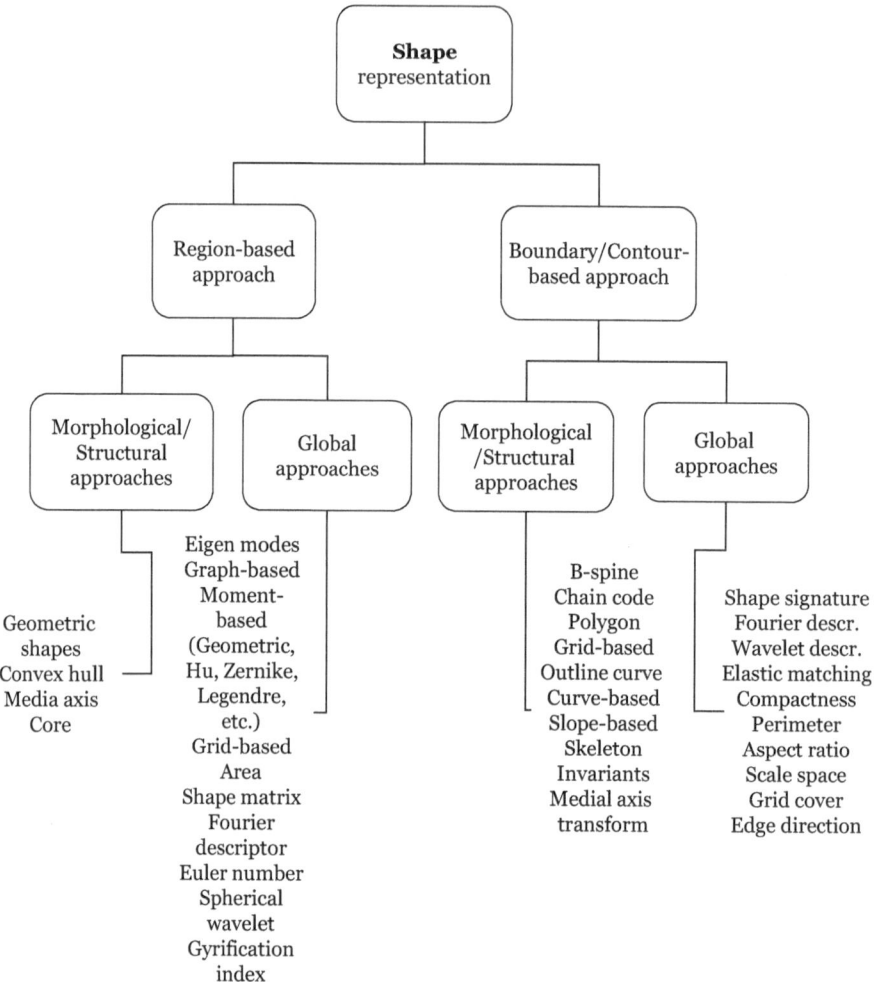

Fig. 5.1: Shape representation — various approaches.

- Transformation-based approaches and
- Measurement-based approaches.

The transformation-based approaches are broken into:

- Functional approaches and
- Structural approaches.

Some drawbacks of this categorization are that it does not distinguish between boundary or region based techniques, and sometimes it miss categorizes some techniques [644]. On the other hand, [644] proposed a taxonomy of shape description techniques based on —

- Boundary-based methods and
- Region-based methods;

— where, the these are again sub-divided as —

- Transform domain and
- Spatial domain (geometric) — Partial (in presence of occlusion) & Complete (no occlusion).

Here, we present a few key approaches for action recognition.

5.2.1 Contour-based Methods

Contour-based methods can be divided into two groups, as mentioned above.

5.2.1.1 Structural Approaches

Some well-known structural approaches are —

- B-spline
- Polygon
- Chain code

5.2.1.2 Global Approaches

Some important contour-based global approaches for shape representations are —

- Fourier descriptors
- Compactness
- Hausdorff distance
- Shape signatures
- Wavelet transform
- Curvature scale space
- Eccentricity

5.2.2 Region-based Methods

Similar to the contour-based methods, region-based approaches can be typified as, global and structural [478].

5.2.2.1 Structural Approaches

Structural approaches cover —

- Convex hull
- Geometrical shape parameters (e.g., form factor, area, Feret's diameter)

5.2.2.2 Global Approaches

Under this group, we can have —

- Hu invariants
- Legendre moments
- Zernike moments
- Shape matrix
- Euler number

In the next section, we present moment invariants, mainly Hu moments and Zernike moments due to their popularity in calculating feature vectors.

5.3 Moment Invariants

5.3.1 Hu Moments for Feature Sets

Geometrical Hu moment invariants are widely used as global-based method for various 2D pattern recognition applications. These moments are invariant to translation, scaling and rotation, though not invariant to changes in illumination [478]. This sub-section presents Hu moment with various sets for feature vectors to compare the performance. The 2D $(p+q)^{\text{th}}$ order moments of a density distribution function $\rho(x, y)$ is defined as,

$$m_{pq} = \iint x^p y^q \rho(x, y) \, dx \, dy \tag{5.1}$$

where,
the limit is from $-\infty$ to ∞;
p and q are the order of the moments in the x and y axes, respectively;
$p, q = 0, 1, 2, \ldots$;

A complete moment set of order n consists of all moments, m_{pq}, such that $p + q \leqslant n$.

M.K. Hu [438] derive relative and absolute combinations of moment values that are invariant with respect to scale, position, and orientation based on the theories of invariant algebra that deal with the properties of certain classes of algebraic expressions, which remain invariant under general linear transformations [202]. Hu's *Uniqueness Theorem* states that if $\rho(x, y)$ is piecewise continuous and has non–zero values only in the finite region of the (x, y) plane, then the moments of all orders exist [438].

It can then be shown that the moment set m_{pq} is uniquely determined by $\rho(x, y)$ and conversely, $\rho(x, y)$ is uniquely determined by m_{pq}. Since an image segment has finite area and, in the worst case, is piecewise continuous, moments of all orders exist and a moment set can be computed that will uniquely describe the information contained in the image segment. To characterize all of the information contained in an image segment requires a potentially infinite number of moment values. The goal is to select a meaningful subset of moment values that contain sufficient information to uniquely characterize the image for a specific application [202].

5.3.1.1 Low-Order Moments

Different orders of moments have different perspectives. Usually, the low-order moment values represent well-known, fundamental geometric properties of a distribution or a body. And the higher orders are more complex and prone to noise. The following paragraphs explain some of these properties [202].

0th Order Moments: Area

Here, m_{00} denotes the area of the object and it represents the total *mass* of the given distribution function or image. When computed for a silhouette image of a segmented object, the 0th moment represents the total object area.

First Order Moments

If the pair (m_{01}, m_{10}) is applied to a binary image and the results are then normalized with respect to the total mass (m_{00}), we get the centre coordinates of the object [202].

Second Order Moments

The second order moments, (m_{11}, m_{20}, m_{02}), known as the *moments of inertia*, may be used to determine several useful object features. The second order moments are used to determine the *principal axes* of the object. The principal axes may be described as the pair of axes about which there is the minimum and maximum second moment (major and minor principal axes, respectively).

Image Ellipse: The first and second order moments also define an inertially equivalent approximation of the original image, referred to as the *image ellipse* [202]. The image ellipse is a constant intensity elliptical disk with the same mass and second order moments as the original image.

Radii of Gyration: Another property that may be determined from the second order moments is the *radii of gyration* (ROG) of an image. The radius of gyration *about an axis* is the distance from the axis to a line where all the mass may be concentrated without change to the second moment about that axis.

Moments of Order Three and Greater

Moments of order three and greater are most easily described using properties of the projection of the image onto the x or y axis rather than properties of the image itself.

Third Order Moments: The two third order central moments, (m_{03}, m_{30}), describe the skewness. Skewness is a classical statistical measure of a distribution's degree of deviation from symmetry about the mean.

These moments are not invariant to geometrical transformations. To achieve invariance under translation, we need to get the central moment. The central moment μ_{pq} can be defined as,

$$\mu_{pq} = \iint (x - \bar{x})^p (y - \bar{y})^q \rho(x, y) \, d(x - \bar{x}) \, d(y - \bar{y}) \tag{5.2}$$

where,
$\bar{x} = m_{10}/m_{00}$ and
$\bar{y} = m_{01}/m_{00}$.

This is essentially a translated Cartesian moment, which means that the centralized moments are invariant under translation [202]. Based on the above equation, we can calculate moments of first four orders (i.e., $(p+q)$ is from 0 to 3),

$$\mu_{00} = m_{00} \equiv \mu$$
$$\mu_{10} = \mu_{01} = 0$$
$$\mu_{20} = m_{20} - \mu\bar{x}^2$$
$$\mu_{11} = m_{11} - \mu\bar{x}\bar{y}$$
$$\mu_{02} = m_{02} - \mu\bar{y}^2$$
$$\mu_{30} = m_{30} - 3m_{20}\bar{x} + 2\mu\bar{x}^3$$
$$\mu_{21} = m_{21} - m_{20}\bar{y} - 2m_{11}\bar{x} + 2\mu\bar{x}^2\bar{y}$$
$$\mu_{12} = m_{12} - m_{02}\bar{x} - 2m_{11}\bar{y} + 2\mu\bar{x}\bar{y}^2$$
$$\mu_{03} = m_{03} - 3m_{02}\bar{y} + 2\mu\bar{y}^3$$

Here, the first three central moments are constant. For the second and third order moments, following seven orthogonal invariants are achieved to calculate feature vectors. The first six moments are rotation, scaling and translation invariants. The 7th moment is skew (and bi-correlations) invariant that enables it to distinguish mirror or otherwise identical images. For the second and third order moments, the following six absolute orthogonal invariants (I_1 to I_6) and one skew orthogonal invariant (I_7) are computed:

$$I_1 = \mu_{20} + \mu_{02}$$
$$I_2 = (\mu_{20} - \mu_{02})^2 + 4\mu_{11}^2$$
$$I_3 = (\mu_{30} - 3\mu_{12})^2 + (3\mu_{21} - \mu_{03})^2$$
$$I_4 = (\mu_{30} + \mu_{12})^2 + (\mu_{21} + \mu_{03})^2$$
$$I_5 = (\mu_{30} - 3\mu_{12})(\mu_{30} + \mu_{12})[(\mu_{30} + \mu_{12})^2 - 3(\mu_{21} + \mu_{03})^2]$$
$$+ (3\mu_{21} - \mu_{03})(\mu_{21} + \mu_{03})[3(\mu_{30} + \mu_{12})^2 - (\mu_{21} + \mu_{03})]$$
$$I_6 = (\mu_{20} - \mu_{02})[(\mu_{30} + \mu_{12})^2 - (\mu_{21} + \mu_{03})^3]$$
$$+ 4\mu_{11}(\mu_{30} + \mu_{12})(\mu_{21} + \mu_{03})$$
$$I_7 = (3\mu_{21} - \mu_{03})(\mu_{30} + \mu_{12})[(\mu_{30} + \mu_{12})^2 - 3(\mu_{21} + \mu_{03})^2] -$$
$$(\mu_{30} - 3\mu_{12})(\mu_{21} + \mu_{03})[3(\mu_{30} + \mu_{12})^2 - (\mu_{21} + \mu_{03})^2]$$

Note that higher order invariants are difficult to derive and quite complex. So usually these seven invariants are considered and higher than these are ignored due to their enhanced complexities and higher tendency toward noise. For example, the MHI method employs these 7 invariants (i.e., 14-dimensional feature vector, comprising seven moments for history image and another seven moments for energy image), which are widely used by most others who employ the MHI for their research. However, in the DMHI method [484], they initially compute normalized 0th order moment for each template, e.g., for $H_\tau^{right}(x, y, t)$ component for an image $f(x, y)$, the 0th order moment is:

$$\mu(H_\tau^{right}(x, y, t)) = \sum_x \sum_y f(x, y) \qquad (5.3)$$

Then they compute normalized 0th order moment for $H_\tau^{right}(x, y, t)$ by employing the following equation (similarly for eight templates):

$$\overline{\mu(H_\tau^{right})} = \frac{\mu(H_\tau^{right})}{\mu(H_\tau^{right}) + \mu(H_\tau^{left}) + \mu(H_\tau^{up}) + \mu(H_\tau^{down})} \qquad (5.4)$$

Having these, a 64-dimensional feature vector (7 Hu moments for each template in addition to normalized 0th order moments) for a motion is computed. However, instead of using seven moments for energy images, one may consider only the 0th order moments, which provide the total object area, and thereby can reduce to 36-D feature vectors.

5.3.2 Zernike Moments for Feature Sets

Several researchers employ Zernike moments [464] to construct better feature vectors instead of employing Hu moments. It is useful due to its orthogonality and rotation invariance property. Moreover, it is robust against the presence of noise [471]. These moments are a set of complex polynomials, which form a complete orthogonal set over the interior of the unit circle, i.e., $x^2 + y^2 = 1$. The form of these polynomials is,

$$V_{nm}(x, y) = V_{nm}(\chi, \theta) = R_{nm}(\chi) \exp(jm\theta) \qquad (5.5)$$

where,

$n \in \mathbb{N}$ (positive integer or zero) is the order of the Zernike moment transform;
$m \in \mathbb{Z}$ (set of integers) is the rotation degree with constraints $n - \|m\|$ even; $\|m\| \leq n$;
χ is the length of vector from the origin to (x, y) pixel;
θ is the angle between vector χ and x-axis in a counter-clockwise direction.
Zernike orthogonal radial polynomials ($R_{nm}(\chi) = R_{n,-m}(\chi)$), can be defined as,

$$R_{nm}(\chi) = \sum_{s=0}^{n-|m|/2} (-1)^s \frac{(n-s)!}{s!(\frac{n+|m|}{2} - s)!(\frac{n-|m|}{2} - s)!} \chi^{n-2s} \qquad (5.6)$$

which satisfy,

$$\iint_{x^2+y^2 \leq 1} [V_{nm}(x, y)]^* V_{pq}(x, y) \, dx \, dy = \frac{\pi}{n+1} \delta_{np} \delta_{mq} \qquad (5.7)$$

with,

$$\delta_{ab} = \begin{cases} 1 & \text{if } a = b, \\ 0 & \text{otherwise} \end{cases}$$

Zernike moments of order n with repetition m for a density distribution function $\rho(x,y)$ that vanishes outside the unit circle can be defined as,

$$A_{nm} = \frac{n+1}{\pi} \iint_{x^2+y^2 \leq 1} \rho(x,y) V_{nm}^*(\chi,\theta) \, dx \, dy \tag{5.8}$$

To compute the Zernike moments of an image, the center of the image is taken as the origin and pixel coordinates are mapped to the range of unit circle with the constraint $x^2 + y^2 \leq 1$.

5.3.2.1 Constraints with Zernike Moments

Usually, Zernike moments are used even though they have a high computational cost and they lack numerical precision. Especially at high orders, it is usually not possible to calculate them accurately in reasonable time — when the desired moment order is high and/or the images to be processed are large [471]. For example, high computational cost (for orders $n = 0$ to 12, hence 49 moments) remains a concern with Zernike moments compared to Hu moment-based feature vectors. Zernike moments are employed by [251, 256, 304, 474, 475]. One case is in the DMHI method [484], where due to the four history and four energy templates, eight times of 49 moments create a large-dimensional feature vector for a video sequence. So it becomes expensive to compute and in the recognition part based on distance-based measurement makes it slower.

5.3.2.2 Hu Moment — Some Points

We address here about the concept of reduced size of Hu moment. From its inception, seven higher orders Hu moments are employed by many researchers without considering why seven always, why not less *numbers!* Various feature sets with different number of Hu moments are analyzed. They rationalize that based on the characteristics of central moments, it is not necessary to employ all the seven moments in every application and in that way, one may reduce the computational cost and make it faster.

Based on various feature vector sets, it is evident that one can use lower dimensional feature vectors for various methods. Hu moments naturally produce higher error rate compared to other moments [478], but Hu moments require less number of moments and hence trade-off is necessary to select the appropriate moments for recognition. Zernike moment might yield higher recognition rates, compare to Hu moment [464]. However, Hu moment invariants have some drawbacks as well [469], e.g.,

- One drawback is their dramatic increase in complexity with increasing order.
- These are not derived from a family of orthogonal functions, and so contain much redundant information about an object's shape.
- Hu moments naturally produce higher error rate compared to other moments [478].
- Hu moments are invariant to translation, scaling and rotation, but are not invariant to changes in illumination [201].
- Any small local disturbance affects all the moments [198].

Even though, Hu moments suffer from these constraints, they require less number of moments and hence trade-off is necessary to select the appropriate moments for recognition. The problem with illumination variation is a challenging task to solve and remains as a future work. However, Maitra [200] introduces contrast change invariance of Hu moments and he uses the first six invariants. Li [199] reformulates Hu moments and introduces some new high-order moment invariants.

A question may arise – are these seven or less moments constitute good features for object recognition? The answer is YES!

- Hu moments are based on a strong mathematical background;
- Hu moments are invariant to many transformations;
- Hu moments have strong discrimination power;
- Hu moments are almost robust to noise;
- Hu moments are global.

5.4 Component Analysis Methods

Which low dimensional features of a template or object image are the most informative or relevant for classification?

5.4.1 *Appropriate Feature Selection*

An appropriate feature selection is a key issue for pattern recognition. The choice of a precise feature vector is always a decisive parameter for a method. However, a framework called Sparse Representation-based Classification (SRC) is proposed, for which no precise choice of feature space is required (for details, [104]).

The following three principles play a critical role in feature selection [79]:

- *Discrimination*: Each selected feature should be as discriminative as possible.
- *Diversity*: The selected features must not be redundant.
- *Reinforcement*: Unless, this redundancy is itself discriminant.

5.4.2 Dimension Reduction

Dimension reduction is the process of mapping high-dimensional data into a low-dimensional space. Since images are often represented as high-dimensional pixel arrays, suitable dimension reduction techniques need to be applied to increase efficiency [374]. Various component analysis methods can be employed to reduce the dimensionality of the feature vectors for better and faster recognition. Historically, subspace methods have been one of the most popular techniques for the dimension reduction of face images. Some of the algorithms are,

- Principal Component Analysis (PCA) [377]
- Kernel Principal Component Analysis (KPCA) [380]
- Multi-linear Principal Component Analysis (MPCA) [378, 379]
- Multi-factor Kernel Principal Component Analysis (MKPCA) [375, 376]
- Regular Discriminant Analysis (RDA) [94]
- Regularized Gaussian Discriminant Analysis (RGDA)
- High-Dimensional Discriminant Analysis (HDDA) [96]
- Linear Discriminant Analysis (LDA)
- Null-space LDA
- Dual-space LDA
- Random Sampling LDA (RS-LDA) [10]
- Fisher's Linear Discriminant Analysis (FLDA) [98]
- Structural two-Dimensional Principal Component Analysis (S2DPCA) [649]
- Independent Component Analysis (ICA) [100]
- Local Nonnegative Matrix Factorization (LNMF) [102]
- Quadratic Discriminant Analysis (QDA)
- Canonical Correlation Analysis (CCA) [577]

- Tensor Canonical Correlation Analysis (TCCA) [577]

5.4.2.1 *Principal Component Analysis (PCA)*

Principal Component Analysis (PCA) [377] is most often cited as the precursor of several subspace methods that have been applied to various action and face recognitions. The basic methodology of the PCA is to first calculate the linear subspace spanned by the principal directions with the largest variations, and then to project a sample vector into it. The PCA approach is not robust to occlusion. There are many variants of the PCA, which are a bit robust to occlusion or incomplete data [99].

5.4.2.2 *Kernel Principal Component Analysis (KPCA)*

Kernel Principal Component Analysis (KPCA) [380], a nonlinear application of the PCA, assumes that there exists a nonlinear map that makes mapped observations linearly separable, and then applies the PCA to them. Thus, the subspace achieved by the KPCA is nonlinear in the input space, which allows the KPCA to be applied to complex real-world data that are not linearly separable.

5.4.2.3 *Multi-linear Principal Component Analysis (MPCA)*

Another variant of the PCA is the Multi-linear Principal Component Analysis (MPCA) or Tensorfaces [378, 379], which is used to analyze the interaction between multiple factors using a tensor framework – a multidimensional generalization of a matrix. After establishing multiple dimensions based on multiple factors, the MPCA computes a linear subspace representing the variation of each factor and an additional subspace is obtained from the image space. By using the MPCA, a data set is represented as a tensor product of multiple orthogonal matrices whose column vectors span the space representing variations of multiple factors. Similarly, an image is represented as a tensor product of multiple parameters that describes the features of multiple factors.

5.4.2.4 *Multifactor Kernel Principal Component Analysis (MKPCA)*

By combining the KPCA and the MPCA, a more advanced subspace method called Multifactor Kernel Principal Component Analysis (MKPCA) is introduced by [375, 376].

5.4.2.5 *Structural two-Dimensional Principal Component Analysis (S2DPCA)*

Structural two-Dimensional Principal Component Analysis (S2DPCA) is proposed for image recognition by [649]. Different from conventional two-dimensional Principal Component Analysis (2DPCA) that only reflects the within-row information of images, the S2DPCA can discover structural discriminative information contained in both within-row and between-row of the images [649]. Computationally, this approach is comparative with the 2DPCA.

5.4.2.6 *Regular Discriminant Analysis (RDA)*

Friedman [94] proposes the Regular Discriminant Analysis (RDA). It is a classification tool to smooth out the effects of poorly–conditioned covariance estimates due to the lack of training measurements. It is a combination of the ridge shrinkage, the Linear Discriminant Analysis (LDA) and the Quadratic Discriminant Analysis (QDA). Though it performs significantly well, it has a constraint that it fails to provide interpretable classification rules [94].

5.4.2.7 *Regularized Gaussian Discriminant Analysis (RGDA)*

The problem of the RDA (i.e., its failure to provide interpretable classification rules) is solved by the Regularized Gaussian Discriminant Analysis (RGDA). The RGDA is proposed by Bensmail [95], where this approach designs classification rules that have also a median position between linear and quadratic discriminant analysis. It is based on the re-parameterization of the covariance matrix of a group in terms of its eigenvalue decomposition [95]. Experimental results show its superiority over the RDA.

5.4.2.8 *High-Dimensional Discriminant Analysis (HDDA)*

One recent update is the High-Dimensional Discriminant Analysis (HDDA) for classification that reduces dimensions for different classes independently and regularizes class covariance matrices by assuming classes are spherical in their eigenspace [96].

5.4.2.9 *Linear Discriminant Analysis (LDA)*

Linear Discriminant Analysis (LDA) is another well-employed approach for classification. It can manage the cases the within–class frequencies are unequal. In the LDA, unlike the QDA, it is necessary to assume that the covariance of each of the classes is identical. Though the PCA and the LDA are very well-known, the PCA does more of feature classification, whereas the LDA concentrates more on data classification.

5.4.2.10 Fisher's Linear Discriminant Analysis (FLDA)

Fisher's Linear Discriminant Analysis (FLDA) is widely employed in many fields. To improve its performance, fractional-step FLDA (FS-FLDA) is developed by introducing a complex weighting function [98]. The FLDA maximizes all KL (Kullback-Leibler) divergences between different pairs of densities with the homoscedastic Gaussian assumption [98]. The Fractional-step FLDA introduces a complex weighting function [98]. However, the linear dimensionality reduction step in the FLDA has a critical problem: for a classification task with c classes, if the dimension of the projected subspace is strictly lower than $c - 1$, the projection to a subspace tends to merge those classes, which are close together in the original feature space [97].

5.4.2.11 Independent Component Analysis (ICA)

Independent Component Analysis (ICA) targets to express the training set as a linear combination of statistically independent basis images. Kim *et al.* [100] explore the ICA in face recognition and demonstrate its robustness to local distortion and partial occlusion.

5.4.2.12 Local Nonnegative Matrix Factorization (LNMF)

Local Nonnegative Matrix Factorization (LNMF) [102] approximates the training set as an additive combination of basis images.

5.4.2.13 Quadratic Discriminant Analysis (QDA)

Quadratic Discriminant Analysis (QDA) is an extension of the Fisherfaces method. The QDA is related to the Linear Discriminant Analysis (LDA), where it is assumed that there are only two classes of points, and that the measurements are normally distributed. In the QDA, it is not necessary to assume that the covariance of each of the classes is identical.

5.4.2.14 Eigenspace

Eigenvectors are a special set of vectors associated with a linear system of equations (i.e., a matrix equation) that are sometimes also known as characteristic vectors, proper vectors, or latent vectors. Each eigenvector is paired with a corresponding so-called eigenvalue. The decomposition of a square matrix **A** into eigenvalues and eigenvectors is known as eigen decomposition, and the fact that this decomposition is always possible as long as the matrix consisting of the eigenvectors of **A** is square, is known as the eigen decomposition theorem (source: http://mathworld.wolfram.com/Eigenvector.html). For a square matrix **A**, a non-zero vector **v** is an *eigenvector* of **A**, if there is a scalar λ term (the λ is called the *eigenvalue* of **A** corresponding to **v**) such that —

$$\mathbf{A}\mathbf{v} = \lambda \mathbf{v}$$

An *eigenspace* of **A** is the set of all eigenvectors with the same eigenvalue together with the zero vector. Due to some similarities with a biological vision system, eigenspace analysis [132] gains much attention for various applications, e.g., object picking [131], obstacle identification [377], face detection [377], objects tracking [130] and recognition, storing/recognizing various events [128], [127], etc. Since the principle of an eigenspace analysis depends on the matching appearance of an object rather than shape, there are a number of traditional difficulties such as geometrical calculation and image segmentation, which can easily be solved by this technique.

It can be explored to some other unexplored areas, such as, not only in tracking and understanding rigid objects but also in flexible objects (e.g., human postures, motions, movements, and gestures). If a real-time eigenspace method is developed, it can be applied for camera monitoring systems in order to help disabled person or security purposes, car navigation systems for tracking obstacles and traffic control purposes, intelligent robotic vision systems for their industrial uses such as object tacking and picking, robotic rescue.

5.5 Pattern Classifications

In pattern classification, classification can be supervised, unsupervised or semi-supervised. A *classifier* is typically trained on data pairs, which are defined by feature vectors and the corresponding class labels. This framework is called *supervised* learning, because the task of inferring a function is done from supervised training data. The training data consist of a set of *training examples*, consisting of a set of instances that have been properly labeled manually with the correct output. In supervised learning, each example is a pair — consisting of an input object (typically a vector) and a desired output value. Figure 5.2 shows a simple black-box for a typical classifier, where features are used as input and the classifier decides the class. Choice of a classifier usually depends on the dataset or features.

- Supervised learning,
- Unsupervised learning, and
- Semi-supervised learning.

Fig. 5.2: Classifier black-box.

5.5.1 *Supervised Learning*

For supervised learning, few approaches are —

- Support Vector Machine (SVM)
- Boosting
- Artificial Neural Network (ANN/NN)
- k-Nearest Neighbor classifier
- Naïve Bayesian classifier
- Decision Tree Learning (e.g., Random Forests, Boosted Trees)
- Learning Vector Quantization (LVQ)
- Linear Discriminant Analysis (LDA)

5.5.1.1 *Support Vector Machine (SVM)*

Support Vector Machine (SVM) [19] is the most popular application for classification in action recognition and understanding. Many researchers employ this classifier due to its robust performance. However, the hyper-plane based classifiers as the basis of the Support Vector Machines provide binary decisions, which is not suitable for many multi-class applications. Hence, multi-class Support Vector Machines are proposed [18].

One-versus-rest multi-class Support Vector Machine formulation [18] is the simplest one and is popular due to its ease to implement and evaluate. However, in some applications, if the number of classes is too large to unbalance the one-versus-rest multi-class SVM, another formation is proposed. It is called *one-versus-one* multi-class SVM. The basic concept of one-versus-one multi-class SVM is —

- Train one SVM per pair of class labels, by using the samples of one class as positive and the samples of the other class as negative training examples.
- Evaluate all SVMs.
- Vote to find the class label that is selected the most often.

Some other variants of the SVM in semi-unsupervised manner are [11] —

- Semi-supervised SVM (S3VM)
- Transductive SVM (TSVM)
- LapSVM (SVM with Laplacian regularization)

Code:
SVM^{light} by T. Joachims is an implementation of SVM in C and the code and detailed formulations are available in http://svmlight.joachims.org/ and is widely used by researchers.

5.5.1.2 *Boosting:*

Boosting is a machine learning meta-algorithm for performing supervised learning. Boosting is based on the question: *can a set of* **weak learners** *create a single* **strong learner**? A *weak* learner is defined to be a classifier, which is only slightly correlated with the true classification (it can label examples better than random guessing). In contrast, a *strong* learner is a classifier that is arbitrarily well-correlated with the true classification [648]. A great collection on boosting can be found in http://www.cs.princeton.edu/~schapire/boost.html. The idea of boosting is to combine simple *rules* to form an ensemble such that the performance of the single ensemble member is improved, i.e., *boosted*. Assume that $h_1, h_2, \ldots, h_I$ be a set of hypothesis. Lets consider the composite ensemble hypothesis,

$$f(x) = \sum_{i=1}^{I} \alpha_i h_i(x) \qquad (5.9)$$

where,
α_i is the coefficient with which the ensemble member h_i is combined;

both α_i and the learner or hypothesis h_i are to be learned within the *boosting* algorithm [647]. Though there are various boosting algorithms, the *AdaBoost* (*Ada*ptive *Boost*ing) algorithm is usually taken as an initial step towards more practical boosting algorithms [647]. A detailed list of applications, codes, tutorials and publications on Boosting can be available from http://www.boosting.org/. Several variants of Boosting algorithms are mentioned below,

- Adaptive Boosting (well-known as *AdaBoost*),
- LPBoost,
- TotalBoost,
- GentleBoost,
- BrownBoost,
- MadaBoost,
- SmoothBoost,
- Localized Boosting (LocBoosting),
- SemiBoost (Semi-supervised boosting) [11].

Code:
Boosting and related algorithms: http://www.fml.tuebingen.mpg.de/boosting.org/software.

Ke *et al.* [440] develop a new event detection framework. This is an extension of the Viola-Jones face detector [129]. The Viola-Jones face detector is based on the AdaBoost algorithm, and Haar-like features are used for weak classifiers of the AdaBoost. AdaBoost algorithm is a good choice to select a small number of features from a very large number of potential features. The classifier trained through AdaBoost algorithm is the combination of a set of simple classifiers (called weak classifier). Each weak classifier uses one feature. The construction of a weak classifier is independent of the AdaBoost algorithm. The basic idea of the AdaBoost algorithm is as follows:

After constructing a weak classifier, the samples are re-weighted in order to emphasize those which are incorrectly classified. Then the next weak classifier is trained with the re-weighted samples. A number of weak classifiers are trained in this way till the given false positive rate is reached. The final classifier (called strong classifier) is constructed by combining these weak classifiers using a set of weights. These weights are determined by classification error of each weak classifier.

5.5.2 *Unsupervised Learning*

In the case of unsupervised learning, the concentration remains in trying to find hidden structure in unlabeled data. It assumes that the training data has not been labeled manually. And it attempts to find inherent patterns in the data that can then be used to determine the correct output value for new data instances. Some approaches for unsupervised learning are —

- Clustering (e.g., K-means clustering, mixture models, hierarchical clustering)
- Blind signal separation using feature extraction techniques for *dimensionality reduction* (e.g., PCA, ICA, Non-Negative Matrix Factorization, Singular Value Decomposition (SVD))
- Self-Organizing Map (SOM)
- Adaptive Resonance Theory (ART)
- Hidden Markov Model (HMM)
- Markov Random Field (MRF)
- Radial Basis Function (RBF)
- Conditional Random Field (CRF)

Clustering algorithms separate a collection of objects into groups that are called *clusters*. A typical example of using unsupervised learning approach is shown in the Figure 5.3. The HMM is one of the most well-used classification methods for sequential pattern recognition aspects. The HMM models a series of observable signals. Few variants and topologies of the HMM are,

- Ensemble of HMM (EoHMM)
- Hierarchical HMM [520, 521]
- Coupled HMM
- Mixture of Transformed HMM (MTHMM)
- Parametric HMM
- Left-right HMM
- Circular HMM
- Semi-jump-in HMM
- Semi-jump-out HMM

- Leave-one-out-testing HMM (LOOT-HMM)
- Multi-Observation HMM
- Parallel-HMM
- Coupled-HMM
- Factorial HMM [516]
- Dynamically Multi-Linked HMM [518]

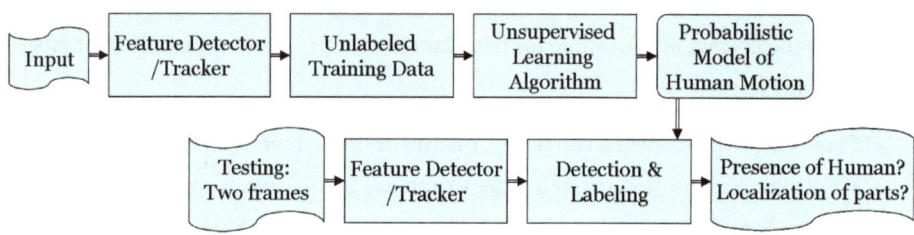

Fig. 5.3: Example of an unsupervised learning by [531].

Most of the pattern classification techniques with numerical inputs can be classified [197] into the following three groups,

- Parametric,
- Semi-parametric, and
- Non-parametric.

All these three techniques use a set of *training patterns* that already have class labels. The parametric and semi-parametric classifiers need a certain amount of a-priori information about the structure of the data in the training set. In many cases, it is difficult to collect this kind of structural information [197]. Therefore, a non-parametric classification technique, called k-nearest neighbor (k-NN) algorithm becomes an attractive approach by many researchers, since its conception in 1951 and 1952 by Fix and Hodges [194–196]. The idea of nearest neighbor classification, one of the oldest and simplest methods for pattern recognition, was first introduced to the research community by Cover and Hart in [539].

5.5.3 *Nearest Neighbor*

Nearest neighbor (NN) methods have traditionally been used as an important pattern recognition tool in many different domains [193]. The NN classifies the test sample based on the best representation in terms of a single training sample. The nearest neighbor and k-NN classifiers are employed by [189, 191–193, 264, 265, 435, 469, 472, 484, 485] as it has been a ubiquitous classification tool with good scalability [190].

A k-nearest neighbor classifier uses the type of the nearest training example to classify a feature vector, according to the following strategy [188, 194]: given an feature vector x, determine the k training examples that are the nearest, $x_1, \ldots, x_k$; (first reorder the data according to increasing Euclidean or other distances [194]). Then determine the class c that has the largest number of representatives in this set, based on the majority of voting. Finally, classify x as c. Note that, in case of a distance tie, the candidate with the smaller index is said to be the closest [194].

The employed k-NN algorithm is very straightforward. In its classical manifestation, for a *test* input sample x, and a training set $X = \{x_1, x_2, \ldots, x_n\}$, the NN rules use a distance metric to compute which k (labeled) training samples are the *nearest* to the sample in question and then casts a majority vote on the labels of the nearest neighbors to decide the class of the test sample [190]. Note that the decision is based upon a majority vote [194].

Parameters of interest are the distance metric being used and k, the number of neighbors to consider. If $k = 1$, then it becomes 1-nearest neighbor (1-NN) rule, where it assigns patterns to the class of the nearest training pattern [267]. For this case, no training is required, and its performance is robust [267]. The most straightforward 1-NN rule can be conveniently used as a benchmark for all the other classifiers since it appears to always provide a reasonable classification performance in most applications [267]. Further, as the 1-NN classifier does not require any user-specified parameters (except perhaps the distance metric is used to find the nearest neighbor, but Euclidean distance is commonly used), its classification results are implementation independent [267].

5.5.3.1 Choice of k

One concern is the choice of k. We know that the single-NN rule has strictly lower probability of error than any other [189]. Past experience has shown that the optimal value of k depends upon the data [190, 195, 196]. According to Fukunaga [187], theoretical treatment to find the optimal k for the Bayes' error estimation is very difficult and very little is known on this subject. In practice, particularly for high dimensional cases, there are very limited choices left other than selecting k to be less than 5 or so [187]. It is obvious that the comparison of any two feature combinations for the same fixed value of k would be incorrect [195]. It is predicted that the large value of k may increase the classification efficiency as there are more bodies of evidence to classify the test pattern [196]. But if the neighborhood is large, then the neighbors may belong to more than one class. It happens especially in the region where two classes overlap, or noise is present. Thus, it may increase the confusion in assigning the class label to the test pattern.

Therefore, the optimal value of k can only be found by a trade-off, which is currently achieved using trial and error procedures [196]. Figure 5.4 depicts an example about this (based on [196]). The conventional 1-nearest (i.e., $k = 1$) neighbor algorithm will classify the test pattern y as positive (+), whereas the conventional 5-nearest (i.e., $k = 5$) neighbor algorithm will classify y as negative (−). Therefore, the classification performance of the k-NN algorithm usually varies significantly with different values of k [196]. Devroye et al. [194] detail variants of the k-NN rule with data-dependent choices of k.

Moreover, when the points are not uniformly distributed, predetermining the value of k becomes difficult [190]. Based on [196], the classification performance fluctuates for different values of k. However, there exists distributions for which, the 1-NN rule is better than the k-NN rule for any $k \geqslant 3$ [189, 194, 196].

Another point related to the selection of k is that the number of computations increases for larger values of k [186]. In practice and convenience, k is usually chosen to be odd, so as to avoid voting ties [194].

Nearest neighbor classifiers are known to be good, in the sense that the risk of using a nearest neighbor classifier with a sufficiently large number of examples lies within quite good bounds of the Bayes' risk. Bayes' risk is the minimum cost of a decision based on the Bayes' criterion. Based on [188], in practice, one seldom uses more than three nearest neighbors. A difficulty in building such classifiers is the choice of distance. For features that are obviously of the same type, such as lengths or moment values, the usual metric may be good enough [188]. But if one feature is a length, one is a color, and an-

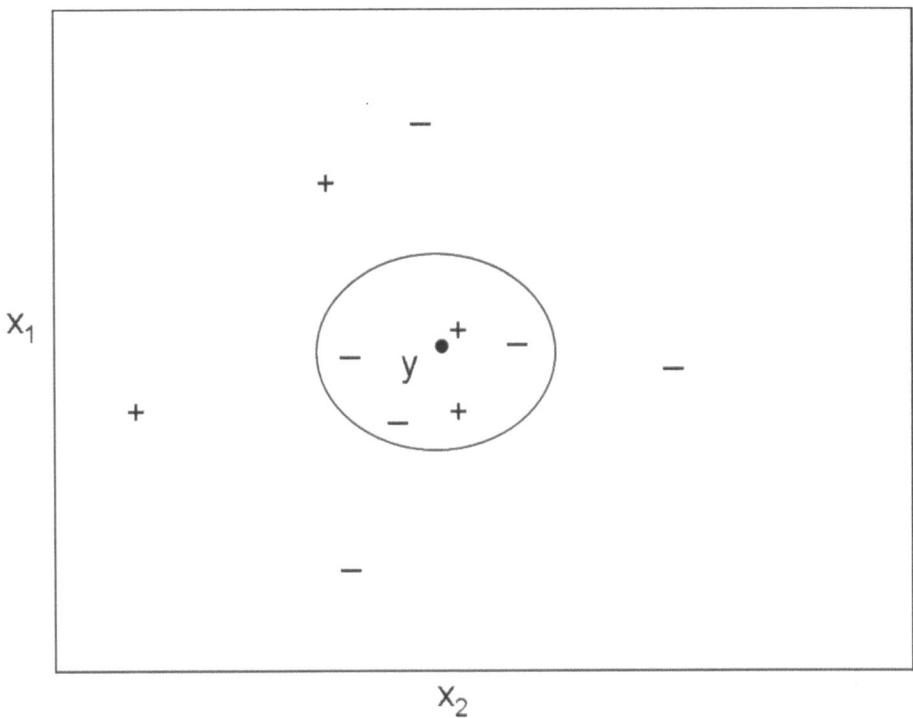

Fig. 5.4: Choice of k: an example. The 1-nearest (i.e., $k = 1$) neighbor algorithm will classify the test pattern y as positive (+), whereas the 5-nearest (i.e., $k = 5$) neighbor algorithm will classify y as negative (–). Thus, the resultant classification depends on the choice of k [196].

other is an angle, and so on – then different distance measures can be considered (e.g., Mahalanobis distance-based Large margin NN [152], Minkowski p-metric, etc.).

Without prior knowledge, the k-NN classifier usually apply Euclidean distances as the distance metric [190]. Let x_i be an input sample with p features $(x_{i1}, x_{i2}, \ldots, x_{ip})$, n be the total number of input samples ($i = 1, 2, \ldots, n$) and p be the total number of features ($j = 1, 2, \ldots, p$) [151]. The Euclidean distance between sample x_i and x_l ($l = 1, 2, \ldots, n$) is defined as,

$$d(x_i, x_l) = \sqrt{(x_{i1} - x_{l1})^2 + (x_{i2} - x_{l2})^2 + \cdots + (x_{ip} - x_{lp})^2} \qquad (5.10)$$

If both training and testing samples do not have equal number of features, one could exploit the chamfer distance [150], as it can provide a distance measure between feature sets with unequal number of features.

5.5.3.2 k-NN and Its Variants

Researchers attempt to propose new approaches to augment the performance of k-NN method [152, 190, 196], e.g.,

- Discriminant Adaptive NN (ADNN),
- Adaptive Metric NN (ADAMENN),
- Weight Adjusted k-NN (WAKNN),
- Large margin NN (LMNN),
- Fuzzy k-NN,
- Locally Informative-k-NN (LI-KNN),
- Globally Informative-k-NN (GI-KNN).

5.5.3.3 Nearest Subspace (NS)

It is measured by the minimum distance to the subspace spanned all training samples from each object class [103]. The nearest subspace classifies the test sample based on the best linear representation in terms of all the training samples in each class and it is not a popular one.

5.5.3.4 Nearest Feature Line (NFL)

Nearest Feature Line (NFL) is a balance between the Nearest Neighbor (NN) and the Nearest Subspace (NS). The NFL classifies data based on the best affine representation in terms of a pair of training samples.

5.5.4 *Cross-validation — Partitioning Scheme*

In splitting dataset for training and testing — various cross-validation schemes are available. For example [267],

- Re-substitution method;
- Holdout method;
- Leave-one-out method;
- Rotation method;

- N-fold cross validation;
- Bootstrap method.

In the *re-substitution method*, the training and test sets are the same. In the *holdout method*, half the data is used for training and the rest data is used for testing).

The *leave-one-out cross validation scheme* (e.g., [188, 266, 484]) is the most usual version of cross-validation [188]. This means that out of N samples from each of the c classes per database, $N-1$ of them are used to train (design) the classifier and the remaining one to test it [464]. This process is repeated N times, each time leaving a different sample out. Therefore, all of the samples are ultimately used for testing. This process is repeated and the resultant recognition rate is averaged. This estimate is unbiased. In short, for *cross-validation* [188], we need to choose some class of subsets of the training set. Afterwards, for each element of that class, a classifier is constructed by omitting that element in training, and the classification errors (or risk) on the omitted subset is computed. Finally, by averaging these errors over the class of subsets, the risk of using the classifier trained on the entire training dataset is estimated.

For the N-fold cross validation, a compromise between leave-one-out method and holdout method is considered, which divides the samples into P disjoint subsets, $1 \leq P \leq N$. In this scheme, $(P-1)$ subsets are used for training and the remaining subset are kept for test.

5.6 Evaluation Matrices

Recall
Recall is the proportion of *all* relevant parts that belong to the cluster. It is a measure of compactness.

Precision
Precision is the *proportion* of relevant parts of interest or information in the cluster that are relevant. Precision and recall are two widely used metrics for evaluating the correctness of various algorithms. By definition, a high recall means that missing rate is low along with the presence of much useless information. On the other hand, high precision means that everything returned was a relevant result. The precision is a measure of exactness. Recall and precision can be defined in terms of *true positive (tp), true nega-*

tive (*tn*), *false positive* (*fp*) and *false negative* (*fn*) information based on the ground truth (or data labeling):

$$\text{Recall} = \frac{tp}{(tp+fn)} \quad (5.11)$$

$$\text{Precision} = \frac{tp}{(tp+fp)} \quad (5.12)$$

Few other related notations are,

True Negative Rate,

$$\text{True Negative Rate} = \frac{tn}{(tn+fp)} \quad (5.13)$$

Accuracy,

$$\text{Accuracy} = \frac{tp+tn}{(tp+tn+fp+fn)} \quad (5.14)$$

F-measure,

$$F_1 = 2 \cdot \frac{\text{Precision} \times \text{Recall}}{(\text{Precision} + \text{Recall})} \quad (5.15)$$

E-measure

E-measure is the combination of the precision and the recall values of a cluster.

Receiver Operating Characteristic (ROC) Curve

Receiver Operating Characteristic (ROC) or ROC curve is a graphical plot of the *true positive rate* (TPR) vs. the *false positive rate* (FPR).

Area Under ROC curve (AUC)

Area Under ROC curve (AUC) offers classification accuracy. It is equal to the probability that a classifier will rank a randomly chosen positive instance higher than a randomly chosen negative one. More on these issues can be read from [9].

Detection Error Trade-off (DET) Graph

Detection Error Trade-off (DET) graph is an alternative to the ROC curve and it plots the *false negative rate* (i.e., the missed detections) vs. the *false positive rate* (i.e., the false alarms). These are sometimes demonstrated on logarithmic scales.

Average Frequency of Convergence (AFC)

Average Frequency of Convergence (AFC) [17] is the number of trials where the alignment converges, divided by the total number of trials. The AFC measures the robustness of alignment.

Histogram of the Resultant Root Mean Square Error

Histogram of the Resultant Root Mean Square Error (HRMSE) [17] of converged trials measures how close the aligned landmarks are with respect to the ground truth. The HRMSE measures the accuracy of alignment.

Equal Error Rate (EER)

Equal Error Rate (EER) is the cross-over error rate when the *false accept rate* becomes equal to the *false reject rate*. Therefore, a lower EER value represents a higher accuracy of a biometric matcher [8].

5.7 Think Ahead!

(1) What are the challenges in feature point correspondence in consecutive frames?
(2) Do an extensive research on various shape representation approaches and find *which* approaches are suitable for *what* kind of applications.
(3) Which dimension reduction approaches are the most-suitable for bag-of-features-based methods?
(4) Why Support Vector Machine is leading? What are the problems and constraints of the SVM and related methods?

Chapter 6

Action Datasets

6.1 Action Datasets

Based on the contents of the previous chapters, it is evident that human action understanding and recognition are exploited for different applications in the field of computer vision and human-machine interaction. However, different researchers experiment with various datasets, having different number of subjects, variations in gender, size, number of action classes, background, number of cameras and their respective positions, image size, illumination, indoor or outdoor, fixed or moving cameras, etc. Due to these various issues, for more than a decade, several datasets have been developed and made open for research communities to explore – to recognize various actions and activities. A recent survey [48] covers the major datasets in a shorter version.

6.2 Necessity for Standard Datasets

Researchers have been exploiting various action datasets along with the *open-access* datasets, and some of those *open-access and free* datasets become prominent in the research community. Due to the presence of some benchmark and free datasets, it becomes easier for the researchers to compare their new approaches with the state-of-the-arts. However, for some methods, existing datasets may not be suitable or may lack severe dimensional and variational issues, specifically for which these methods are proposed. Therefore, the demand for a new dataset for a specific method is necessary, and based on this context, every year — we find few more datasets, typically, more challenging and with more variability. This chapter covers important and well-known datasets along with some recent datasets, which will be explored in more papers as expected in the future.

However, the demand for new and challenging datasets remains as an important area of contribution for the vision community. Among the existing datasets, most of the cases, digital video cameras are employed to capture videos, though various other sensors (e.g., wireless sensors [76], body-markers, gyro-sensors, etc.) are used as well.

6.2.1 *Motion Capture System*

Motion capture or *mocap* system is an important technique for capturing and analyzing human articulations, though it is very expensive to buy professional motion capture systems (e.g., Vicon (http://vicon.com), Animazoo (http://www.animazoo.com/), Xsens (http://www.xsens.com/), Optotrak). The *mocap* is widely used to animate computer graphics in motion pictures and video games [85]. A typical layout is shown in Figure 6.1.

A motion capture system is a special arrangement of very high-specific camera arrangements and their coordination — to record human body configuration and movement in digital model. In film industry and animation — expensive motion capture systems are used. Various markers are placed in tight-fit clothing or on body parts, face, wrist, etc. as per the requirement and then these are tracked. Some markers are based on optical systems. Some of these are —

- Passive markers (passive optical system uses markers coated with a retro-reflective material to reflect light that is generated near the cameras lens).
- Active markers (e.g., flashing IR lights).
- Time modulated active marker.
- Semi-passive imperceptible marker.

There are some non-optical sensors based on,

- Inertial systems,
- Mechanical systems,
- Magnetic systems,

— to aid motion capture. However, recently, marker-less motion capture systems are being developed by some groups. Microsoft's Kinect (http://www.xbox.com/en-US/Kinect), released for the XBOX 360, is capable of Marker-less motion capture as well. A good description on motion capture systems is available in [20].

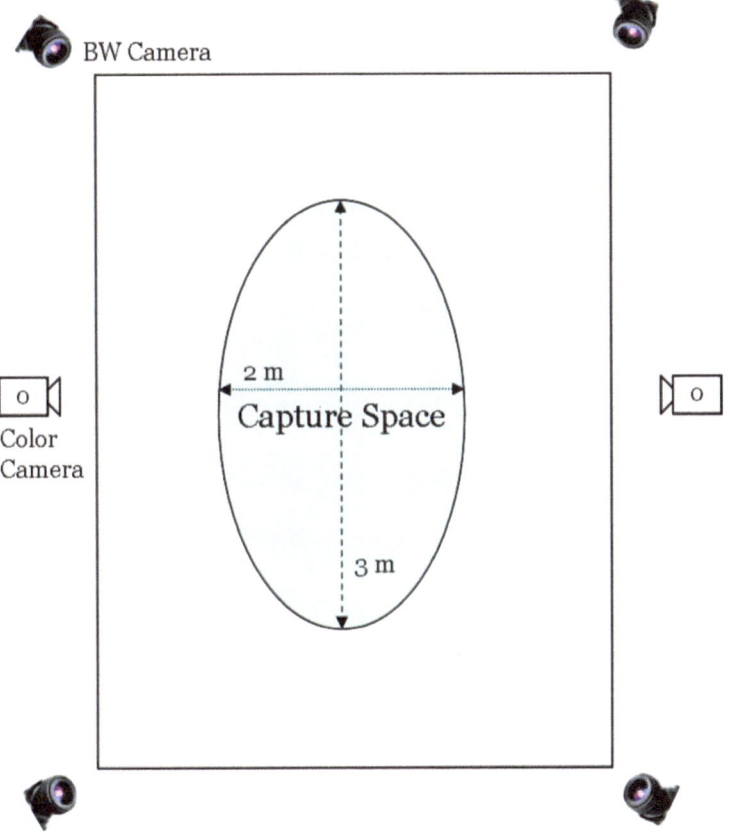

Fig. 6.1: A typical motion capture system layout. The setting may vary based on the number of cameras and the target of the acquisition.

6.3 Datasets on Single-person in the View

This section presents dominant datasets on action and gesture that has mainly one-subject in action or in the scene. We provide short information about these and some comparative recognition results for dominant datasets.

6.3.1 *KTH Dataset*

The most widely used dataset is the KTH dataset [592]. The KTH human action dataset has 6 action classes of a single person. The actions are — walking, running, jogging, boxing, hand-waving, and hand-clapping. Each type of action is performed by 25 actors in indoor and outdoor settings (in four sets). There are 600 video sequences in the dataset. For the common KTH dataset, results are often non-comparable due to the different experimental settings used by different papers [587]. Figure 6.2 shows some sample frames of this dataset. From this Fig., we can understand that even though the dataset has single-subject in the views, it is a difficult dataset. Moreover, the presence of *run, walk* and *jog* turn this dataset to a more challenging one. However, several recent methods achieve good recognition results, as shown in Table 6.1.

Fig. 6.2: Sample frames for KTH action dataset. Each row represents one set out of four settings.

6.3.2 Weizmann Dataset

The Weizmann dataset [542] is an easy dataset. It consists of 90 low-resolution (180 × 144) videos of 9 different subjects, each performing 10 natural actions. The actions are — bend, jumping jack, jump forward, jump in place, run, gallop sideways, skip, walk, wave one hand and wave both hands. This dataset uses a fixed camera setting and a simple background. Figure 6.3 shows some sample frames of this dataset. Table 6.2 presents some comparative results of different methods on this dataset.

Table 6.1

Approach	Recognition (in %)
[110]	81.50
[1]	97.40
[87]	95.10
[593]	80.00
[415]	80.99
[86]	87.70
[584]	81.50
Relative Motion Descriptor [590]	84.00
Relative Motion Descriptor + RANSAC [590]	89.30
[592]	71.72
[394]	90.50
[599]	91.40
[579]	91.80
[578]	94.50
[81]	94.50
[573]	97.00
[583]	97.00
[577]	95.00
[587]	86.60

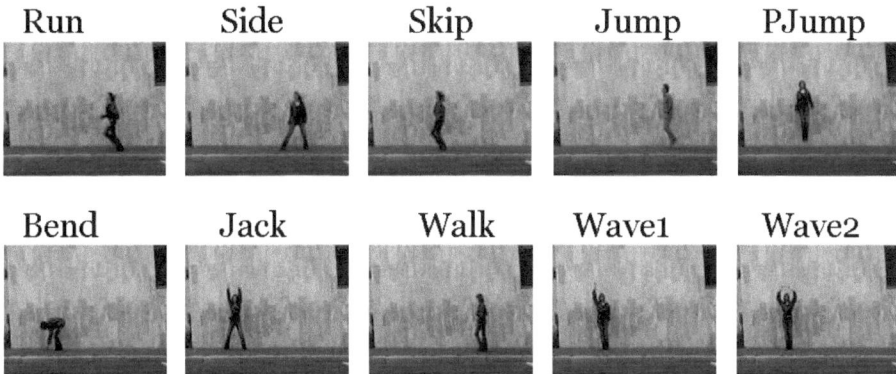

Fig. 6.3: Sample frames for Weizmann action dataset.

6.3.3 *IXMAS Dataset*

The IXMAS dataset records in a controlled environment [473] by 11 actors, each performing 13 actions for 3 times. These are — check watch, cross arms, scratch-head, sit-down, get-up, turn-around, walk, wave, punch, kick, point, pick up, and throw. Multiple views of 5 synchronized and calibrated cameras are employed in this case. This dataset can be used for view-invariant analysis.

Table 6.2

Approach	Recognition (in %)
[88]	95.33
[87]	97.50
[86]	94.74

6.3.4 CASIA Action Database

The CASIA action dataset is a collection of sequences of human activities captured by video cameras outdoors from different angles of view [72, 74]. There are 1446 sequences in all containing eight types of actions of a single person. The actions are — walk, run, bend, jump, crouch, faint, wander and punching a car. These are performed by 24 subjects. It also includes seven types of two person interactions (i.e., rob, fight, follow, follow and gather, meet and part, meet and gather, overtake) performed by every 2 subjects [73].

6.3.5 UMD Dataset

The UMD dataset [44] contains 100 sequences of 10 activities (e.g., pick up object, jog in place, push, squat, wave, kick, bend on the side, throw, turn around, talk on cellphone) performed 10 times each by only one actor. These activities are captured using two synchronized cameras that were about 45 degrees apart.

6.3.6 ICS Action Database

The ICS Action Database [78] is used for human action recognition and segmentation. The ICS database has 25 different actions, which are — get-up, lying, lookup, turn, walk, run, stand-up, sit-down, sitting, etc. Each action has five trials.

6.3.7 Korea University Gesture Database

The Korea University Gesture (KUG) database [77, 204] is created by 20 subjects. It includes 14 normal gestures (such as — sitting, walking), 10 abnormal gestures (different forms of falling such as forward, backward, or from a chair), and 30 command gestures (well-defined and commonly used in gesture based studies such as yes, no, pointing, and drawing numbers). As of today, it is not free of cost like other datasets and one should pay for the dataset to get it.

6.3.8 Wearable Action Recognition Database (WARD)

The Wearable Action Recognition Database [76] consists of continuous sequences of human actions that are measured by a network of wearable and wireless motion sensors. These sensors are located on the two wrists, the waist, and two ankles. It has 13 male and 7 female subjects and they produce a rich set of 13 action categories that covers some of the most common actions in a human's daily activities, such as standing, sitting, walking, and jumping [75].

6.3.9 Biological Motion Library (BML)

The Biological Motion library [71] is built to analyze and identify features such as gender, identity, and affects. This dataset is structured and evenly distributed across these parameters. There are 15 male and 15 female non-professional actors who perform: walk, arm motions (knocking, throwing, and lifting), and sequences of a walk; as well as their affective styles.

6.3.10 HDM05 (Hochschule der Medien) Motion Capture Database

The Hochschule der Medien (HDM05) database [70] has more than 70 motion classes in 10–50 realizations executed by five actors. Most of the motion sequences are performed several times as per fixed guidelines.

6.4 Gesture Datasets

6.4.1 Cambridge Gesture Dataset

The Cambridge Gesture dataset [577] contains nine classes of gestures. In total, there are 900 video sequences, which are partitioned into five different illumination subsets (Set1, Set2, Set3, Set4, and Set5).

6.4.2 Naval Air Training and Operating Procedures Standardization (NATOPS) Dataset

The Naval Air Training and Operating Procedures Standardization (NATOPS) aircraft handling signals database [69] is a body-and-hand gesture dataset containing an official gesture vocabulary used for communication between carrier deck personnel and Navy pilots (e.g., yes/no signs, taxing signs, fueling signs, etc.). The dataset contains 24

Table 6.3

Approach	Recognition (in %)
Baseline [HOG/SVM]	46.98
MultiSVM [115]	59.35
(Best) [115]	63.61
Latent Pose [124]	50.58
Binary representation of node tests [590]	61.10
Quaternary representation of node tests [590]	71.30

gestures, with each gesture performed by 20 subjects 20 times, resulting in 400 samples per gesture. Each sample has a unique duration. Unlike previous gesture databases, this data requires knowledge about both body and hand in order to distinguish gestures.

6.4.3 Keck Gesture Dataset

The Keck gesture dataset [581] consists of 14 different gesture classes. It is performed by three people, repeated three times, which are a subset of military signals. Hence there are 126 video sequences for training, which are captured using a fixed camera with the person viewed against a simple, static background. There are 168 video sequences for testing, which are captured from a moving camera and in the presence of background clutter and other moving objects. Another dataset consisting of 14 army signaling gestures is developed by [68], where each gesture is performed 5 times by 5 subjects.

6.5 Datasets on Social Interactions

Most of the above-mentioned single-subject datasets are not good enough for real-life activities and social interactions. Moreover, these are not much challenging — considering background, camera movements, cluttered environment, presence of multiple subjects and other moving objects, noisy data, etc. Therefore, recently a good number of datasets are developed and this section will cover these.

6.5.1 Youtube Dataset

The YouTube dataset [67] contains actions obtained from YouTube, TV broadcast, and personal video collections and are captured under uncontrolled conditions. The videos are of varying resolution, and contain significant variations. There are 11 action categories. Table 6.4 presents some comparative results of different methods on this dataset.

6.5.2 Youtube Video Dataset

There is another *youtube video dataset*, which is collected by Niebles *et al.* [65]. It is publicly available in `http://vision.stanford.edu/projects/extractingPeople.html`

6.5.3 Hollywood2 Human Action (HOHA) Datasets

The Hollywood2 actions dataset [601] has been collected from 69 different Hollywood movies. There are 12 action classes: answering the phone, driving car, eating, fighting, getting out of the car, hand shaking, hugging, kissing, running, sitting down, sitting up, and standing up. Since action samples in Hollywood2 are collected from movies, they contain many shot boundaries, which cause many artificial interest points. Figure 6.4 shows some sample frames of this dataset.

Hug   Kiss   Answering Phone   Opening Door

Fig. 6.4: Few action samples for HOHA2 actions dataset.

6.5.4 UCF Sports Dataset

The UCF sport action dataset [387] consists of ten categories of human actions including swinging on the pommel horse, driving, kicking, lifting weights, running, skateboarding, swinging at the high bar, swinging golf clubs, and walking. This dataset has various diverse actions from real sports broadcasts. The number of videos for each action varies from 6 to 22 and there are 150 video sequences in total. Furthermore, the videos presented in this dataset have non-uniform backgrounds and both the camera and the subject are moving in some actions. This dataset has strong scene correlations among videos, and some videos are captured in exactly the same location. Table 6.5 presents some comparative results of different methods on this dataset.

Table 6.4

Approach	Recognition (in %)
[573]	88.00
Hierarchy of Discriminative Space-Time Neighborhood (HDN) [578]	87.27
Orientation-Magnitude Descriptor (OMD) [84]	86.90
Histograms of 3D Gradient Orientations (HOG3D) [587]	86.60

Table 6.5

Approach	Recognition (in %)
[435]	67.00
[394]	71.00
[4]	66.00

6.5.5 Soccer Dataset

The Soccer dataset is a low-resolution dataset of World Cup soccer game [435]. It contains 66 action sequences from 8 classes. The classes are defined as — run left 45 degree, run left, walk left, walk in/out, run in/out, walk right, run right, run right 45 degree. Table 6.6 presents some comparative results of different methods on this dataset.

6.5.6 Figure-skating Dataset — Caltech Dataset

The Figure-skating dataset contains 32 video sequences of seven people each with three actions: stand-spin, camel-spin and sit-spin [118].

6.5.7 ADL — Assisted Daily Living Dataset

The ADL dataset [80] consists of high resolution videos of activities performed in daily living. Actions include: answer phone, chop banana, dial phone, look up in directory, write on whiteboard, drink water, eat snack, peel banana, eat banana, and eat with silverware. Table 6.7 presents some comparative results of different methods on this dataset.

6.5.8 Kisses/Slaps Dataset

The Kisses/Slaps dataset [387] contains actions of two classes — (i) Kissing and (ii) Hitting/Slapping. These are compiled from various movies, covering 92 samples of *Kissing* and 112 samples of *Hitting/Slapping*. These actions are performed by different actors,

Table 6.6

Approach	Recognition (in %)
Binary representation of node tests [590]	87.90
Quaternary representation of node tests [590]	91.20
Velocity histories [80]	63.00
Latent velocity histories [80]	63.00
Tracklets [83]	82.70
Augmented velocity histories with relative and absolute position [80]	89.00
Relative Motion Descriptor [590]	84.00
Relative Motion Descriptor + RANSAC [590]	89.30

Table 6.7

Approach	Recognition (in %)
Binary representation of node tests [590]	67.70
Quaternary representation of node tests [590]	74.60
Action MACH [387]	66.80
Local Trinary Pattern (LTP) [82]	80.75
Relative Motion Descriptor [590]	74.60
Relative Motion Descriptor + RANSAC [590]	79.80

at different scales, and in a wide range of scenes. Table 6.8 presents some comparative results of different methods on this dataset.

6.5.9 UIUC Action Dataset

The UIUC action dataset [45] has two different items — some actions and badminton sequences. The dataset-1 consists of 532 high resolution sequences of 14 activities performed by 8 actors. The dataset-2 has one single and two double matches of the Badminton World Cup 2006 (taken from youtube), with various labels (e.g., jump, walk, hop, unknown, various shots, etc.). It is available in http://vision.cs.uiuc.edu/projects/activity/

6.6 Datasets on Other Arenas

This section present various datasets related to action understanding and recognition in different dimensions.

Table 6.8

Approach [111]	Recognition in % [112]
Structure-level approach	67.4
Feature-level approach	60.3
Root + SVM	52.4
Minimum spanning tree	62.3

6.6.1 Actions in Still Images

Still image action dataset is collected by [114, 115]. This dataset contains five action classes (running, walking, playing golf, sitting and dancing). It has 2458 images. The images of this dataset are downloaded from the Internet. So there are a lot of pose variations and cluttered backgrounds in the dataset. Yang *et. al.* [116] further increase the size and pose variability of the dataset by mirror-flipping all the images. Most of actions in the dataset do not have axial symmetry. For example, running-to-left and running-to-right appear very different in the image. So mirror-flipping makes the dataset more diverse. The baseline HOG/SVM approach shows 52% per class accuracy, whereas the latent pose approach by [116] shows 62% per class accuracy [116]. Action recognition from still images is important mainly in news and sports image retrieval and analysis.

6.6.2 Nursing-home Dataset

This is one of the rare but very important real-life action datasets. However, due to privacy issue, till-to-date, these are not available as open-access. It is developed for *fall* analysis in nursing-home surveillance videos [111], to find the causes of falls by elderly residents in order to develop strategies for prevention. This is recorded in a dining room of a nursing home by a low resolution fish-eye camera. Typical activities happening in nursing homes include — people walking, sitting, standing, falling and people helping the fallen person to stand up, etc. This dataset contains ten 3-minutes video clips without falls and another ten short clips with falls [111]. Figure 6.5 and Figure 6.6 show some sample frames of this dataset. Table 6.9 presents some comparative results of different methods on this dataset.

6.6.3 Collective Activity Dataset

This dataset contains five different collective activities: crossing, walking, waiting, talking, and queuing and 44 short video sequences, some of which are recorded by con-

Action Datasets

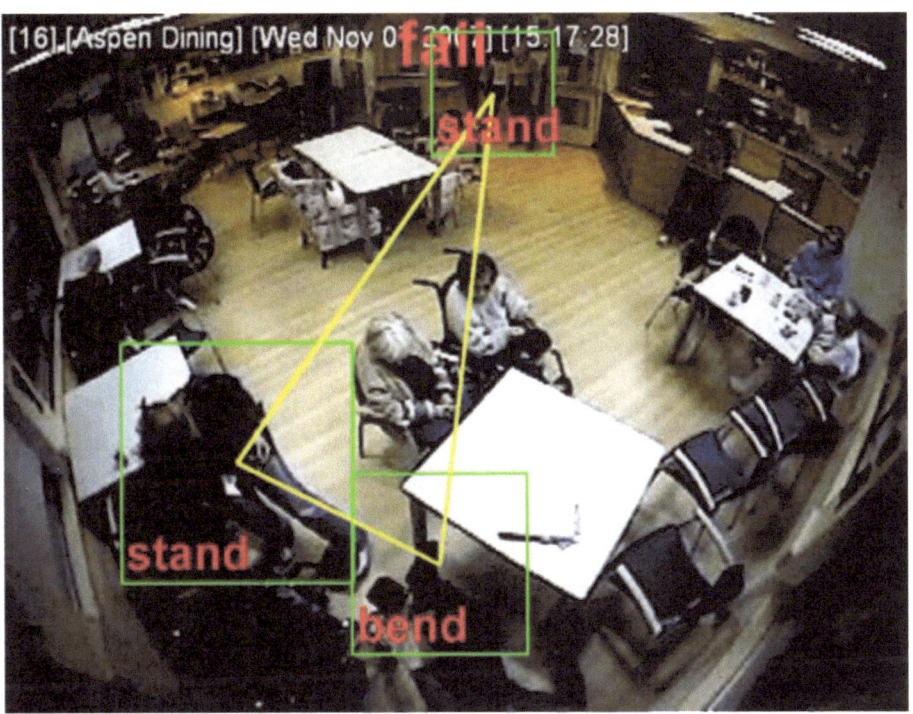

Fig. 6.5: Nursing-home dataset: Samples with some results. Image courtesy to G. Mori, SFU for his permission.

sumer hand-held digital camera with varying view point. Every 10th frame in all video sequences is annotated with an image location of the person, activity ID, and pose direction. The average number of people per frame performing a certain activity is 5.22 persons. The average number of different activities in a short video sequence and hence represents the activity contamination is 1.37.

They later augment the dataset by adding two more categories (dancing and jogging). Since the Walking activity is rather an isolated activity than a collective activity, in another augmented dataset, they remove it and include the following two categories: dancing and jogging activities. Annotation file has the same format as original dataset and the dancing/jogging activities are labeled as 7 and 8 respectively. Figure 6.7 shows some sample frames of this dataset. Table 6.10 presents some comparative results of differ-

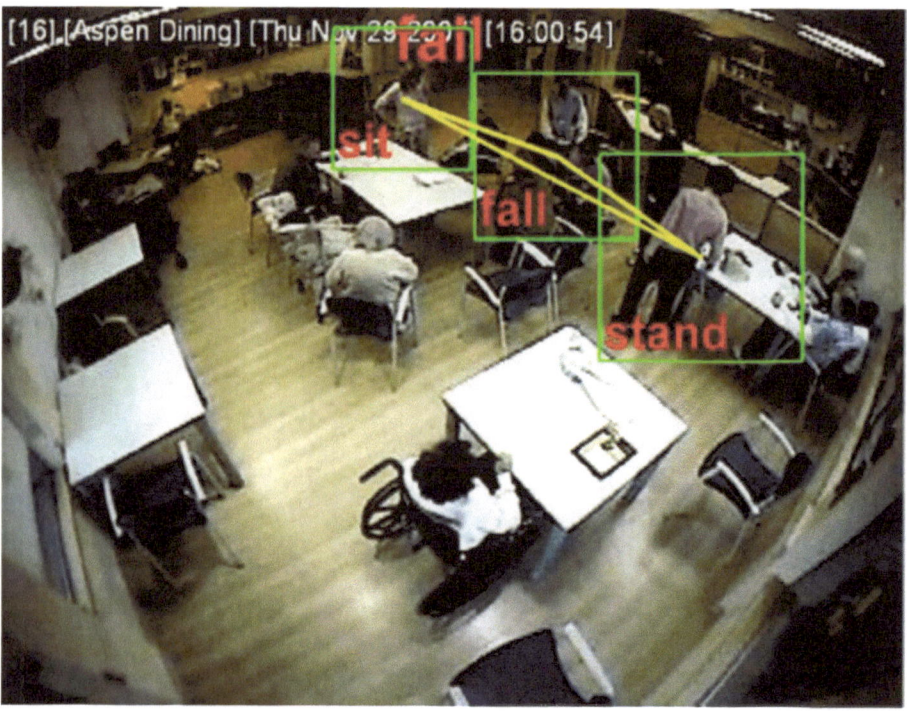

Fig. 6.6: Nursing-home dataset: Samples with some results of *fall* detection. Image courtesy to G. Mori, SFU for his permission.

Table 6.9

Approach	Recognition in %
STV (Spatio-Temporal Volume) [126]	64.3
STV (Spatio-Temporal Volume)+MC [126]	65.9
STV (Spatio-Temporal Volume)+RF (Random Forest) [125]	64.4
RSTV (Randomized Spatio-Temporal Volume) [125]	67.2
RSTV (Randomized Spatio-Temporal Volume)+MRF (Markov Random Field) [125]	70.9
AC (Action Context) [111]	68.2

ent methods on this dataset. It is available in http://www.eecs.umich.edu/vision/activity-dataset.html

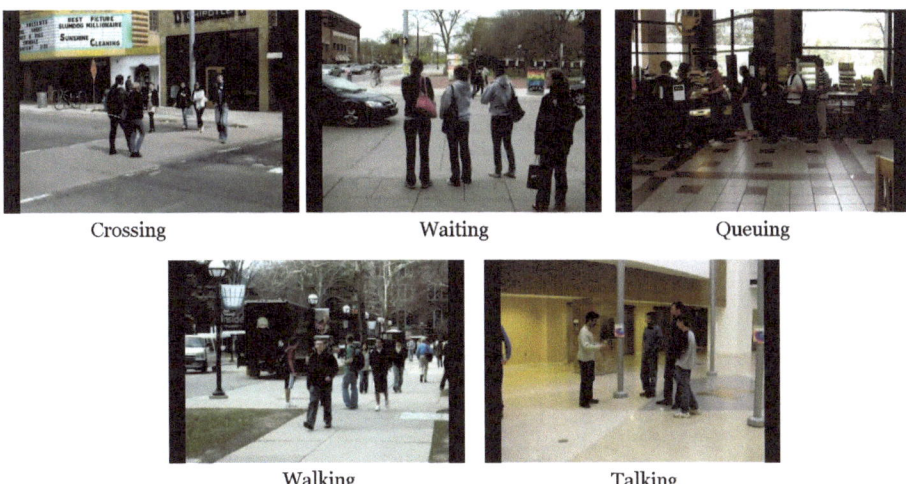

Fig. 6.7: Sample images from the collective activity dataset from http://www.eecs.umich.edu/vision/activity-dataset.html

6.6.4 Coffee and Cigarettes Dataset

Another recent benchmark for temporal action detection is called *Coffee and Cigarettes* [91]. It consists of a single movie composed of 11 short stories, each with different scenes and actors [600].

6.6.5 People Playing Musical Instrument (PPMI)

The *People Playing Musical Instrument* (PPMI) [117] is a dataset of human and object interaction activities. The PPMI dataset contains images of humans interacting with twelve different musical instruments. These are: bassoon, cello, clarinet, flute, French horn, guitar, harp, recorder, saxophone, trumpet, and violin. Different interactions are with the same object. For each instrument, there are images that contain a person playing the instrument (PPMI+), as well as images that contain a person holding the instrument without playing (PPMI-). On each image, they also crop image neighborhood of the face(s) of the target person(s), then normalize the image neighborhood so that the size of human face is 32x32 pixels. All images are downloaded from Internet. Resources of the images include image search engines Google, Yahoo, Baidu, and Bing, and photo hosting websites Flickr, Picasa and Photobucket. Therefore, these images are real-world images and backgrounds are cluttered. It is available in http://ai.stanford.edu/~bangpeng/ppmi.html

6.6.6 DARPA's Mind's Eye Program

DARPA's Mind's Eye Program covers animated videos, multi-camera, multi-view, intensity variations, challenging dataset, variability in object sizes, depth, illumination, context, view-angle, presence of serious occlusion, low-intensity and contrast, etc. *Action-verb!* – 48 action-verbs are maintained in this dataset. It is extremely difficult dataset for analysis, and has huge impact in real-life applications.

6.6.7 VIRAT Video Dataset

The dataset [66] is designed to be realistic, natural and challenging for video surveillance domains in terms of its resolution, background clutter, diversity in scenes, and human activity/event categories than existing action recognition datasets, with a large number of examples (> 30) per action class. Here, both ground camera videos and aerial videos are collected. The 1st workshop on this dataset was held with IEEE CVPR 2011 and the papers and challenges are available in http://www.umiacs.umd.edu/conferences/cvpr2011/ARC/

6.6.8 UMN Dataset: Unusual Crowd Activity

In this dataset, unusual crowd activities are collected in 11 videos, from 3 scenes. Videos contain a normal starting section and an abnormal ending section [106]. Figure 6.8 shows some sample frames of this dataset.

6.6.9 Web Dataset

This dataset contains eight videos of real-life escape panic, clash, fight (as abnormal scenes) and 12 videos of normal pedestrians (as normal scenes) [106, 107]. Figure 6.9 shows some images for normal behaviors of crowd and abnormal scenes from real-life video (image courtesy: R. Mehran, UCF).

6.6.10 HumanEva Dataset

The HumanEva-I dataset contains 7 calibrated video sequences (4 grayscale and 3 color) that are synchronized with 3D body poses obtained from a motion capture system. The

Table 6.10

Features	HumanEva-I	HumanEva-II
Synchronization	Software	Hardware
Number of video cameras	7	4
Types of video cameras	3 color + 4 grayscale	4 color
Number of motion capture cameras	6	8
Types of data	Training, Validation, Testing	Testing
Actions	Walking, jogging, gesturing, throwing	catching a ball, boxing, combo
# of subjects	4	2
# of frames	6800 frames (training [synchronized]),37000 frames (training [MoCap only]), 6800 frames (validation),	24000 (testing) 2460 frames (testing)

database contains 4 subjects performing a 6 common actions (e.g. walking, jogging, gesturing, etc.). The error metrics for computing error in 2D and 3D pose are provided to participants. The dataset contains training, validation and testing (with withheld ground truth) sets [49].

The HumanEva database [49] provides ground-truth data to assist in the evaluation of algorithms for pose estimation and tracking of human motion. For every video of a human figure performing some action, there is the corresponding motion capture data of the same performance. The dataset also provides a standard evaluation metric, which can be used to evaluate algorithms using the data. There are six actions performed by four subjects in the HumanEva dataset. Figure 6.10 shows some sample frames of this dataset. Table 6.11 presents some comparative features for HumanEva-I and HumanEva-II datasets.

Based on these datasets, two workshops were organized with NIPS and IEEE CVPR:

EHuM: Evaluation of Articulated Human Motion and Pose Estimation workshop at NIPS (Neural Information Processing System Conference) 2006.

EHuM$_2$: 2nd Workshop on Evaluation of Articulated Human Motion and Pose Estimation workshop at IEEE CVPR 2007. More than 50 papers utilize the HumanEva dataset, and publish those papers in reputed journals and conference/workshop.

6.6.11 University of Texas Dataset of Interaction, Aerial-view and Wide-area Activity

The University of Texas develops three different datasets, for the *ICPR 2010 Contest on Semantic Description of Human Activities* (SDHA 2010 http://cvrc.ece.utexas.edu/SDHA2010/). These are described below.

6.6.11.1 Interaction Dataset for High-level Human Interaction Recognition Challenge

The UT-Interaction dataset contains videos of continuous executions of 6 classes of human-human interactions: shake-hands, point, hug, push, kick and punch. Figure 6.11 shows some sample frames of this dataset.

6.6.11.2 Aerial-view for Aerial View Activity Classification Challenge

It has human actions in low-resolution videos. The average height of human figures in this dataset is about 20 pixels. It contains total nine classes: pointing, standing, digging, walking, carrying, running, wave1, wave2, and jumping. Figure 6.12 shows some sample frames of this dataset. For details, http://cvrc.ece.utexas.edu/SDHA2010/Aerial_View_Activity.html

6.6.11.3 Wide-area Activity for Wide-Area Activity Search and Recognition Challenge

The Videoweb dataset consists of about 2.5 hours of video observed from 4-8 cameras. The data is divided into a number of scenes that are collected over many days. Each scene is observed by a camera network, where the actual number of cameras changes by scene due the nature of the scene. The dataset contains several types of activities including — throwing a ball, shaking hands, standing in a line, handing out forms, running, limping, getting into/out of a car, and cars making turns. Figure 6.13 shows some sample frames of this dataset.
Source: http://cvrc.ece.utexas.edu/SDHA2010/Wide_Area_Activity.html

6.6.12 Other Datasets

There are several other datasets available for the research community. Here, the name and reference of these are mentioned.

- MSR Action Dataset of 63 actions [55];

- CMU motion capture database http://mocap.cs.cmu.edu;
- Human Motion Database (HMD) at University of Texas at Arlington [64];
- Interactive Emotional Dyadic MoCo (IEMOCAP) Database [63];
- Multi-camera Human Action Video Data [62];
- Manually Annotated Silhouette Data from the MuHAVi Dataset [62];
- Virtual Human Action Silhouette (ViHASi) Dataset [60, 61, 266];
- POETICON Enacted Scenario Corpus [59];
- TMU Kitchen Dataset [58];
- Carnegie Mellon University Multimodal Activity (CMUMMAC) Database [57];
- i3DPost Multi-view Dataset [56];
- CHIL 2007 Evaluation Dataset [54];
- OpenDoor and SitDown-StandUp Dataset [53];
- Visual Geometry Gr. opens up several datasets in [52], e.g., TV human interactions dataset; available in http://www.robots.ox.ac.uk/~vgg/data/
- Yilmaz and Shah develop a dataset having 18 sequences of 8 actions [51];
- PETS has sequences of datasets, e.g., PETS2006 benchmark data-sets are multi-sensor sequences containing unattended luggage scenarios with increasing scene complexity [50];
- PETS2007 contains the following 3 scenarios, with increasing scene complexity: loitering, attended luggage removal (theft), and unattended luggage. Based on these datasets, workshops are organized [50].

There are a few sign language datasets. Sign language recognition has more problems than action datasets, as the former lacks of large corpuses of labeled training data. Moreover, it consists of hand motions and the position of it varies depending on the Interpreter.

6.7 Challenges Ahead on Datasets

In this chapter, a survey of various important action/activity datasets for the computer vision community is presented. However, a systematically constructed gesture database in carefully controlled environment is essential due to the fact that it can help to find or analyze the characteristics of human motion and verify or evaluate the developed algorithm and its application system [48]. Few datasets consider mainly upper body gestures, whereas, in some cases, lower-body movements are systematically collected, mainly for gait recognition and analysis. Despite clear advances in the field of action recognition and understand, evaluation of these methods remains mostly heuristic and qualitative [77]. Different datasets have different perspectives, and are suitable for different methods. For example, it is found that local descriptors are more suitable for the KTH dataset; whereas, the holistic features are more suitable for Weizmann dataset [48].

Ashbrook and Starner [350, 351] introduce a gesture creation and testing tool called *Multiple Action Gesture Interface Creation* (MAGIC) for motion gestures from wrist mounted accelerometers. The MAGIC combines interactive recognizer building with a false positive testing method. It encourages iterative design and attempts to predict the number of false positives by a module called 'Everyday Gesture Library' (EGL), where the EGL is a large database of users' movements recorded from everyday life. At the top of the MAGIC, [349] develop a prototype of MAGIC 2.0 grounded by the task of creating a gesture set for Android phones using their built-in accelerometer. However, the MAGIC 2.0 can handle all kinds of gestures recorded as a time series of any dimension. The Gesture Interface Designer (GID) [352] allows users to design a physical interface on a screen that responds to pointing and finger gestures. Long's *Quill* [357], a pen gesture system, enables users to create pen gestures by example. Furthermore, Quill offers an aid for improving recognition. However, Long discovered that many Quill users do not understand basic error sources and have difficulties in understanding suggestions from the aid system. Another design tool called SUEDE [356] is designed to focus on speech-based user interfaces. It supports a design/test/analyze iterative work flow that inspired MAGIC [350]. Other existing tools include Crayons [354], Eyepatch [358] and aCapella [353]. Numerous machine learning tools like Weka (http://www.cs.waikato.ac.nz/ml/weka/) and GART (Gesture and Activity Recognition Toolkit) [355] are often used for gesture recognition but acted more as a library than a design tool for interaction designers.

Most of the datasets do not include ground-truth and detailed pose information for the researchers. Hence, a researcher may not think and consider beyond the conventional approaches in analyzing actions (e.g., developing mathematical foundation for computer vision based on new approaches or existing physics-based approaches). Sigal *et al.* [49] define a standard set of error measures to evaluate their action datasets. More efforts on this similar track are required [48].

One important area is the development of smart data structure approaches for storing and extracting human motion data [47]. It is necessary to understand the involvement of the cerebral structures in processing the *how, what,* and *why* of other people's actions [46]. Datasets that can somehow relate to research on neuron system is a due now. How monkey's brain acts in doing something — is under study in computer vision recently. It is necessary to investigate various scaling aspects for large motion capture databases as well as reconstructing multiple people and handling occlusions and different observation representations [48]. Development of action datasets in few areas are still in the list to do; e.g.,

- Action datasets at night or darker areas (e.g., by employing IR camera);
- Action datasets from far distance (e.g., by manipulating PNZ cameras);
- Abnormal activities understanding in cluttered outdoor scene (even though a few datasets are available lately);
- Action datasets along with face and emotion (few datasets are partly having these);
- Action datasets — considering the notion of how brain works and thinks;
- Action datasets in rehabilitation and nursing-home environment (however, privacy issue may be a concern in some places);
- Action datasets in various sports' activities for automatic sports analysis; etc.

Usually, most of the datasets are — cropped, isolated, not having much context, have limited cluttered scenes in the background, do not capture real surveillance scenarios, and some of their performances are already saturated (e.g., KTH dataset, Weizmann dataset). It is necessary to have datasets which,

- Do not have any spatio-temporal crop in videos (end-to-end examples),
- Diversity in events (e.g., cars, human, facilities, etc.),
- Detailed annotations,
- Natural scenes and variability (not acted scenes but realistic and spontaneous),
- Variations in sites, subjects, view angles, samples, etc.

The community needs a noble dataset. But question comes – what is *noble* in creating dataset? This depends on various applications and research dimensions. Therefore, researchers are free to develop based on their applications. However, a key point to keep in mind towards a *noble* dataset is that — the *diversity* and *dimensions* should be incorporated. We need to find some meaningful datasets and areas to work, rather than keeping our engagement in trivial action recognition datasets. The community is also struggling to decipher a *right-size* problem in this arena. We may consider multi-modality or cross-modality to learn our systems. By multi-modes, we mean information from audio, video and the contexts.

6.8 Think Ahead!

(1) 'KTH or Weizmann datasets are *beaten to death* (!!!) by research communities in terms of achieved recognition rates' — Do you agree on this point? Why or why not?
(2) 'The real-life applications usually have more people in the view and have complex background with different actions/activities' — So do we need datasets with single person and regular simple actions?
(3) What are the key parameters a benchmark dataset should have?
(4) 'Some groups developed a dataset for their papers and because the papers/works have become important or well-known, the datasets also have become well-known and are used by other researchers' — Do you think that *all* of the existing datasets fulfill the necessary requirements of *being* a benchmark dataset?
(5) List up the problems of the existing datasets and make a guideline for future datasets to develop.
(6) If you want to make a new dataset for the computer vision community — then what kind of dataset(s) do you want to develop? Why?
(7) 'Dataset should be application-oriented and goal-oriented' — What do you think about this statement?

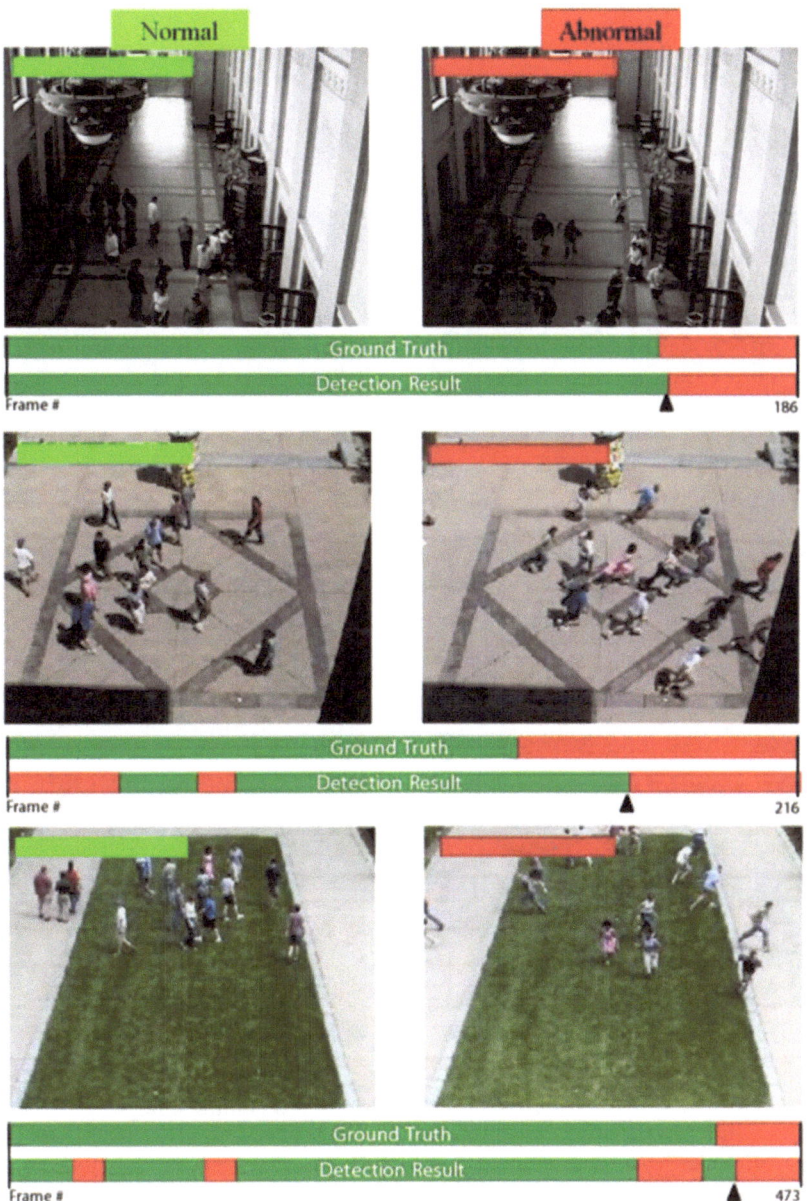

Fig. 6.8: UMN dataset: Unusual Crowd Activity — few sample images with proper detection. Image courtesy to R. Mehran for the permission.

Fig. 6.9: Abnormal crowd dataset — few sample images.

Action Datasets

Fig. 6.10: Sample frames from HumanEva dataset.

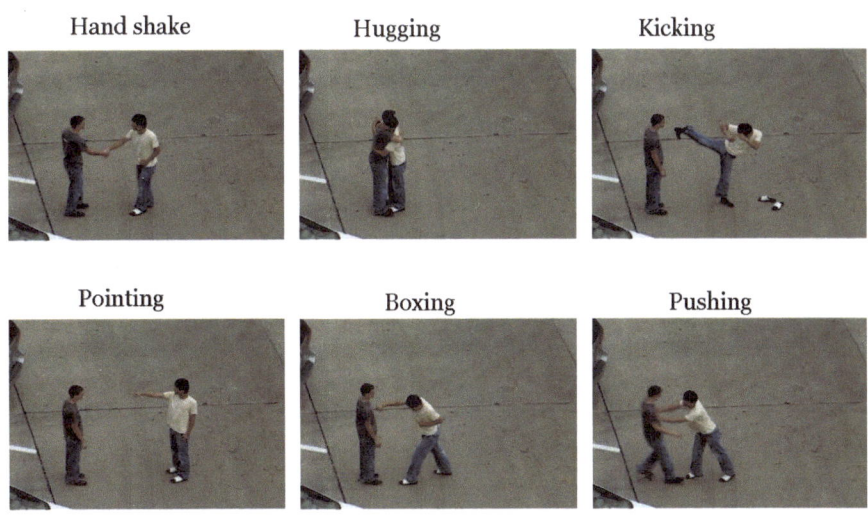

Fig. 6.11: Human interaction dataset.
Source: http://cvrc.ece.utexas.edu/SDHA2010/Human_Interaction.html

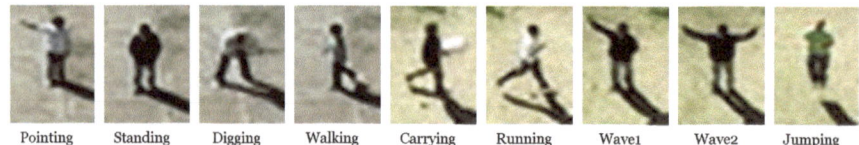

Fig. 6.12: Aerial-view activity dataset — person extraction from each class.
Source: http://cvrc.ece.utexas.edu/SDHA2010/Aerial_View_Activity.html

Fig. 6.13: Wide-area activity dataset.
Source: http://cvrc.ece.utexas.edu/SDHA2010/Wide_Area_Activity.html

Chapter 7

Challenges Ahead

7.1 Challenges Ahead

This last chapter illustrates some future issues based on the present progress of action recognition and understanding. Some of the aspects mentioned here may seem very difficult to accomplish soon, but due to the presence of growing research community in this arena, we can be very hopeful about the future.

7.2 Key Challenges Ahead in Action Recognition

The challenges are manifold. We have covered some of these sparsely in earlier chapters. Few more issues are added here and some of these are related to pre-processing steps. One important area is stereo vision and stereo reconstruction — especially when it comes to understand pedestrian's behavior. Some major challenges in dealing with stereo reconstruction are:

- Occlusion
- Estimations of outliers
- Dealing with image noise
- Presence of texture-less regions
- Static vs. moving object's depth analysis while the camera is moving
- In video, having coherent recovered dense depth maps
- Depth or disparity estimation
- Smoothing vs. over-smoothing (or blending artifact)
- Dealing with false segmentation

It is necessary to develop the segmentation methods for segmenting moving objects from cluttered background and moving camera. The correspondence problem in stereo system is still an open problem. If there are *inconsistent* or *extremeness* or *outlier-prone* data, which are deviant significantly from the *normal* data, these are called as *outliers* [93]. Outlier detection is an important issue in computer vision along with other arenas like network security, remote sensing, anthropology, zoology, — for researchers from statistics, machine learning and data mining communities [93]. Outlier detection is also called as novelty detection or anomaly detection or fault detection [93]. An outlier detector detects samples that deviate significantly (i.e., outliers) from the normal samples. Random Sample Consensus (RANSAC) [92] is widely used to handle outliers.

In multi-camera system, optimal camera arrangement is necessary to maximize the performance. Silhouette resolution, observation view, and its local and global changes affect the recognition performance [359]. There are several observation conditions affecting action and gait recognition performance, such as observation view and distance between the subjects and the camera [359]. Since these observation conditions are dependent on the camera arrangement, the optimal camera arrangement is required for better recognition.

For action recognition in complex scenes, dimensional variations matter a lot. For example,

- Static vs. dynamic scenes;
- Multi-objects' identification or recognition;
- Analyzing the context of scene;
- Goal-directed behavior analysis;

— are important and if all of these issues can be handled at the same time, then we can hope for smart applications of action understanding. *Conversational action* is going to be a new terminology in this field and to understand *goal-directed* behavior — we need to analyze the main context of the scenes (not just object recognition) and relate the objects with *action verbs*. It is also necessary to consider *action-context*. The term *action-context* means to define an action based on the various actions or activities around the person of interest in a scene having multiple subjects. Also, use *adverb, adjective*, etc. to explain an action from the context.

We need to observe people and their movements in videos. To understand familiar activities, we are more or less expert by now due to having various algorithms and approaches for action understanding. But there are many unfamiliar activities and these are numerous. And we are still trying to define, classify and understand these unfamiliar activities.

We need to know what is going to happen afterwards based on the present scenes. For security and other issues, we need to know —

- What is going to happen soon? / What action do we expect next?
- How will it affect the scene and the subjects in it?
- Who is important in the multi-person scene?
- How about the people around?
- How do they feel and what will be there responses?
- Choosing what to report based on the context?

— based on the present understanding. And these are important questions to cover in future. Scene context helps a lot in identifying action. We need to understand *where* the action is happening in the video — whether it is occurring in indoor or outdoor, or inside a car, or in a corner of the booth, or elsewhere.

So far, we can find mainly two kinds of compositions –

- Temporal (temporal chunks or actoms or temporal-based models) and
- Compositions across the body (body-parts analysis and linking body chunks).

Under adverse conditions (e.g., in highly cluttered scenes), saliency mechanism is a good point. Saliency mechanisms improve robustness. Most of the saliency mechanisms have focused on the extraction of image locations (i.e., interest points). These saliency detection mechanisms are widely exploited in various purposes – e.g., in object tracking, recognition, and other applications. Saliency detection can detect specific visual attributes (e.g., edges, contours, local symmetries, corners, blobs) optimally. One of the generic principles is to define saliency by the variance of Gabor filter responses over multiple orientations, wavelet image decomposition, and entropy of the distribution of local intensities. One of the key constraints is that the detected salient points or locations do not necessarily co-occur with the objects to be detected or tracked. For example, the SURF or the SIFT approaches consume plenty of interest points in the image scene and of them a number of points are not the required ones and not salient feature points.

The effect of varying subject's resolution (e.g., more than 30 pixels are reasonable) should be explored — especially in videos with the presence of many people. It is necessary to detect and segment people in the context to understand *where* the subject is, what kind of environment, what sort of activities the person is undertaking, etc. Because activity occurs in *context* and as we move around, it changes with gaze, posture, and goals. Describing people is important but very difficult till-to-date. Methods based on *stick figures* may not work well when it will fail to differentiate a limb and a non-limb to find a stick to correspond to a body-part. This makes it more challenging in cluttered environments. Moreover, this is not pixel-friendly. The key problem of body-parts modeling is that if correlations among the parts are not done smartly, then the entire recognition may be compromised. One could consider the timing of the attributes. However, different bodies have different styles in performing the same action. Hence, body-parts, context, kinematics among the parts are key in dealing with this kind of scenario. Also, various poses or shapes change along with the sitting or standing or steps in between some interactions. These issues make the recognition a difficult task.

Moreover, we need to know *where* the body is in the scene. It is because we need to know the contexts, and need to understand unfamiliar actions. One strategy may appear by building a set of basic labels and make a composite activity models at the end. However, this may not work in a wider set of activities. Hence, a new representation is required to deal with unfamiliar activities. By defining *action attributes*, then adding them for appropriate descriptions, we may focus on solving this problem.

Song *et al.* [123] describe a method for learning the structure and parameters of a decomposable triangulated graph in an unsupervised fashion from unlabeled data. It is based on *unlabeled data*, i.e., the training features include both useful foreground parts and background clutter and the correspondence between the parts and detected features are unknown [123]. They apply this method to learn models of biological motion that can be used to reliably detect and label biological motion [123].

Another concern is the effect of dress. Guan *et al.* [43] describe a new 2D model of the human body contour that combines an underlying naked body with a low-dimensional clothing model. The naked body is represented as a Contour Person that can take on a wide variety of poses and body shapes. Clothing is represented as a deformation from the underlying body contour. This deformation is learned from training examples using principal component analysis to produce eigen clothing [43].

Regarding learning features, the target is to extract motion-sensitive features from the pairs of frames. However, this is a challenging task. And hence, in many cases, due to plenty of outliers and less important motion cues cause the damage in action understanding. Regarding features, it is necessary to look into why some features are more repeatable than others, and which features seem more important and have repeatability for moving scenes.

7.3 Few Points for New Researchers

At the top of above discussions, in this section, few more points are added for a new researcher. To start with action recognition and understanding, few points may juggle in the mind — e.g.,

- Single-person vs. multi-person?
- Single-camera vs. multi-camera?
- Indoor vs. outdoor?
- Fixed camera vs. moving camera?
- Few action classes vs. lots of action instances?
- Separate class vs. continuous actions?
- Static and simple background vs. cluttered and moving background?
- For a new concept — start with simpler task vs. complex scenes?
- Concentrate on recognition results vs. the nobility of the approach?
- Always try with existing benchmark/available datasets to compare a new approach vs. to develop a new dataset that will be suitable to judge the method?
- Instead of exploring existing ideas — may I explore something new and challenging as well as application-oriented?
- Short-term vs. long-term research goal?
- Which application(s) to explore?
- etc.!

Some of these questions pop up while working on new challenging areas. One may develop a balanced approach based on the target of his/her research, and step by step, one can develop and move towards difficult tasks. Many issues are still unsolved and hence, the challenges are open for enthusiastic researchers to explore. For example, it is necessary to come up the following questions and work out –

- Can we build upon the success of faces and pedestrians for action recognition and pose estimation?
- Can we borrow from other ideas, like face recognition, where illumination or pose are managed significantly — by any smart model, or in 3D domain, or by considering stereo, or by taking depth information, or by other means?
- Could we have a FACS (*Facial Action Coding System*)-like description of body movement so that we can work on that?

The answers of the above questions are very much unknown, though a YES would be very much praiseworthy. FACS is a research tool, which is useful for measuring any facial expression a human being can make and it is well-established and organized. A similar approach is considered recently by [91], where they segment an action in the similar concept of segmenting facial expressions of FACS. But FACS-like description will be very challenging due to the dimensional varieties of action and limb/muscle movements. A key concern is the fact that muscles move and act in groups. However, a trial can be done – by recording and predicting the activity of the muscles, which are mainly responsible for activity.

It is necessary to capture patterns that are common and visually characteristics. *Poselet* is one successful approach though it is not the optimum solution. *What do poselets tell us about an image*? A poselet is a set of patches not only with similar pose configuration, but also from the same action class. It provides key point prediction after having an expected person in bound. However, not all poses or elements of poses are equally important. It is also important to find out the latent pose from an image. Moreover, development of an integrated learning framework to estimate pose for action recognition is necessary. Poses could be important cues for video-based action recognition. So, once pose estimations can be managed smartly, the action recognition could be easier (Figure 7.1).

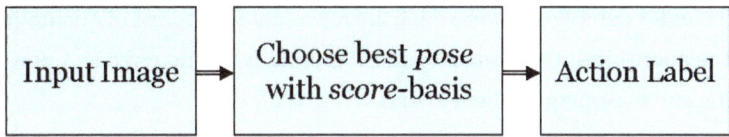

Fig. 7.1: Choose the best-*pose* based on some *score*.

Regarding gesture analysis, *cultural gestures* are important to look into as it varies from culture to region significantly. To understand gestures, especially in continuous and having very slight movements of head and hands, we need to consider cultural gestures (e.g., *WH*-questions by moving head up a bit and down, etc.). Sign language varies apparently along with gestures. A few studies noticed that the people in USA or UK usually gesture with eye contact, they have more animated gestures, more facial expressions, shrugging, hands are apart or crossed, etc. On the other hand, gestures in some Eastern cultures are introvert and self-controlled nature, where avoidance of eye contacts are more evident; in some cases, women cover their mouths (full or part) when talk or smile, less movement of hands (and in many cases, they perform by holding both hands together). So these distinctions must be incorporated and studied for a universal approach to develop for action and gesture understanding.

Another area of deeper study is to learn on how human neuron system functions for activity. Understanding human activity needs the understanding of human nervous system. The primary motor cortex is directly involved with activity. Our motor system is active even when we passively observe other persons' activities. So the obvious questions that come to mind – whether our motor system is necessary to recognize action; or whether our understanding of the neural code can help us to understand human activity. These issues may solve some bigger problems in future. For example, in applications related to patients who are affected with paralysis — understanding the neural activity will aid a lot in digging out some unknown reasons and remedies of human movement and actions of an affected patient. Note that *biological vision system* has a good future but still very challenging.

How to find the events that constitute an activity? It is challenging as several events may occur in parallel. Moreover, overlapping events may share participating objects. Sridhar *et al.* [42] propose a graph mining-based approach to mine a taxonomy of events from activities for complex videos, which are represented in terms of qualitative spatio-temporal relationships. Qualitative spatio-temporal relations provide a powerful way for learning and reasoning about activities.

7.3.1 *Intelligent Transport System*

Intelligent Transport System (ITS) is progressing rapidly and attracting interest to more people due to its importance. Many new researchers can find it interesting and some significant developments will lead towards better traffic security for human life.

Every year more than 1.17 million people die in road crashes around the world, about 70% occur in developing countries [135]. 65% of deaths involve pedestrians and 35% of pedestrian deaths are children. Over 10 million are crippled or injured each year [135]. Road crashes cost approximately 1-3% of a country's annual Gross National Product (GNP) [135]. In European countries, more than 150,000 pedestrians are injured and more than 6000 are killed yearly and in USA, 12% of casualties in traffic accidents are pedestrians [135]. Persons killed in road traffic accidents are 5,744 and injured cases are 1,034,445 in Japan, based on the reports of the Ministry of Internal Affairs and Communications [134]. 77,412 traffic accidents between motor vehicle and pedestrian had occurred in 2006 where 1,990 persons were killed. The offenses of drivers are failure in stopping at crossing, safe passing at the junction, obstruction to pedestrian (all traffic accidents are 865,257 cases and traffic accidents with deaths are 5,906); whereas pedestrians are also responsible for their negligence to signals, crossing, wandering in intoxication, playing on the road, running out, etc. and 185 casualties occurred in 2006 [134]. The majority of traffic accidents involving pedestrians and bicycles occur near intersections [133]. Though the number of the traffic accidents, the injured person, and casualties decreases every year, this is still a big number [134].

Therefore, accurate, robust and real-time Automated Pedestrian Detection (APD) system has high demand as an answer to help drivers to avoid fatal accidents. Also low-cost is a crucial parameter to develop any system so that developing countries can also afford it. Accidents occur near roadside or in the zebra crossing (pedestrian cross-walk) frequently, especially near schools, kindergarten or parks and it is very imperative to reduce the number of accidental injury or collision or even fatality. Though some groups are working in this field after understanding various behaviors and movements of pedestrians, the progress is still slow. Therefore, a plenty to do – to achieve safety driving, and to develop driver awareness systems, concentrating on the activity analyzes of pedestrians. Aim should direct to develop robust systems for the safety of human lives on the streets or pathway or cross-walk or near-by.

Few key objectives of research in this arena could be,

- To establish a robust system for human activity detection and behavior analysis of pedestrians from dynamic and cluttered background (e.g., across the cross-walks, corner of crossings, etc.).
- To create a system that makes a driver aware of a danger through some means — so that the driver can take early precaution for any sudden and risky movement that may cause accident of pedestrians.
- To develop a robust system so that safety driving can be ensured for reduced number of accidents of the pedestrians.

One of the most challenging tasks in computer vision is analysis of human activity in crowded scenes [106]. In addition, research in sociology and behavioral sciences provide mathematical models of pedestrian behavior patterns such as Social Force Model. Though [106] introduce a computer vision method based on particle advection to detect and localize abnormal crowd behavior using the Social Force model, this area has not been explored much. In Social Force Model, an individual is subject to long-ranged forces and his/her dynamics follow the equation of motion, similar to Newtonian mechanics. The velocity of an individual is described as the result of a personal desire force and interaction forces [106]. Future works can be directed in this direction too. However, regarding crowd behavior analysis, one should note the following challenges [106] in mind,

- Crowd scenes suffer various levels of occlusion;
- Cluttered environment;
- Low resolution for human (in some cases, a few pixels tall for a subject to detect or analyze);
- Having various types of social interactions of the people in the scene.

These issues are challenging. It is well-known that occlusion corrupts a measured image, introducing errors that can be [104],

- Large in magnitude in the value of pixels affected (gross errors);
- Concentrated only on relatively small portion of pixels of the image (sparse errors); and
- Unpredictable in location of the pixels affected (randomly supported errors).

Ensuring robust recognition performance despite such errors incurred by occlusion is undoubtedly a challenging task [104].

7.4 Conclusion

In this chapter, several challenging and unsolved issues are explored. The last section presents few ideas for new researchers. I close this chapter by *opening various new* avenues for research communities. Let's hope that better methodologies in future will lead us towards more human-oriented real-life applications for *better life*. With this high-toned yearning, I would like to conclude this book!

7.5 Think Ahead!

(1) List up the challenges that *you think* still existing in action recognition field.
(2) List up the major approaches that you feel best-suited for your *target* application or research area.
(3) Find out the *constraints* of your enlisted methods to solve the issues you feel in your specific target research.
(4) How to solve each of your enlisted *constraints* with the existing different concepts?
(5) Can you find a clue from other methods to solve the problem? If yes, why and how? If not, then how to solve your research problem within a time period?
(6) What are the challenging areas ahead to work and solve the problems?
(7) Make several panel discussions (in a place, or over teleconferences (e.g., by *skype*)) with your friends who are working in similar/related research objectives, and do brain-storming on the points that hammer you. Do you find new ideas from these discussions?

Bibliography

[1] Guo K, Ishwar P, Konrad J (2010) Action recognition using sparse representation on covariance manifolds of optical flow. IEEE International Conference on Advanced Video and Signal Based Surveillance.
[2] Ahad M, Tan J, Kim H, Ishikawa S (2011) Approaches for global-based action representations for games and action understanding. IEEE Automatic Face and Gesture Recognition 753–758.
[3] Rosten E, Drummond T (2005) Fusing points and lines for high performance tracking. International Conference on Computer Vision.
[4] Chen C, Aggarwal J (2009) Recognizing human action from a far field of view. IEEE Workshop on Motion and Video Computing.
[5] Willamowski J, Arregui D, Csurka G, Dance C, Fan L (2004) Categorizing nine visual classes using local appearance descriptors. IWLAVS.
[6] Matikainen P, Hebert M, Sukthankar R (2009) Trajectons: Action recognition through the motion analysis of tracked features. VOEC Workshop.
[7] Bosch A, Zisserman A, Munoz X (2007) Image classification using random forests and ferns. International Conference on Computer Vision.
[8] Sun Z, Tan T (2009) Ordinal measures for iris recognition. IEEE Trans. Pattern Analysis and Machine Intelligence.
[9] Fawcett T (2006) An introduction to ROC analysis. Pattern Recognition Letters **27**:861–874.
[10] Wang X, Tang X (2004) Random sampling LDA for face recognition. IEEE Computer Vision and Pattern Recognition.
[11] Mallapragada P, Rong J, Jain A, Yi L (2009) SemiBoost: boosting for semi-supervised learning. IEEE Trans. Pattern Analysis and Machine Intelligence.
[12] Pavlidis I, Morellas V, Tsiamyrtzis V, Harp S (2001) Urban surveillance systems: from the laboratory to the commercial world. Proceedings of the IEEE 1478–1497.
[13] Lo B, Velastin S (2001) Automatic congestion detection system for underground platforms. International Symp. on Intell. Multimedia, Video and Speech Processing 158–161.
[14] Cucchiara R, Grana C, Piccardi M, Prati A (2003) Detecting moving objects, ghosts and shadows in video streams. IEEE Trans. Pattern Analysis and Machine Intelligence **25(10)**:1337–1342.
[15] Han B, Comaniciu D, Davis L (2004) Sequential kernel density approximation through mode propagation: applications to background modeling. Asian Conference on Computer Vision.
[16] Oliver N, Rosario B, Pentland A (2000) A Bayesian computer vision system for modeling human interactions. IEEE Trans. Pattern Analysis and Machine Intelligence **22(8)**:831–843.
[17] Liu X (2009) Discriminative face alignment. IEEE Trans. Pattern Analysis and Machine Intelligence.

[18] Hsu C, Lin C (2002) A comparison of methods for multiclass, support vector machines. IEEE Trans. Neural Networks **13(2)**.
[19] Vapnik V (1998) Statistical learning theory. Wiley Pub.
[20] Gleicher M (1999) Animation from observation: motion capture and motion editing. Computer Graphics **33**:51–54.
[21] Horn B (2000) Tsai's camera calibration method revisited. http://people.csail.mit.edu/bkph/articles/Tsai_Revisited.pdf
[22] Abdel-Aziz Y, Karara H (1971) Direct linear transformation from comparator coordinates into object space coordinates in close-range photogrammetry. Symp. on Close-Range Photogrammetry 1–18.
[23] Hartley R, Zisserman A (2004) Multiple view geometry in computer vision. Cambridge University Press.
[24] Chum O, Matas J (2005) Matching with PROSAC — progressive sample consensus. IEEE Computer Vision and Pattern Recognition **1**.
[25] Nister D (2003) Preemptive RANSAC for live structure and motion estimation. International Conference on Computer Vision **1**.
[26] Matas J, Chum O, Urba M, Pajdla T (2002) Robust wide baseline stereo from maximally stable extremal regions. British Machine Vision Conference.
[27] Belongie S, Malik J (2000) Matching with shape contexts. IEEE Workshop on Contentbased Access of Image and Video Libraries.
[28] Viola P, Jones M (2001) Rapid object detection using boosted cascade of simple features. IEEE Computer Vision and Pattern Recognition.
[29] Piccardi M (2004) Background subtraction techniques: a review. IEEE International Conference on Systems, Man and Cybernetics.
[30] Bouwmans T (2009) Subspace learning for background modeling: a survey. Recent Patents on Computer Science **2(3)**.
[31] Elhabian S, El-Sayed E, Ahmed S (2008) Moving object detection in spatial domain using background removal techniques-state-of-art. Recent Patents on Computer Science.
[32] Sarfraz S, Hellwich O (2008) Head pose estimation in face recognition across pose scenarios. International conference on Computer Vision Theory and Applications 235–242.
[33] Kim S, Yoon K, Kweon I (2006) Object recognition using a generalized robust invariant feature and Gestalt's law of proximity and similarity. IEEE Computer Vision and Pattern Recognition Workshop.
[34] Lazebnik S, Schmid C, Ponce J (2004) Semi-local affine parts for object recognition. British Machine Vision Conference.
[35] Lowe D (1999) Object recognition from local scale-invariant features. International Conference on Computer Vision **2**:1150–1157.
[36] Deng H, Zhang W, Mortensen E, Dietterich T, Shapiro L (2007) Principal curvature-based region detector for object recognition. IEEE Computer Vision and Pattern Recognition.
[37] Wang H, Brady M (1995) Real-time corner detection algorithm for motion estimation. Image and Vision Computing **13(9)**:695–703.
[38] Mikolajczyk K, Schmid C (2004) Scale and affine invariant interest point detectors. International Journal of Computer Vision **60(1)**:63–86.
[39] Harris C, Stephens M (1988) A combined corner and edge detector. 4th Alvey Vision Conference 147–151.
[40] Trajkovic M, Hedley M (1998) Fast corner detection. Image and Vision Computing **16(2)**:75–87.
[41] Smith S, Brady J (1997) SUSAN — a new approach to low level image processing. International Journal of Computer Vision **23**:45–78.

[42] Sridhar M, Cohn A, Hogg D (2010) Discovering an event taxonomy from video using qualitative spatio-temporal graphs. European Conference on Artificial Intelligence.
[43] Guan P, Freifeld O, Black M (2010) A 2D human body model dressed in eigen clothing. European Conference on Computer Vision.
[44] Veeraraghavan A, Chellappa R, Roy-Chowdhury A (2006) The function space of an activity. IEEE Computer Vision and Pattern Recognition.
[45] Tran D, Sorokin A (2008) Human activity recognition with metric learning. European Conference on Computer Vision.
[46] Thioux M, Gazzola V, Keyesers C (2008) Action understanding: how, what and why. Current Biology **18(10)**.
[47] Yamane K, Nakamura Y (2010) Human motion database with a binary tree and node transition graphs. J. of Autonomous Robots **29(2)**.
[48] Ahad M, Tan J, Kim H, Ishikawa S (2011) Action dataset — a survey. SICE Annual Conference.
[49] Sigal L, Balan A, Black M (2010) HumanEva: Synchronized video and motion capture dataset and baseline algorithm for evaluation of articulated human motion. International Journal of Computer Vision **87(1-2)**.
[50] PETS (2007) Workshops on Performance Evaluation of Tracking & Surveillance (PETS). http://www.cvg.rdg.ac.uk/PETS2007/data.html
[51] Yilmaz A, Shah M (2005) Recognizing human actions in videos acquired by uncalibrated moving cameras. International Conference on Computer Vision.
[52] Patron-Perez A, Marszalek M, Zisserman A, Reid I (2010) High five: recognising human interactions in TV shows. British Machine Vision Conference.
[53] Duchenne O, Laptev I, Sivic J, Bach F, Ponce J (2009) Automatic annotation of human actions in video International Conference on Computer Vision.
[54] Burger S (2008) The CHIL RT07 evaluation data. Multimodal Technologies for Perception of Humans.
[55] MSR action dataset. http://research.microsoft.com/en-us/um/people/zliu/actionrecorsrc/default.htm
[56] Gkalelis N, Kim H, Hilton A, Nikolaidis N, Pitas I (2009) The i3DPost multi-view and 3D human action/interaction database. Conference on Visual Media Production.
[57] Hodgins F, Macey J (2009) Guide to the Carnegie Mellon University multimodal activity (cmu-mmac) database. CMU-RI-TR-08-22.
[58] Tenorth M, Bandouch J, Beetz M (2009) The TUM kitchen data set of everyday manipulation activities for motion tracking and action recognition. IEEE International Workshop on Tracking Humans for the Evaluation of their Motion in Image Sequences with International Conference on Computer Vision.
[59] Wallraven C, Schultze M, Mohler B, Vatakis A, Pastra K (2011) The POETICON enacted scenario corpus — a tool for human and computational experiments on action understanding. IEEE Automatic Face and Gesture Recognition http://poeticoncorpus.kyb.mpg.de
[60] Ragheb H, Velastin S, Remagnino P, Ellis T (2008) ViHASi: Virtual human action silhouette data for the performance evaluation of silhouette-based action recognition methods Workshop on Activity Monitoring by Multi-Camera Surveillance Systems.
[61] ViHASi Virtual Human Action Silhouette (ViHASi) database. http://dipersec.king.ac.uk/VIHASI/
[62] MuHAVi. http://dipersec.king.ac.uk/MuHAVi-MAS/
[63] Busso C, Bulut M, Lee C, Kazemzadeh A, Mower E, Kim S, Chang J, Lee S, Narayanan S (2008) IEMOCAP: Interactive emotional dyadic motion capture database. Language Resources and Evaluation **42(4)**:335–359.
[64] G.-Filho G, Biswas A (2011) The human motion database: A cognitive and parametric sampling of human motion. IEEE Automatic Face and Gesture Recognition.

[65] Niebles J, Han B, Ferencz B, Fei-Fei L (2008) Extracting moving people from internet videos. European Conference on Computer Vision.
[66] VIRAT (2011) VIRAT database. http://www.viratdata.org/
[67] Liu J, Luo J, Shah M (2009) Recognizing realistic actions from videos "in the wild". IEEE Computer Vision and Pattern Recognition.
[68] Keck gesture database
http://www.umiacs.umd.edu/~shivnaga/supplmat_ActionRecBallisticDyn_CVPR08/action_rec_using_ballistic_dynamics.html#gesture_rec
[69] Song Y, Demirdjian D, Davis R (2011) Tracking body and hands for gesture recognition: NATOPS aircraft handling signals database. IEEE Automatic Face and Gesture Recognition.
[70] Muller M, Ryder T, Clausen M, Eberhardt B, Kruger B, Weber A (2007) Documentation: Mocap database HDM05. Universitat Bonn, Tech. Report **CG-2007-2**.
[71] Ma Y, Paterson H, Pollick F (2006) A motion capture library for the study of identity, gender, and emotion perception from biological motion. Behavior Research Methods **38**:134–141.
[72] CASIA Database. http://www.cbsr.ia.ac.cn/english/Action%20Databases%20EN.asp
[73] Zhang Z, Huang K, Tan T (2008) Multi-thread parsing for recognizing complex events in videos. European Conference on Computer Vision.
[74] Wang Y, Huang K, Ta T (2007) Human activity recognition based on R transform. IEEE Computer Vision and Pattern Recognition.
[75] WAR. http://www.eecs.berkeley.edu/~yang/software/WAR/
[76] Yang A, Jarafi R, Kuryloski P, Iyengar S, Sastry S, Bajcsy R (2008) Distributed segmentation and classification of human actions using a wearable motion sensor network. Workshop on Human Communicative Behavior Analysis with Computer Vision and Pattern Recognition.
[77] Hwang B, Kim S, Lee S (2006) A full-body gesture database for automatic gesture recognition. IEEE Automatic Face and Gesture Recognition.
[78] ICS Action Database, The University of Tokyo. http://www.ics.t.u-tokyo.ac.jp/action/
[79] Vasconcelos M, Vasconcelos N (2009) Natural image statistics and low-complexity feature selection. IEEE Trans. Pattern Analysis and Machine Intelligence **31(2)**.
[80] Messing R, Pal C, Kautz H (2009) Activity recognition using the velocity histories of tracked keypoints. International Conference on Computer Vision.
[81] Gilbert A, Illingworth J, Bowden R (2010) Action recognition using mined hierarchical compound features. IEEE Trans. Pattern Analysis and Machine Intelligence.
[82] Yaffet L, Wolf L (2009) Local trinary patterns for human action. International Conference on Computer Vision.
[83] Raptis M, Soatto S (2010) Tracklet descriptors for action modeling and video analysis. European Conference on Computer Vision.
[84] Bregonzio M, Li J, Gong S, Xiang T (2010) Discriminative topics modelling for action feature selection and recognition. British Machine Vision Conference.
[85] Liu G, Zhang J, Wang W, McMillan L (2005) A system for analyzing and indexing human-motion databases. SIGMOD.
[86] Ali S, Shah M (2010) Human action recognition in videos using kinematic features and multiple instance learning. IEEE Trans. Pattern Analysis and Machine Intelligence **32(2)**.
[87] Seo H, Milanfar P (2011) Action recognition from one example. IEEE Trans. Pattern Analysis and Machine Intelligence.
[88] Junejo I, Dexter E, Laptev I, Perez P (2011) View-independent action recognition from temporal self-similarities. IEEE Trans. Pattern Analysis and Machine Intelligence **33**:172–185.
[89] Satkin S, Hebert M (2010) Modeling the temporal extent of actions. European Conference on Computer Vision.

[90] Schindler K, Van Gool L (2008) Action snippets: How many frames does human action recognition require. IEEE Computer Vision and Pattern Recognition.
[91] Gaidon A, Harchaoui Z, Schmid C (2011) Actom sequence models for efficient action detection. IEEE Computer Vision and Pattern Recognition.
[92] Fischler M, Bolles R (1981) Random Sample Consensus: a paradigm for model fitting with applications to image analysis and automated cartography. Communications of the ACM **24(6)**:381–395.
[93] Chen Y, Dang X, Peng H, Bart H (2009) Outlier detection with the kernelized spatial depth function. IEEE Trans. Pattern Analysis and Machine Intelligence.
[94] Friedman J (1989) Regularized discriminant analysis. J. Am. Statistical Assoc.
[95] Bensmail H, Celeux G (1996) Regularized Gaussian discriminant analysis through Eigenvalue decomposition. J. Am. Statistical Assoc.
[96] Bouveyron C, Girard S, Schmid C (2007) High dimensional discriminant analysis. Comm. in Statistics: Theory and Methods.
[97] Tao D, Ji X, Wu X, Maybank S (2009) Geometric mean for subspace selection. IEEE Trans. Pattern Analysis and Machine Intelligence.
[98] Lolitkar R, Kothari R (2000) Fractional-step dimensionality reduction. IEEE Trans. Pattern Analysis and Machine Intelligence.
[99] Sanja F, Skocaj D, Leonardis A (2006) Combining reconstructive and discriminative subspace methods for robust classification and regression by subsampling. IEEE Trans. Pattern Analysis and Machine Intelligence.
[100] Kim J, Choi J, Yi J, Turk M (2005) Effective representation using ICA for face recognition robust to local distortion and partial occlusion. IEEE Trans. Pattern Analysis and Machine Intelligence **27(12)**:1977–1981.
[101] Belhumeur P, Hesanha J, Kreigman D (1997) Eigenfaces vs. Fisherfaces: Recognition using class specific linear projection. IEEE Trans. Pattern Analysis and Machine Intelligence.
[102] Li S, Hou X, Zhang H, Cheng Q (2001) Learning spatially localized, parts-based representation. IEEE Computer Vision and Pattern Recognition.
[103] Ho J, Yang M, Lim J, Lee K, Kriegman D (2003) Clustering appearances of objects under varying illumination conditions. IEEE Computer Vision and Pattern Recognition.
[104] Wright J, Yang A, Ganesh A, Sastry S, Ma Y (2009) Robust face recognition via sparse representation. IEEE Trans. Pattern Analysis and Machine Intelligence.
[105] Zhang X, Fan G (2010) Dual gait generative models for human motion estimation from a single camera. IEEE Trans. on Systems, Man, and Cybernetics, Part B: Cybernetics **40(4)**:1034–1049.
[106] Mehran R, Oyama A, Shah M (2009) Abnormal crowd behavior detection using social force model. IEEE Computer Vision and Pattern Recognition.
[107] Web dataset, UCF Web Dataset. http://www.cs.ucf.edu/~ramin/?page_id=24#2._Experiments_on_Web_Dataset
[108] Mehran R, Moore B, Shah M (2010) A streakline representation of flow in crowded scenes. European Conference on Computer Vision.
[109] Mehran R, Courtesy: Ramin Mehran for his permission to use the materials. http://www.cs.ucf.edu/~ramin/?page_id=99
[110] Niebles J, Wang H, Fei-Fei L (2006) Unsupervised learning of human action categories using spatial-temporal words. British Machine Vision Conference.
[111] Lan T, Wang Y, Mori G, Robinovitc S (2010) Retrieving actions in group contexts. International Workshop on Sign Gesture Activity with European Conference on Computer Vision.
[112] Lan T, Wang Y, Yang W, Mori G (2010) Beyond actions: Discriminative models for contextual group activities. Neural Information Processing Systems (NIPS)

[113] Lan T, Wang Y, Mori G (2011) Discriminative figure-centric models for joint action localization and recognition. International Conference on Computer Vision.
[114] Ikizler N, Cinbis R, Pehlivan S, Duygulu P (2008) Recognizing actions from still images. International Conference on Pattern Recognition.
[115] Ikizler N, Cinbis R, Sclaroff S (2009) Learning actions from the web. International Conference on Computer Vision.
[116] Yang W, Wang Y, Mori G (2010) Recognizing human actions from still images with latent poses. IEEE Computer Vision and Pattern Recognition.
[117] Yao B, Fei-Fei L (2010) A structured image representation for recognizing human and object interactions. IEEE Computer Vision and Pattern Recognition.
[118] Wang Y, Jiang H, Drew M, Li Z, Mori G (2008) Unsupervised discovery of action classes. IEEE Computer Vision and Pattern Recognition.
[119] Fanti C (2008) Towards automatic discovery of human movemes. PhD Thesis, California Institute of Technology. http://www.vision.caltech.edu/publications/phdthesis_fanti.pdf
[120] Del Vecchio D, Murray R, Perona P (2002) Primitives for human motion: a dynamical approach. IFAC World Congress on Automatic Control.
[121] Bregler C, Malik J (1997) Learning and recognizing human dynamics in video sequences. IEEE Computer Vision and Pattern Recognition 568–674.
[122] Goncalves L, Di Bernardo E, Perona P (1998) Reach out and touch space (motion learning). IEEE Automatic Face and Gesture Recognition 234–239.
[123] Song Y, Goncalves L, Perona P (2001) Unsupervised learning of human motion models. Advances in Neural Information Processing Systems (NIPS).
[124] Wang Y, Mori G (2011) Hidden part models for human action recognition: probabilistic vs. max-margin. IEEE Trans. Pattern Analysis and Machine Intelligence.
[125] Choi W, Shahid K, Savarese S (2011) Learning context for collective activity recognition. IEEE Computer Vision and Pattern Recognition.
[126] Choi W, Shahid K, Savarese S (2009) What are they doing? : collective activity classification using spatio-temporal relationship among people. International Workshop on Visual Surveillance (VSWS09) with International Conference on Computer Vision.
[127] Murase H, Lindenbaum M (1995) Partial eigenvalue decomposition of large images using spatial temporal adaptive method. IEEE Trans. on Image Processing **4(5)**:622–629.
[128] Rahman M, Ishikawa S (2005) Human posture recognition: eigenspace tuning by mean eigenspace. International Journal of Image and Graphics **5(4)**:825–837.
[129] Viola P, Jones M (2000) Robust real-time object detection. IEEE Workshop on Statistical and Computational Theories of Vision.
[130] Black M, Jepson A (1998) Eigen tracking: robust matching and tracking of articulated objects using view-based representation. International Journal of Computer Vision **26(1)**:63–84.
[131] Ohba K, Ikeuchi K (1997) Detectability, uniqueless and reliability of eigen windows for stable verifications of partially occluded objects. IEEE Trans. Pattern Analysis and Machine Intelligence **9**:1043–1047.
[132] Murase H, Nayar K (1995) Visual learning and recognition of 3-D objects from appearance. International Journal of Computer Vision **14**:39–50.
[133] Li Z, Wang K, Li L, Wang F (2006) A review on vision-based pedestrian detection for intelligent vehicles. ICVES 57–62.
[134] MIAC-JP. Ministry of Internal Affairs and Communications, JAPAN. http://www.stat.go.jp/english/data/nenkan/1431-26.htm
[135] The World Bank. http://www.worldbank.org/html/fpd/transport/roads/safety.htm

[136] Krotosky S, Trivedi M (2007) On color-, infrared-, and multimodal-stereo approaches to pedestrian detection. IEEE Trans. ITS **8(4)**:619–629.
[137] Zhang Z, Faugeras O (1992) Three-dimensional motion computation and object segmentation in a long sequence of stereo frames. International Journal of Computer Vision **7**:211–241.
[138] Chang Y, Aggarwal J (1991) 3D structure reconstruction from an ego motion sequence using statistical estimation and detection theory. Workshop on Visual Motion.
[139] Sethi I, Jain R (1987) Finding trajectories of feature points in a monocular image sequence. IEEE Trans. Pattern Analysis and Machine Intelligence **9**:56–73.
[140] Cui N, Weng J, Cohen P (1990) Extended structure and motion analysis from monocular image sequences. International Conference on Computer Vision 222–229.
[141] Weng J, Ahuja N, Huang T (1992) Matching two perspective views. IEEE Trans. Pattern Analysis and Machine Intelligence **14**:806–825.
[142] Tomasi C, Kanade T (1991) Detection and tracking of point features. Carnegie Mellon University, Tech. Report **CMU-CS-91-132**.
[143] Hager G, Belhumeur P (1996) Real-time tracking of image regions with changes in geometry and illumination. IEEE Computer Vision and Pattern Recognition 403–410.
[144] Tommasini T, Fusiello A, Trucco E, Roberto V (1998) Making good features track better. IEEE Computer Vision and Pattern Recognition.
[145] Shi J, Tomasi C (1994) Good features to track. IEEE Computer Vision and Pattern Recognition.
[146] Yao Y, Chellappa R (1995) Tracking a dynamic set of feature points. IEEE Trans. Image Processing **4(10)**:1382–1395.
[147] Yao Y, Chellappa R (1994) Dynamic feature point tracking in an image sequence. IAPR Computer Vision and Pattern Recognition **1**:654-657.
[148] Naito Y, Okatani T, Deguchi K (2003) Comparison of the feature point tracking method in image sequences. SICE Annual Conference 1326-1331.
[149] Wang Y, Cao L, Huang W (2003) 3-D human motion estimation using regularization with 2-d feature point tracking. International Conference on Machine Learning and Cybernetics 2931-2935.
[150] Borgefors G (1988) Hierarchical chamfer matching: a parametric edge matching algorithm. IEEE Trans. Pattern Analysis and Machine Intelligence **10(6)**:849–865.
[151] Peterson L (2009) K-nearest neighbor. http://www.scholarpedia.org/article/K-nearest_neighbor **4:2**.
[152] Weinberger K, Blitzer J, Saul L (2005) Distance metric learning for large margin nearest neighbor classification. Annual Conference on Neural Information Processing Systems.
[153] Aguiar P, Moura J (2000) Weighted factorization. International Conference on Image Processing 549–562.
[154] Li Y, Brooks M (1999) An efficient recursive factorization method for determining structure from motion. IEEE Computer Vision and Pattern Recognition 138–143.
[155] Fujiki J, Kurata T (2000) Recursive factorization method for the paraperspective model based on the perspective projection. International Conference on Pattern Recognition 406–410.
[156] Fujiki J, Kurata T, Tanaka M (1998) Iterative factorization method for object recognition. International Symp. on Electronic Imaging 192–201.
[157] Quan L, Kanade T (1996) A factorization method for affine structure from line correspondences. IEEE Computer Vision and Pattern Recognition 803–808.
[158] Ueshiba T, Tomita F (1998) A factorization method for projective and Euclidean reconstruction from multiple perspective views via iterative depth estimation. European Conference on Computer Vision 296–210.

[159] Sturm P, Triggs B (1996) A factorization based algorithm for multi-image projective structure and motion. European Conference on Computer Vision 709–720.
[160] Christy S, Horaud R (1996) Euclidean reconstruction: from paraperspective to perspective. European Conference on Computer Vision **2**:129–140.
[161] Aguiar P, Moura J (1999) Factorization as a rank 1 problem. IEEE Computer Vision and Pattern Recognition **1**:178–184.
[162] Aguiar P, Moura J (1999) A fast algorithm for rigid structure from image sequences. International Conference on Image Processing **3**:125–129.
[163] Aguiar P, Moura J (1998) Video representation via 3D shaped mosaics. International Conference on Image Processing **1**:823–827.
[164] Guerreiro R, Aguiar P (2002) Factorization with missing data for 3D structure recovery. IEEE Workshop on Multimedia Signal Processing 105-108.
[165] Aguiar P, Moura J (2001) Three-dimensional modeling from two-dimensional video. IEEE Trans. Image Processing **10**:1541–1551.
[166] Nakamura K, Saito H, Ozawa S (2000) 3D reconstruction of book surface taken from image sequence with handy camera. International Conference on Pattern Recognition **4**:575–578.
[167] Costeria J, Kanade T (1998) A multi-body factorization method for independently moving objects. International J. on Computer Vision **29**:159–178.
[168] Sugaya Y, Kanatani K (2002) Outlier removal for feature tracking by subspace separation. Symp. on Sensing via Imaging Info 603-608.
[169] Huynh D, Hartley R, Heyden A (2003) Outlier correction in image sequences for the affine camera. International Conference on Computer Vision 585–590.
[170] Huynh D, Heyden A (2001) Outlier detection in video sequences under affine projection. IEEE Computer Vision and Pattern Recognition 695–701.
[171] Ke Q, Kanade T (2003) A robust subspace approach to extracting layers from image sequences. Ph.D. Thesis, Carnegie Mellon University, USA.
[172] Hawkins D, Liu L, Young S Robust singular value decomposition. http://www.niss.org/technicalreports/tr122.pdf
[173] Hwang K, Yokoya N, Takemura H, Yamazawa K (1998) A factorization method using 3-D linear combination for shape and motion recovery. International Conference on Pattern Recognition **2**:959-963.
[174] Yu H, Chen Q, Xu G, Yachida M (1996) 3D shape and motion by SVD under higher-order approximation of perspective projection. International Conference on Pattern Recognition 456–460.
[175] Xi L (2004) 3D orthographic reconstruction based on robust factorization method with outliers. International Conference on Image Processing 1927–1930.
[176] Morita T, Kanade T (1997) A sequential factorization method for recovering shape and motion from image streams. IEEE Trans. Pattern Analysis and Machine Intelligence **19**:858–867.
[177] Branco C, Costeira J (1998) A 3D image mosaicing system using the factorization method. IEEE International Symp. on Industrial Electronics **2**:674–678.
[178] Guerreiro R, Aguiar P (2002) 3D structure from video streams with partially overlapping images. International Conference on Image Processing **3**:897–900.
[179] Tan J, Ishikawa S (1999) Extracting 3-D motions of individuals at work by uncalibrated multiple video cameras. International Conference on Systems, Man, and Cybernetics **3**:487-490.
[180] Kurata T, Fujiki J, Kourogi K, Sakaue K (2000) A fast and robust approach to recovering structure and motion from live video frames. IEEE Computer Vision and Pattern Recognition **2**:528–535.
[181] Yamaguchi J, Tan J, Ishikawa S (2005) A mobile motion capture system employing image transfer. IEEE TENCON.

[182] Poelman C, Kanade T (1997) A paraperspective factorization method for shape and motion recovery. IEEE Trans. Pattern Analysis and Machine Intelligence **19**:206–218.
[183] Tan J, Ishikawa S (2001) Deformable shape recovery by factorization based on a spatiotemporal measurement matrix. Computer Vision and Image Understanding **82**:101–109.
[184] Tan J, Ishikawa S (2000) On modeling three-dimensional objects by uncalibrated cameras. IEEE TENCON **1**:59–63.
[185] Tomasi C, Kanade T (1992) Shape and motion from image streams under orthography: a factorization method. International J. on Computer Vision **9**:137–154.
[186] Djouabi A, Bouktache E (1997) A fast algorithm for the nearest-neighbor classifier. IEEE Trans. Pattern Analysis and Machine Intelligence **19**:277–281.
[187] Fukunaga K (1985) The estimation of the Bayes error by the k-nearest neighbor approach. Progress in Pattern Recognition, L. Kanal and A. Rosenfeld (Eds.), Elsevier Science Publishers **2**:169–187.
[188] Forsyth D, Ponce J (2003) Computer vision — a modern approach. Prentice-Hall, NJ
[189] Cover T, Hart P (1967) Nearest neighbor pattern classification. IEEE Trans. Information Theory **13**:21–27.
[190] Song Y, Huang J, Zhou D, Zha H, Giles C (2007) IKNN: Informative k-nearest neighbor pattern classification. LNAI **4702**:248–264.
[191] Prokop R, Reeves A (1992) A survey of moment-based techniques for unoccluded object representation and recognition. CVGIP: Graphical Models and Image Processing **54**:438-460.
[192] Dudani S, Breeding K, McGhee R (1977) Aircraft identification by moment invariants. IEEE Trans. Computers **26**:39–45.
[193] Sanz P, Marin R, Sanchez J (2005) Including efficient object recognition capabilities in online robots: from a statistical to a neural-network classifier. IEEE Trans. SMC – Part C: Applications and Reviews **35**:87–96.
[194] Devroye L, Gyorfi L, Lugosi G (1996) A probabilistic theory of pattern recognition. Applications of Mathematics — Stochastic Modelling and Applied Probability.
[195] Jozwik A, Serpico S, Roli F (1998) A parallel network of modified 1-NN and k-NN classifiers — application to remote-sensing image classification. Pattern Recognition Letters **19**:57–62.
[196] Sarkar M (2007) Fuzzy-rough nearest neighbor algorithms in classification. Fuzzy Sets and Systems **158**:2134–2152.
[197] Bishop C (1995) Neural networks for pattern recognition. Oxford University Press, Oxford
[198] Flusser J, Zitova B, Suk T, Moments and moment invariants in image analysis. http://staff.utia.cas.cz/zitova/tutorial/
[199] Li Y (1992) Reforming the theory of invariant moments for pattern recognition. Pattern Recognition **25**:723–730.
[200] Maitra S (1979) Moment invariants. IEEE **67**:697-699.
[201] Reiss T (1991) The revised fundamental theorem of moment invariants. EEE Trans. Pattern Analysis and Machine Intelligence **13**:830–834.
[202] Shutler J, Statistical moments, University of Southampton, UK, Tutorial http://homepages.inf.ed.ac.uk/rbf/CVonline/LOCAL_COPIES/SHUTLER3/CVonline_moments.html
[203] Sziranyi T, with other partners UPC, SZTAKI, Bilkent and ACV. Real time detector for unusual behavior. http://www.muscle-noe.org/content/view/147/64/
[204] Full-body gesture database. http://gesturedb.korea.ac.kr/
[205] Kellokumpu V, Pietikainen M, Heikkila J (2005) Human activity recognition using sequences of postures. Machine Vision and Applications 570–573.
[206] Yu S, Tan D, Tan T (2004) A framework for evaluating the effect of view angle, clothing and carrying condition on gait recognition. International Conference on Pattern Recognition 441–444.

[207] Sarkar S, Phillips P, Liu Z, Vega I, Grother P, Bowyer K (2005) The Humanid Gait Challenge Problem: data sets, performance, and analysis. IEEE Trans. Pattern Analysis and Machine Intelligence **27**:162–177.
[208] The Inria XMAS (IXMAS) motion acquisition sequences. https://charibdis.inrialpes.fr
[209] Ahad A, Ogata T, Tan J, Kim H, Ishikawa S (2007) A smart automated complex motion recognition technique. Workshop on Multi-dimensional and Multi-view Image Processing with Asian Conference on Computer Vision 142–149.
[210] Spengler M, Schiele B (2003) Towards robust multi-cue integration for visual tracking. Machine Vision and Applications **14**:50–58.
[211] Piater J, Crowley J (2001) Multi-modal tracking of interacting targets using Gaussian approximations. IEEE Workshop on Performance Evaluation of Tracking and Surveillance with Computer Vision and Pattern Recognition 141–147.
[212] Kumar S, Kumar D, Sharma A, McLachlan N (2003) Classification of hand movements using motion templates and geometrical based moments. International Conference on Intelligent Sensing and Information Processing 299–304.
[213] Ryu W, Kim D, Lee H, Sung J, Kim D (2006) Gesture recognition using temporal templates. International Conference on Pattern Recognition, Demo Program.
[214] Ruiz-del-Solar J, Vallejos P (2004) Motion detection and tracking for an AIBO robot using camera motion compensation and Kalman filtering. RoboCup International Symp. 619–627.
[215] Valstar M, Patras I, Pantic M (2004) Facial action recognition using temporal templates. IEEE Workshop on Robot and Human Interactive Communication 253–258.
[216] Leman K, Ankit G, Tan T (2005) PDA-based human motion recognition system. International J. Software Engineering and Knowledge **2**:199–205.
[217] Dollar P, Rabaud V, Cottrell G, Belongie S (2005) Behavior recognition via sparse spatiotemporal features. International Workshop on Visual Surveillance and Performance Evaluation of Tracking and Surveillance 65–72.
[218] Shin H, Lee S, Lee S (2005) Real-time gesture recognition using 3D motion history model. Conference on Intelligent Computing, LNCS **3644**:888–898.
[219] Davis J (2004) Sequential reliable-inference for rapid detection of human actions. IEEE Workshop on Detection and Recognition of Events in Video.
[220] Lo C, Don H (1989) 3-D moment forms: their construction and application to object identification and positioning. IEEE Trans. Pattern Analysis and Machine Intelligence **11**:1053–1063.
[221] Weinland D, Ronfard R, Boyer E (2006) Automatic discovery of action taxonomies from multiple views. IEEE Computer Vision and Pattern Recognition 1639-1645.
[222] Canton-Ferrer C, Casas J, Pardas M, Sargin M, Tekalp A (2006) 3D human action recognition in multiple view scenarios. Jornades de Recerca en Automatica, Visi. Robotica.
[223] Petras I, Beleznai C, Dedeoglu Y, Pardas M, et al. (2007) Flexible test-bed for unusual behavior detection. ACM Conference Image and video retrieval 105–108.
[224] Dalal N, Triggs B (2005) Histograms of oriented gradients for human detection. IEEE Computer Vision and Pattern Recognition 886–893.
[225] Dalal D, Triggs B, Schmid C (2006) Human detection using oriented histograms of flow and appearance. European Conference on Computer Vision 428–441.
[226] Kadir T, Brady M (2001) Scale, saliency and image description. International J. of Computer Vision **45(1)**:83–105.
[227] Davis J (1998) Recognizing movement using motion histograms. MIT Media Lab. Perceptual Computing Section Tech. Report **487**.
[228] Senior A, Tosunoglu S (2005) Hybrid machine vision control. Florida Conference on Recent Advances in Robotics.

[229] Wong S, Cipolla R (2005) Continuous gesture recognition using a sparse Bayesian classifier. International Conference on Pattern Recognition **1**:1084–1087.
[230] Wong S, Cipolla R (2005) Real-time adaptive hand motion recognition using a sparse Bayesian classifier. International Conference on Computer Vision Workshop 170–179.
[231] Ng J, Gong S (2001) Learning pixel-wise signal energy for understanding semantics. British machine Vision Conference 695–704.
[232] Ng J, Gong S (2003) Learning pixel-wise signal energy for understanding semantics. Image and Vision Computing **21**:1183–1189.
[233] Albu A, Trevor B, Naznin V, Beach C (2007) Analysis of irregularities in human actions with volumetric motion history images. IEEE Workshop on Motion and Video Computing.
[234] Alahari K, Jawahar C (2006) Discriminative actions for recognizing events. Indian Conference on Computer Vision, Graphics and Image Processing 552–563.
[235] Meng H, Pears N, Freeman M, Bailey C (2009) Motion history histograms for human action recognition. Embedded Computer Vision (Advances in Pattern Recognition), Springer London **2**:139–162.
[236] Vafadar M, Behrad A (2008) Human hand gesture recognition using motion orientation histogram for interaction of handicapped persons with computer. ICISP, LNCS **5099**:378–385.
[237] Forbes K (2004) Summarizing motion in video sequences. http://thekrf.com/projects/motionsummary/MotionSummary.pdf
[238] Tan J, Ishikawa S (2007) High accuracy and real-time recognition of human activities. Annual Conference of IEEE Industrial Electronics Society 2377–2382.
[239] Han J, Bhanu B (2003) Gait Energy Image representation: comparative performance evaluation on USF HumanID database. Joint International Workshop VS-PETS 133–140.
[240] Han J, Bhanu B (2006) Individual recognition using gait energy image. IEEE Trans. Pattern Analysis and Machine Intelligence **28(2)**:133–140.
[241] Bashir K, Xiang T, Gong S (2008) Feature selection on gait energy image for human identification. IEEE International Conference on Acoustics, Speech and Signal Processing 985–988.
[242] Bashir K, Xiang T, Gong S (2008) Feature selection for gait recognition without subject cooperation. British Machine Vision Conference.
[243] Yang X, Zhang T, Zhou Y, Yang J (2008) Gabor phase embedding of gait energy image for identity recognition. IEEE International Conference on Computer and Information Technology 361–366.
[244] Chen C, Liang J, Zhao H, Hu H, Tian J (2009) Frame difference energy image for gait recognition with incomplete silhouettes. Pattern Recognition Letters **30(11)**:977–984.
[245] Ma Q, Wang S, Nie D, Qiu J (2007) Recognizing humans based on Gait Moment Image. ACIS International Conference on Software Engineering, Artificial Intelligence, Networking, and Parallel/Distributed Computing 606–610.
[246] Yu C, Cheng H, Cheng C, Fan H (2010) Efficient human action and gait analysis using multiresolution motion energy histogram. EURASIP J. on Advances in Signal Processing.
[247] Ogata T, Tan J, Ishikawa S (2006) High-speed human motion recognition based on a motion history image and an eigenspace. IEICE Trans. Information & Systems **E89-D(1)**:281–289.
[248] Jin T, Leung M, Li L (2004) Temporal human body segmentation. IASTED International Conference Visualization, Imaging, and Image Processing 1482-7921.
[249] Singh R, Seth B, Desai U (2006) A real-time framework for vision based human robot interaction. IEEE/RSJ Conference on Intelligent Robots and Systems 5831-5836.
[250] Davis J, Morison A, Woods D (2007) Building adaptive camera models for video surveillance. IEEE Workshop on Applications of Computer Vision.
[251] Ahmad M, Parvin I, Lee S (2010) Silhouette history and energy image information for human movement recognition. J. of Multimedia **5(1)**:12-21.

[252] Watanabe K, Kurita T (2008) Motion recognition by higher order local auto correlation features of motion history images. Bio-inspired, Learning and Intelligent Systems for Security 51–55.
[253] Chen D, Yan R, Yang J (2007) Activity analysis in privacy-protected video. www.informedia.cs.cmu.edu/documents/T-MM_Privacy_J2c.pdf
[254] Ahad A, Tan J, Kim H, Ishikawa S (2010) Action recognition by employing combined directional motion history and energy Images. IEEE Computer Vision and Pattern Recognition Workshop.
[255] Kindratenko V (1997) Development and application of image analysis techniques for identification and classification of microscopic particles. PhD Thesis, University of Antwerp, Belgium http://www.ncsa.uiuc.edu/~kindr/phd/index.pdf
[256] Ahmad M, Hossain M (2008) SEI and SHI representations for human movement recognition. International Conference on Computer and Information Technology 521–526.
[257] Chandrashekhar V, Venkatesh K (2006) Action energy images for reliable human action recognition. Asian Symp. on Information Display 484–487.
[258] Chen D, Yang J (2006) Exploiting high dimensional video features using layered Gaussian mixture models. International Conference on Pattern Recognition.
[259] Meng H, Pears N, Bailey C (2007) A human action recognition system for embedded computer vision application. Workshop on Embedded Computer Vision with Computer Vision and Pattern Recognition.
[260] Meng H, Pears N, Bailey C (2006) Human action classification using SVM_2K classifier on motion features. Multimedia Content Representation, Classification and Security, LNCS **4105**:458–465.
[261] Meng H, Pears N, Bailey C (2007) Motion information combination for fast human action recognition. Conference Computer Vision Theory and Applications.
[262] Meng H, Pears N, Bailey C (2006) Recognizing human actions based on motion information and SVM. IEE International Conference Intelligent Environments 239–245.
[263] Babu R, Ramakrishnan K (2003) Compressed domain human motion recognition using motion history information. International Conference on Image Processing **2**:321–324.
[264] Pantic M, Patras I, Valstar M (2005) Learning spatio-temporal models of facial expressions. International Conference on Measuring Behaviour 7–10.
[265] Babu R, Ramakrishnan K (2004) Recognition of human actions using motion history information extracted from the compressed video. Image Vision Computing **22**:597–607.
[266] Orrite C, Martinez-Contreras F, Herrero E, Ragheb H, Velastin S (2008) Independent viewpoint silhouette-based human action modelling and recognition. Workshop on Machine Learning for Vision-based Motion Analysis with European Conference on Computer Vision.
[267] Jain A, Duin R, Mao J (2000) Statistical pattern recognition: a review. IEEE Trans. Pattern Analysis and Machine Intelligence **22(1)**:4–37.
[268] Shan C, Wei Y, Qiu X, Tan T (2004) Gesture recognition using temporal template based trajectories. International Conference on Pattern Recognition **3**:954–957.
[269] Kellokumpu C, Zhao G, Pietikainen M (2008) Texture based description of movements for activity analysis. Conference Computer Vision Theory and Applications **2**:368–374.
[270] Albu A, Beugeling T (2007) A three-dimensional spatiotemporal template for interactive human motion analysis. J. of Multimedia **2(4)**:45–54.
[271] Jan T (2004) Neural network based threat assessment for automated visual surveillance. IEEE Joint Conference on Neural Networks **2**:1309–1312.
[272] Liu J, Zhang N (2007) Gait history image: a novel temporal template for gait recognition. IEEE International Conference Multimedia and Expo 663–666.
[273] Xiang T, Gong S (2006) Beyond tracking: modelling activity and understanding behaviour. International J. of Computer Vision **67(1)**:21–51.

[274] Bobick A, Davis J (1996) An appearance-based representation of action. International Conference on Pattern Recognition 307–312.
[275] Davis J (1996) Appearance-based motion recognition of human actions. M.I.T. Media Lab Perceptual Computing Group Tech. Report **387**.
[276] Essa I, Pentland S (1995) Facial expression recognition using a dynamic model and motion energy. IEEE Computer Vision and Pattern Recognition.
[277] Haritaoglu I, Harwood D, Davis L (2000) W4: real-time surveillance of people and their activities. IEEE Trans. Pattern Analysis and Machine Intelligence **22(8)**:809–830.
[278] Mittal A, Paragois N (2004) Motion-based background subtraction using adaptive kernel density estimation. IEEE Computer Vision and Pattern Recognition.
[279] Kilger M (1992) A shadow handler in a video-based real-time traffic monitoring system. IEEE Workshop on Applications of Computer Vision 1060–1066.
[280] Yang Y, Levine M (1992) The background primal sketch: an approach for tracking moving objects. Machine Vision and Applications **5**:17–34.
[281] Wren C, Azarbayejani A, Darrell T, Pentland A (1997) Pfinder: real-time tracking of the human body. IEEE Trans. Pattern Analysis and Machine Intelligence **19(7)**:780–785.
[282] Stauffer C, Grimson W (1999) Adaptive background mixture models for real-time tracking. IEEE Computer Vision and Pattern Recognition **2**:246–252.
[283] McKenna S, Jabri S, Duric Z, Wechsler H, Rosenfeld A (2000) Tracking groups of people. Computer Vision and Image Understanding **80(1)**:42–56.
[284] Arseneau S, Cooperstock J (1999) Real-time image segmentation for action recognition. IEEE Pacific Rim Conference on Communications, Computers and Signal Processing 86–89.
[285] Sun H, Feng T, Tan T (2000) Robust extraction of moving objects from image sequences. Asian Conference on Computer Vision 961–964.
[286] Elgammal A, Harwood D, David L (2000) Nonparametric background model for background subtraction. European Conference on Computer Vision.
[287] Collins R, Lipton A, Kanade T, et al. (2000) A system for video surveillance and monitoring. Carnegie Mellon University, Tech. Report **CMU-RI-TR-00-12**.
[288] Wang C, Brandstein M (1998) A hybrid real-time face tracking system. International Conference on Acoustics, Speech, and Signal Processing.
[289] Lipton A, Fujiyoshi H, Patil R (1998) Moving target classification and tracking from real-time video. IEEE Workshop on Applications of Computer Vision 8–14.
[290] Anderson C, Bert P, Wal G (1985) Change detection and tracking using pyramids transformation techniques. SPIE-Intelligent Robots and Computer Vision **579**:72–78.
[291] Bergen J, Burt P, Hingorani R, Peleg S (1992) A three frame algorithm for estimating two-component image motion. IEEE Trans. Pattern Analysis and Machine Intelligence **14(9)**:886–896.
[292] Kameda Y, Minoh M (1996) A human motion estimation method using 3-successive video frames. International Conference on Virtual Systems and Multimedia.
[293] Beauchemin S, Barron J (1995) The computation of optical flow. ACM Computing Surveys **27(3)**:443–467.
[294] McCane B, Novins K, Crannitch D, Galvin B (2001) On benchmarking optical flow. Computer Vision and Image Understanding **84**:126–143.
[295] Horn B, Schunck B (1981) Determining optical flow. Artificial Intelligence **17**:185–203.
[296] Papenberg N, Bruhn A, Brox T, Didas S, Weickert J (2006) Highly accurate optic flow computation with theoretically justified warping. International J. of Computer Vision **67(2)**:141–158.
[297] Wixson L (2000) Detecting salient motion by accumulating directionally-consistent flow. IEEE Trans. Pattern Analysis and Machine Intelligence **22(8)**:774–780.

[298] Talukder A, Goldberg S, Matthies L, Ansar A (2003) Real-time detection of moving objects in a dynamic scene from moving robotic vehicles. IEEE/RSJ International Conference on Intelligent Robots and Systems 1308–1313.
[299] Bimbo A, Nesi P (1993) Real-time optical flow estimation. International Conference on Systems Engineering in the Service of Humans, Systems, Man and Cybernetics **3**:13–19.
[300] Wei J, Harle N (1997) Use of temporal redundancy of motion vectors for the increase of optical flow calculation speed as a contribution to real-time robot vision. IEEE TENCON 677–680.
[301] Christmas W (1998) Spatial filtering requirements for gradient-based optical flow. British Machine Vision Conference 185–194.
[302] Rosales R, Sclaroff S (1999) 3D trajectory recovery for tracking multiple objects and trajectory guided recognition of actions. IEEE Computer Vision and Pattern Recognition **2**:117–123.
[303] Zou X, Bhanu B (2006) Human activity classification based on gait energy image and co-evolutionary genetic programming. International Conference on Pattern Recognition **3**:555–559.
[304] Ahmad M, Lee S (2008) Recognizing human actions based on silhouette energy image and global motion description. IEEE Automatic Face and Gesture Recognition 523–588.
[305] Inamura T, Toshima I, Tanie H, Nakamura Y (2004) Embodied symbol emergence based on mimesis theory. International J. of Robotics Research **23(4-5)**:363–377.
[306] Takano W, Yamane K, Sugihara T, Yamamoto K, Nakamura Y (2006) Primitive communication based on motion recognition and generation with hierarchical mimesis model. International Conference on Robotics and Automation 3602–3608.
[307] Takano W, Nakamura Y (2006) Humanoid robot's autonomous acquisition of proto-symbols through motion segmentation. IEEE-RAS Conference Humanoid Robotics 425–431.
[308] Kim T, Park S, Shin S (2003) Rhythmic-motion synthesis based on motion-beat analysis. ACM Trans. Graphics **22**:392–401.
[309] Shiratori T, Nakazawa A, Ikeuchi K (2004) Detecting dance motion structure through music analysis. IEEE Automatic Face and Gesture Recognition 857–862.
[310] Arikan O, Forsyth D, O'Brien J (2003) Motion synthesis from annotations. ACM Annual Conference Series Computer Graphics (SIGGRAPH).
[311] Bradski G, Davis J (2002) Motion segmentation and pose recognition with motion history gradients. Machine and Vision Applications **13(3)**:174–184.
[312] Griesbeck C (1996) Introduction to Labanotation. http://user.uni-frankfurt.de/~griesbec/LABANE.html
[313] Barbic J, Safonova A, Pan J, Faloutsos C, Hodgins J, Pollard N (2004) Segmenting motion capture data into distinct behaviors. Graphics Interface 185–194.
[314] Kadone H, Nakamura Y (2006) Segmentation, memorization, recognition and abstraction of humanoid motions based on correlations and associative memory. IEEE-RAS International Conference on Humanoid Robots.
[315] Peker K, Alatan A, Akansu A (2000) Low-level motion activity features for semantic characterization of video. IEEE Conference on Multimedia and Expo 801–804.
[316] Vitaladevuni S, Kellokumpu V, Davis L (2008) Action recognition using ballistic dynamics. IEEE Computer Vision and Pattern Recognition.
[317] Wang T, Shum H, Xu Y, Zheng N (2001) Unsupervised analysis of human gestures. IEEE Pacific Rim Conference on Multimedia 174–181.
[318] Ihara M, Watanabe N, Nishimura K (1999) A gesture description model based on synthesizing fundamental gestures. IEEE SouthEast Conference 47–52.
[319] Badler N, Costa M, Zhao L, Chi D (2000) To gesture or not to gesture: what is the question? Comp Graphics International 3–9.

[320] Osaki R, Shimada M, Uehara K (1999) Extraction of primitive motion for human motion recognition. International Conference on Discovery Science, LNCS.
[321] Mahalingam G, Kambhamettu C (2011) Can discriminative cues aid face recognition across age? IEEE Automatic Face and Gesture Recognition.
[322] Zhang W, Shan S, Qing L, Chen X, Gao W (2009) Are Gabor phases really useless for face recognition? Pattern Analysis Applications **12**:301–307.
[323] Guo Y, Zhao G, Chen J, Pietikainen M, Xu Z (2009) A new Gabor phase difference pattern for face and ear recognition. Computer Analysis of Images and Patterns **5702**:41–49.
[324] Perez C, Cament L, Castillo L (2011) Local matching Gabor entropy weighted face recognition. IEEE Automatic Face and Gesture Recognition.
[325] Wiskott L, Fellous J, Kruger N, Malsburg C (1997) Face recognition by elastic bunch graph matching. IEEE Trans. Pattern Analysis and Machine Intelligence **19(7)**:775–779.
[326] Liu H (2002) Gabor feature based classification using the enhanced fisher linear discriminant model for face recognition. IEEE Trans. Image Processing **11(4)**:467–476.
[327] Lei Z, Li S, Chu R, Zhu X (2007) Face recognition with local Gabor textons. International Conference on Advances in Biometrics 49–57.
[328] Xie S, Shan S, Chen X, Meng X, Gao W (2009) Learned local gabor patterns for face representation and recognition. Signal Processing **89**:2333–2344.
[329] Nguyen H, Bai L, Shen L (2009) Local Gabor binary pattern whitened PCA: a novel approach for face recognition from single image per person. International Conference on Advances in Biometrics 269–278.
[330] Zou J, Ji Q, Nagy G (2007) A comparative study of local matching approach for face recognition. IEEE Trans. Image Processing **16(10)**:2617–2628.
[331] Chen Y, De la Torre F (2011) Active conditional models. IEEE Automatic Face and Gesture Recognition.
[332] Leordeanu M, Hebert M (2009) A spectral technique for correspondence problems using pairwise constraints. International Conference on Computer Vision 1482–1489.
[333] Leordeanu M, Hebert M (2009) Unsupervised learning for graph matching. IEEE Computer Vision and Pattern Recognition 864–871.
[334] Duchennel O, Bach F, Kweon I, Ponce J (2009) A tensor-based algorithm for high-order graph matching. IEEE Computer Vision and Pattern Recognition 1980–1987.
[335] Caetano T, McAuley J, Cheng L, Le Q, Smola A (2009) Learning graph matching. IEEE Trans. Pattern Analysis and Machine Intelligence **31**:1048–1058.
[336] Mikolajczyk K, Tuytelaars T, Schmid C, Zisserman A, Matas J, Schaffalitzky F, Kadir T, Gool L (2005) A comparison of affine region detectors. International J. of Computer Vision **65**:43–72.
[337] Zass R, Shashua A (2008) Probabilistic graph and hypergraph matching. IEEE Computer Vision and Pattern Recognition.
[338] Torresani L, Kolmogorov V, Rother C (2008) Feature correspondence via graph matching: models and global optimization. European Conference on Computer Vision 596–609.
[339] Tola E, Lepetit V, Fua P (2008) A fast local descriptor for dense matching. IEEE Computer Vision and Pattern Recognition.
[340] Ke Y, Sukthankar R (2004) PCA-SIFT: a more distinctive representation for local image descriptors. IEEE Computer Vision and Pattern Recognition 506–513.
[341] Bay H, Tuytelaars T, Gool L (200) SURF: speeded up robust features. European Conference on Computer Vision 404–417.
[342] Cootes T, Taylor C, Cooper D, Graham J (1995) Active shape models: their training and application. Computer Vision and Image Understanding **61**:38–59.
[343] Cootes T, Edwards G, Taylor C (2001) Active appearance models. IEEE Trans. Pattern Analysis and Machine Intelligence **23**:681–685.

[344] Blanz V, Vetter T (1999) A morphable model for the synthesis of 3D faces. Annual Conference on Computer Graphics and Interactive Techniques 187–194.
[345] Asthana A, Goecke R, Quadrianto N, Gedeon T (2009) Learning-based automatic face annotation for arbitrary poses and expressions from frontal images only. IEEE Computer Vision and Pattern Recognition 1635–1642.
[346] De la Torre F, Nguyen M (2008) Parameterized kernel principal component analysis: theory and applications to supervised and unsupervised image alignment. IEEE Computer Vision and Pattern Recognition.
[347] Morel J, Yu G (2009) ASIFT — a new framework for fully affine invariant image comparison. SIAM J. on Imaging Sciences **2**:438–469.
[348] Liu C, Hertzmann A, Popovic Z (2005) Learning physics-based motion style with nonlinear inverse optimization. ACM Trans. on Graph **24**:1071–1081.
[349] Kohlsdorf D, Starner T, Ashbrook D (2011) MAGIC 2.0: a web tool for false positive prediction and prevention for gesture recognition systems. IEEE Automatic Face and Gesture Recognition.
[350] Ashbrook D, Clawson J, Lyons K, Starner T, Patel N (200) Quickdraw: the impact of mobility and on-body placement on device access time. SIGCHI Conference on Human Factors in Computing Systems 219–222.
[351] Ashbrook D and Starner T (2010) MAGIC: a motion gesture design tool. CHI 2159–2168.
[352] Dannenberg A (1989) A gesture based user interface prototyping system. ACM Symp. on User Interface Software and Technology.
[353] Dey A, Hamid R, Beckmann C, Li I, Hsu D (2004) A CAPpella: programming by demonstration of context aware applications. CHI.
[354] Fails J, Olsen D (2003) A design tool for camera-based interaction. SIGCHI Conference on Human Factors in Computing Systems.
[355] Brashear H, Kim J, Lyons K, Starner T, Westeyn T (2007) GART: The gesture and activity recognition toolkit. International Conference on Human-Computer Interaction.
[356] Klemmer S, Sinha A, Chen J, Landay J, Aboobaker N, Wang A (2000) SUEDE: a wizard of oz prototyping tool for speech user interfaces. ACM Symp. on User Interface Software and Technology.
[357] Long A, Landay J, Rowe L (2001) Quill: a gesture design tool for pen-based user interfaces. http://quill.sourceforge.net/
[358] Maynes-Aminzade D, Winograd T, Igarashi T (2007) Eyepatch: prototyping camera-based interaction through examples. ACM Symp. on User Interface Software and Technology 33–42.
[359] Akae N, Makihara Y, Yagi Y (2011) The optimal camera arrangement by a performance model for gait recognition. IEEE Automatic Face and Gesture Recognition.
[360] Yu S, Tan D, Tan T (2006) Modelling the effect of view angle variation on appearance-based gait recognition. Conference on Computer Vision **1**:807–816.
[361] Makihara Y, Sagawa R, Mukaigawa Y, Echigo T, Yagi Y (2006) Which reference view is effective for gait identification using a view transformation model? IEEE Computer Society Workshop on Biometrics.
[362] Wang Y, Yu S, Wang Y, Tan T (2006) Gait recognition based on fusion of multi-view gait sequences. IAPR International Conference on Biometrics 605–611.
[363] Sugiura K, Makihara Y, Yagi Y (2007) Gait identification based on multi-view observations using omnidirectional camera. Asian Conference on Computer Vision 452–461.
[364] Mori A, Makihara Y, Yagi Y (2010) Gait recognition using periodbased phase synchronization for low frame-rate videos. International Conference on Pattern Recognition 2194–2197.
[365] Mowbray S, Nixon M (2003) Automatic gait recognition via Fourier descriptors of deformable objects. IEEE Conference on Advanced Video and Signal Based Surveillance 566–

573.
[366] Maturana D, Mery D, Soto A (2011) Learning discriminative local binary patterns for face recognition. IEEE Automatic Face and Gesture Recognition.
[367] Mikolajczyk K, Schmid C (2005) Performance evaluation of local descriptors. IEEE Trans. Pattern Analysis and Machine Intelligence **27(10)**:1615–1630.
[368] Liao S, Chung A (2007) Face recognition by using elongated local binary patterns with average maximum distance gradient magnitude. Asian Conference on Computer Vision 672–679.
[369] Liao S, Zhu X, Lei Z, Zhang L, Li S (2007) Learning multiscale block local binary patterns for face recognition. Advances in Biometrics 828–837.
[370] Wolf L, Hassner T, Taigman Y (2008) Descriptor based methods in the wild. Real-Life Images Workshop with European Conference on Computer Vision.
[371] Heikkil M, Pietikinen M, Schmid C (2009) Description of interest regions with local binary patterns. Pattern Recognition **42(3)**:425–436.
[372] Xie S, Shan S, Chen X, Gao W (2008) V-LGBP: volume based local gabor binary patterns for face representation and recognition. International Conference on Pattern Recognition.
[373] Vu N, Caplier A (2010) Face recognition with patterns of oriented edge magnitudes. European Conference on Computer Vision 316–326.
[374] Park S, Savvides M (2011) The multifactor extension of Grassmann manifolds for face recognition. IEEE Automatic Face and Gesture Recognition.
[375] Li Y, Du Y, Lin X (2005) Kernel-based multifactor analysis for image synthesis and recognition. International Conference on Computer Vision **1**:114–119.
[376] Park S, Savvides M (2007) Individual kernel tensor-subspaces for robust face recognition: a computationally efficient tensor framework without requiring mode factorization. IEEE Trans. on Systems, Man and Cybernetics – Part B: Cybernetics **37(5)**:1156–1166.
[377] Turk M, Pentland A (1991) Eigenfaces for recognition. J. of Cognitivie Neurosicence **3**:71–86.
[378] Vasilescu M, Terzopoulos D (2002) Multilinear image analysis for facial recognition. International Conference on Pattern Recognition **1**:511–514.
[379] Vasilescu M, Terzopoulos D (2005) Multilinear independent components analysis. IEEE Computer Vision and Pattern Recognition **1**:547–553.
[380] Scholkopf B, Smola A, Muller K (200) Nonlinear component analysis as a kernel eigenvalue problem. Neural Computation 1299–1319.
[381] O'Hara A, Lui Y, Draper B (2011) Unsupervised learning of human expressions, gestures, and actions. IEEE Automatic Face and Gesture Recognition.
[382] Laptev I (2005) On space-time interest points. International J. of Computer Vision **64(2)**:107–123.
[383] Rapantzikos K, Avrithis Y, Kollias S (2009) Dense saliency-based spatiotemporal feature points for action recognition. IEEE Computer Vision and Pattern Recognition.
[384] Ponce J, Berg T, Everingham M, Forsyth D, Hebert M, Lazebnik S, et al. (2006) Dataset issues in object recognition. Toward Category-Level Object Recognition, LNCS **4170**:29–48.
[385] Pinto N, DiCarlo J, Cox D (2009) How far can you get with a modern face recognition test set using only simple features? IEEE Computer Vision and Pattern Recognition.
[386] Lv F, Nebatia R (2007) Single view human action recognition using key pose matching and viterbi path searching. IEEE Computer Vision and Pattern Recognition.
[387] Rodriguez M, Ahmed J, Shah M (2008) Action MACH: a spatio-temporal maximum average correlation height filter for action recognition. IEEE Computer Vision and Pattern Recognition.
[388] Yuan C, Li X, Hu W, Wang H (2009) Human action recognition using pyramid vocabulary tree. Asian Conference on Computer Vision.

[389] Weinland D, Boyer E (2008) Action recognition using exemplar-based embedding. IEEE Computer Vision and Pattern Recognition.
[390] Liu J, Ali S, Shah M (2008) Recognizing human actions using multiple features. IEEE Computer Vision and Pattern Recognition.
[391] Perronnin F (2008) Universal and adapted vocabularies for generic visual categorization. IEEE Trans. Pattern Analysis and Machine Intelligence **30(7)**:1243–1256.
[392] Wang Y, Jiang H, Drew M, Li Z, Mori G (2006) Unsupervised discovery of action classes. IEEE Computer Vision and Pattern Recognition.
[393] Liu J, Shah M (2008) Learning human actions via information maximazation. IEEE Computer Vision and Pattern Recognition.
[394] Fathi A, Mori G (2008) Action recognition by learning mid-level motion features. IEEE Computer Vision and Pattern Recognition.
[395] Jia K, Yeung D (2008) Human action recognition using local spatio-temporal discriminant embedding. IEEE Computer Vision and Pattern Recognition.
[396] Wang L, Suter D (2007) Recognizing human activities from silhouettes: motion subspace and factorial discriminative graphical model. IEEE Computer Vision and Pattern Recognition.
[397] Lucena M, Blanca N, Fuertes J (2010) Human action recognition based on aggregated local motion estimates. Machine Vision and Applications.
[398] Brox T, Bruhn A, Papenberg N, Weickert J (2004) High accuracy optical flow estimation based on a theory for warping. European Conference on Computer Vision.
[399] Bruhn A, Weickert J, Schnorr C (2005) Lucas/Kanade meets Horn/Schunck: combining local and global optic flow methods. International J. of Computer Vision **61(3)**:211–231.
[400] Farneback C (2003) Two-frame motion estimation based on polynomial expansion. Scandinavian Conference on Image Analysis 363–370.
[401] Lucena M, Blanca N, Fuertes J, Marin-Jimenez M (2009) Human action recognition using optical flow accumulated local histograms. IbPRIA 32–39.
[402] Polana R, Nelson R (1993) Detecting activities. IEEE Computer Vision and Pattern Recognition 2–7.
[403] Shechtman E, Irani M (2007) Space-time behavior-based correlation or how to tell if two underlying motion fields are similar without computing them? IEEE Trans. Pattern Analysis and Machine Intelligence **29(11)**:2045–2056.
[404] Zelnik-Manor L, Irani M (2001) Event-based analysis of video. IEEE Computer Vision and Pattern Recognition **2**:123–130.
[405] Ahmad M, Lee S (2006) HMM-based human action recognition using multiview image sequences. International Conference on Pattern Recognition.
[406] Babu R, Anantharaman B, Ramakrishnan K, Srinivasan S (2002) Compressed domain action classification using HMM. Pattern Recognition Letter **23(10)**:1203–1213.
[407] Brand M, Oliver N, Pentland A (1997) Coupled hidden Markov models for complex action recognition. IEEE Computer Vision and Pattern Recognition.
[408] Cuntoor N, Yegnanarayana B, Chellappa R (2005) Interpretation of state sequences in HMM for activity representation. IEEE ICASSP.
[409] Mendoza M, Perez de la Blanca N (2007) HMM-based action recognition using contour histograms. Iberian Conference on Pattern Recognition and Image Analysis.
[410] Morency L, Quattoni A, Darrell T (2007) Latent-dynamic discriminative models for continuous gesture recognition. M.I.T., Tech. Report.
[411] Wang S, Quattoni A, Morency L, Demirdjian D, Darrel T (2006) Hidden conditional random fields for gesture recognition. IEEE Computer Vision and Pattern Recognition.
[412] Yamato J, Ohya J, Ishii K (1992) Recognizing human action in time sequential images using hidden Markov model. IEEE Computer Vision and Pattern Recognition.

[413] Mikolajczyk K, Uemura H (2008) Action recognition with motion appearance vocabulary forest. IEEE Computer Vision and Pattern Recognition.
[414] Schindler K, Gool L (2008) Action snippets: how many frames does human action recognition require? IEEE Computer Vision and Pattern Recognition.
[415] Wong S, Cipolla R (2007) Extracting spatiotemporal interest points using global information. International Conference on Computer Vision.
[416] Kienzle W, Scholkopf B, Wichmann F, Franz M (2007) How to find interesting locations in video: a spatiotemporal interest point detector learned from human eye movements. DAGM Symp. 405–414.
[417] Bay H, Ess A, Tuytelaars T, Gool L (2008) Speeded-up robust features (SURF). Computer Vision and Image Understanding **110(3)**:346–359.
[418] Kameda Y, Ohta Y (2010) Image retrieval of first-person vision for pedestrian navigation in urban area. International Conference on Pattern Recognition.
[419] Lindeberg T (1998) Feature detection with automatic scale selection. International J. of Computer Vision **30(2)**:79–116.
[420] Ehsan S, McDonald-Maier K (2009) Exploring integral image word length reduction techniques for SURF detector. International Conference on Computer and Electrical Engineering 635–639.
[421] Schweiger F, Zeisl B, Georgel P, Schroth G, Steinbach E, Navab N (2009) Maximum detector response markers for SIFT and SURF. Vision, Modeling and Visualization Workshop.
[422] BenAbdelkader C, Cutler R, Davis L (2002) Motion-based recognition of people in eigengait space. IEEE Automatic Face and Gesture Recognition 378–384.
[423] Fihl P, Moeslund T (2008) Invariant gait continuum based on the duty-factor. Signal, Image and Video Processing, Springer, London.
[424] Masoud O, Papanikolopoulos N (2003) A method for human action recognition. Image Vision Computing **21(8)**:729–743.
[425] Lee L, Grimson W (2002) Gait analysis for recognition and classification. IEEE Automatic Face and Gesture Recognition.
[426] Zhang R, Vogler C, Metaxas D (2004) Human gait recognition. IEEE Computer Vision and Pattern Recognition Workshop.
[427] Ben-Arie J, Wang Z, Pandit P, Rajaram S (2002) Human activity recognition using multidimensional indexing. IEEE Trans. Pattern Analysis and Machine Intelligence **24(8)**:1091–1104.
[428] Rahman M, Ishikawa S (2005) Human motion recognition using an eigenspace. Pattern Recognition Letters **26**:687–697.
[429] Wang L, Tan T, Ning H, Hu W (2003) Silhouette analysis-based gait recognition for human identification. IEEE Trans. Pattern Analysis and Machine Intelligence **25(12)**:505–1518.
[430] Liu Z, Sarkar S (2007) Outdoor recognition at a distance by fusing gait and face. Image and Vision Computing **6**:817–832.
[431] Boulgouris V, Plataniotis K, Hatzinakos D (2006) Gait recognition using linear time normalization. Pattern Recognition **39(5)**:969–979.
[432] Foster J, Nixon M, Bennett A (2003) Automatic gait recognition using area-based metrics. Pattern Recognition Letters **24(14)**:2489–2497.
[433] Andrade E, Fisher R, Blunsden S (2006) Detection of emergency events in crowded scenes. IEE International Symp. on Imaging for Crime Detection and Prevention 528–533.
[434] Bobick A, Davis J (2001) The recognition of human movement using temporal templates. IEEE Trans. Pattern Analysis and Machine Intelligence **23(3)**:257–267.
[435] Efros A, Berg A, Mori G, Malik J (2003) Recognizing action at a distance. International Conference on Computer Vision 726–733.

[436] Gavrila D (1999) The visual analysis of human movement: a survey. Computer Vision and Image Understanding **73(1)**:82–98.
[437] Grimson W, Stauffer C, Romano R, Lee L (1998) Using adaptive tracking to classify and monitor activities in a site. IEEE Computer Vision and Pattern Recognition 22–29.
[438] Hu M (1962) Visual pattern recognition by moment invariants. IRE Trans. Information Theory **8(2)**:179–187.
[439] Iwai Y, Hata T, Yachida M (1998) Gesture recognition from image motion based on subspace method and HMM. Asian Conference on Computer Vision **2**:639–646.
[440] Ke Y, Sukthankar R, Hebert M (2005) Efficient visual event detection using volumetric features. International Conference on Computer Vision 166–173.
[441] Micilotta A, Ong E, Bowden R (2005) Detection and tracking of humans by probabilistic body part assembly. British machine Vision Conference 429–438.
[442] Mitchelson J, Hilton A (2003) Simultaneous pose estimation of multiple people using multiple-view cues with hierarchical sampling. British machine Vision Conference.
[443] Robertson N, Reid I (2005) Behaviour understanding in video: a combined method. International Conference on Computer Vision 808–815.
[444] Roh M, Shin H, Lee S, Lee S (2006) Volume motion template for view-invariant gesture recognition. International Conference on Pattern Recognition 1229–1232.
[445] Weinland D, Ronfard R, Boyer E (2005) Motion history volumes for free viewpoint action recognition. IEEE International Workshop on modeling People and Human Interaction.
[446] Zivkovic Z, Heijden F, Petkovic M, Jonker W (2001) Image processing and feature extraction for recognizing strokes in tennis game videos. Annual Conference of the Advanced School for Computing and Imaging 262–267.
[447] Aggarwal J, Cai Q (1999) Human motion analysis: a review. Computer Vision and Image Understanding **73**:428–440.
[448] Aggarwal J, Cai Q (1997) Human motion analysis: a review. IEEE Nonrigid and Articulated Motion Workshop 90–102.
[449] Bobick A, Intille S, Davis J, Baird F, Pinhanez C, Campbell L, et al. (1999) The Kidsroom: a perceptually-based interactive and immersive story environment. Presence: Teleoperators and Virtual Environments **8**:367–391.
[450] Borshukov G, Bozdagi G, Altunbasak Y, Tekalp A (1997) Motion segmentation by multistage affine classification. IEEE Trans. Image Processing **6(11)**:1591–1594.
[451] Canton-Ferrer C, Casas J, Pardas M (2006) Human model and motion based 3D action recognition in multiple view scenarios. EU. Sig. Conference.
[452] Cedras C, Shah M (1995) Motion-based recognition: a survey. Image and Vision Computing **13**:129–154.
[453] Davis J (2001) Hierarchical motion history images for recognizing human motion. IEEE Workshop on Detection and Recognition of Events in Video 39–46.
[454] Davis J, Bradski G (1999) Real-time motion template gradients using Intel CVLib. International Conference on Computer Vision Workshop on Frame-rate Vision 1–20.
[455] Davis J, Bobick A (1998) Virtual PAT: a virtual personal aerobics trainer. Perceptual User Interfaces 13–18.
[456] Davis J, Bobick A (1997) The representation and recognition of action using temporal templates. IEEE Computer Vision and Pattern Recognition 928–934.
[457] Gao J, Collins R, Hauptmann A, Wactlar H (2004) Articulated motion modeling for activity analysis. International Conference on Image and Video Retrieval, Workshop on Articulated and Nonrigid Motion.
[458] Gheissari N, Bab-Hadiashar A (2003) Motion analysis: model selection and motion segmentation. International Conference on Image Analysis and Processing 442–447.
[459] http://gaijin-in-japan.com/2007/08/11/rajio-taiso-radio-exercise/

[460] Hu M (1961) Pattern recognition by moment invariants. IRE **49**:1218.
[461] Kahol K, Tripathi P, Panchanathan P, Rikakis T (2003) Gesture segmentation in complex motion sequences. International Conference on Image Processing 105–108.
[462] Kahol K, Tripathi P, Panchanathan P (2006) Documenting motion sequences with a personalized annotation system. IEEE J. Multimedia. **13(1)**:37–45.
[463] Kahol K, Tripathi P, Panchanathan P (2004) Automated gesture segmentation from dance sequences. IEEE Automatic Face and Gesture Recognition 883–888.
[464] Khotanzad A, Hong Y (1990) Invariant image recognition by Zernike moments. IEEE Trans. Pattern Analysis and Machine Intelligence **12(5)**:489–497.
[465] Li L, Zeng Q, Jiang Y, Xia H (2006) Spatio-temporal motion segmentation and tracking under realistic condition. International Symp. on Systems and Control in Aerospace and Astronautics 229–232.
[466] Lo C, Don H (1990) Pattern recognition using 3-D moments. International Conference on Pattern Recognition **1**:540–544.
[467] Mangin J, Poupon F, Duchesnay E, Riviere D, et al. (2004) Brain morphometry using 3D moments invariants. Med. Image Anal. **8(3)**:187–196.
[468] Rosales R (1998) Recognition of human action using moment-based features. Boston University, Tech. Report **98-020**:1–19.
[469] Shen D, Ip H (1999) Discriminative wavelet shape descriptors for recognition of 2-D patterns. Pattern Recognition **32**:151–165.
[470] Son D, Dinh T, Nam V, Hanh T, Lam H (2005) Detection and localization of road area in traffic video sequences using motion information and Fuzzy-Shadowed sets. IEEE International Symp. on Multimedia 725–732.
[471] Teh C, Chin R (1988) On image analysis by the methods of moments. IEEE Trans. Pattern Analysis and Machine Intelligence **10**:496–513.
[472] Valstar M, Pantic M, Patras I (2004) Motion history for facial action detection in video. International Conference on SMC **1**:635–640.
[473] Weinland D, Ronfard R, Boyer E (2006) Free viewpoint action recognition using motion history volumes. Computer Vision and Image Understanding **104(2-3)**:249–257.
[474] Yau W, Kumar D, Arjunan S, Kumar S (2006) Visual speech recognition using image moments and multiresolution Wavelet. International Conference on Computer Graphics, Imaging and Visualization 194–199.
[475] Yau W, Kumar D, Arjunan S (2006) Voiceless speech recognition using dynamic visual speech features. HCSNet Workshop Use of Vision in HCI 39–101.
[476] Yin Z, Collins R (2006) Moving object localization in thermal imagery by forward-backward MHI. Workshop on Object Tracking and Classification 133–140.
[477] Yuan C, Medioni G, Kang J, Cohen I (2007) Detecting motion regions in the presence of a strong parallax from a moving camera by multiview geometric constraints. IEEE Trans. Pattern Analysis and Machine Intelligence **29(9)**:1627–1641.
[478] Zhang D, Lu G (2004) Review of shape representation and description techniques. Pattern Recognition **37**:1–19.
[479] Ahad A, Tan J, Kim H, Ishikawa S (2010) A simple approach for low-resolution activity recognition. International J. for Computational Vision and Biomechanics **3(1)**.
[480] Ahad A, Tan J, Kim H, Ishikawa S (2008) Action recognition with various speeds and timed-DMHI feature vectors. International Conference on Computer and Info. Tech 213–218.
[481] Ahad A, Tan J, Kim H, Ishikawa S (2008) Human activity recognition: various paradigms. International Conf Control, Automation and Systems 1896–1901.
[482] Ahad A, Ogata T, Tan J, Kim H, Ishikawa S (2008) Complex motion separation and recognition using directional motion templates. Image Analysis – from Theory to Applications, Research Publishing, Singapore 73–82.

[483] Ahad A, Uemura H, Tan J, Kim H, Ishikawa S (2008) A simple real-time approach for action separation into action primitives. International Workshop on Tracking Humans for the Evaluation of Their Motion in Image Sequences with British machine Vision Conference 69–78.

[484] Ahad A, Tan J, Kim H, Ishikawa S (2009) Temporal motion recognition and segmentation approach. International J. of Imaging Systems & Technology **19**:91–99.

[485] Ahad A, Tan J, Kim H, Ishikawa S (2010) Analysis of motion self-occlusion problem due to motion overwriting for human activity recognition. J. of Multimedia **5(1)**:36–46.

[486] Ahad A, Tan J, Kim H, Ishikawa S (2008) Solutions to motion self-occlusion problem in human activity analysis. International Conference on Computer and Info. Tech. 201–206.

[487] Ahad A, Tan J, Kim H, Ishikawa S (2008) Directional motion history templates for low resolution motion recognition. Annual Conference of the IEEE Industrial Electronics Society (IECON) 1875–1880.

[488] Sigal L, Black M (2006) HumanEva: Synchronized video and motion capture dataset for evaluation of articulated human motion. Dept. of Comp. Science, Brown University, Tech. Report **CS-06-08**.

[489] Moeslund T (1999) Summaries of 107 computer vision-based human motion capture papers. University of Aalborg, Tech. Report **LIA 99-01**.

[490] Zhou H, Hu H (2004) A survey–human movement tracking and stroke rehabilitation. Dept. of Computer Sciences, University of Essex, Tech. Report **CSM-420**.

[491] Pavlovic V, Sharma R, Huang T (1997) Visual interpretation of hand gestures for human-computer interaction: a review. IEEE Trans. Pattern Analysis and Machine Intelligence **19(7)**:677–695.

[492] Pantic M, Pentland A, Nijholt A, Hunag T (2006) Human computing and machine understanding of human behavior: a survey. International Conference on Multimodal Interfac 239–248.

[493] Pantic M, Pentland A, Nijholt A, Hunag T (2007) Human computing and machine understanding of human behavior: a survey. Human Computing, LNAI **4451**:47–71.

[494] Marcel S (2002) Gestures for multi-modal interfaces: a review. IDIAP Research Report **02-34**.

[495] Tangelder J, Veltkamp R (2004) A survey of content based 3D shape retrieval methods. Shape Modeling Applications 145–156.

[496] LaViola J (1999) A survey of hand posture and gesture recognition techniques and technology. Brown University, Tech. Report **CS-99-11**.

[497] Jaimes A, Sebe N (2007) Multimodal human-computer interaction: a survey. Computer Vision and Image Understanding **108(1-2)**:116–134.

[498] Varga E, Horvath I, Rusak Z, Broek J (2004) Hand motion processing in applications: a concise survey and analysis of technologies. International Design Conference.

[499] Poppe R (2007) Vision-based human motion analysis: an overview. Computer Vision and Image Understanding **108(1-2)**:4–18.

[500] Moeslund T, Hilton A, Kruger V (2006) A survey of advances in vision-based human motion capture and analysis. Computer Vision and Image Understanding **104**:90-126.

[501] Wang J, Singh S (2003) Video analysis of human dynamics—a survey. Real-Time Imaging **9(5)**:321–346.

[502] Buxton H (2003) Learning and understanding dynamic scene activity: a review. Image and Vision Computing **21(1)**:125–136.

[503] Aggarwal J, Park S (2004) Human motion: modeling and recognition of actions and interactions. International Symp. on 3D Data Processing, Visualization and Transmission 640–647.

[504] Prati A, Mikic I, Trivedi M, Cucchiara R (2003) Detecting moving shadows: algorithms and evaluation. IEEE Trans. Pattern Analysis and Machine Intelligence **25(7)**:918–923.

[505] Mitra S, Acharya T (2007) Gesture recognition: a survey. IEEE Trans. on SMC: Part C **37(3)**:311–324.

[506] Moeslund T, Granum E (2001) A survey of computer vision-based human motion capture. Computer Vision and Image Understanding **81**:231–268.
[507] Hu W, Tan T, Wang L, Maybank S (2004) A survey on visual surveillance of object motion and behaviors. IEEE Trans. on SMC Part C: Applications and Reviews **34(3)**:334–352.
[508] Boulay B, Bremond F, Thonnat M (2006) Applying 3D human model in a posture recognition system. Pattern Recognition Letters **27 1788–1796**.
[509] Wang L, Hu W, Tan T (2003) Recent developments in human motion analysis. Pattern Recognition **36**:585–601.
[510] Joshi M (2006) Digital Image Processing—An Algorithmic Approach. Prentice-Hall of India.
[511] Teknomo K, Tutorial on normalization methods. http://people.revoledu.com/kardi/tutorial/Similarity/Normalization.html
[512] Dubes R (2009) Cluster analysis and related issues. Handbook of Pattern Recognition and Computer Vision, World Scientific, 4th Edition 3–32.
[513] Davis J, Tyagi A (2006) Minimal-latency human action recognition using reliable-inference. Image and Vision Computing **24**:455–472.
[514] Chen H, Chen H, Chen Y, Lee S (2006) Human action recognition using star skeleton. ACM International Workshop on Video Surveillance and Sensor Networks 171–174.
[515] Jin N, Mukhtarian F (2006) A non-parametric HMM learning method for shape dynamics with application to human motion recognition. International Conference on Pattern Recognition **2**:29–32.
[516] Kulic D, Takano W, Nakamura Y (2007) Representability of human motions by Factorial Hidden Markov Models. IEEE/RSJ International Conference on Intelligent Robots and Systems 2388–2393.
[517] Peursum P, Bui H, Venkatesh S, West G (2005) Robust recognition and segmentation of human actions using HMMs with missing observations. EURASIP J. on Applied Signal Processing **2005(1)**:2110–2126.
[518] Song S, Xing T (2003) Recognition of group activities using dynamic probabilistic networks. International Conference on Computer Vision **2**:742–749.
[519] Sminchisescu C, Kanaujia A, Li Z, Metaxas D (2005) Conditional models for contextual human motion recognition. International Conference on Computer Vision **2**:1808–1815.
[520] Nguyen N, Phung D, Venkatesh S, Bui H (2006) Learning and detecting activities from movement trajectories using the Hierarchical Hidden Markov Models. IEEE Computer Vision and Pattern Recognition 955–960.
[521] Park S, Aggarwal J (2004) Semantic-level understanding of human actions and interactions using event hierarchy. International Workshop with IEEE Computer Vision and Pattern Recognition 12–20.
[522] Ryoo M, Aggarwal J (2006) Recognition of composite human activities through context-free grammar based representation. IEEE Computer Vision and Pattern Recognition 1709–1718.
[523] Shi Y, Huang Y, Minnen D, Bobick A, Essa I (2004) Propagation networks for recognition of partially ordered sequential action. IEEE Computer Vision and Pattern Recognition 862–869.
[524] Shi Y, Bobick A, Essa I (2006) Learning temporal sequence model from partially labeled data. IEEE Computer Vision and Pattern Recognition 1631–1638.
[525] Ahmad M, Lee S (2006) Human action recognition using multi-view image sequences features. IEEE Automatic Face and Gesture Recognition 523–528.
[526] Leo M, D'Orazio T, Gnoni I, Spagnolo P, Distante A (2004) Complex human activity recognition for monitoring wide outdoor environments. International Conference on Pattern Recognition 913–916.
[527] Davis J, Gao H (2003) Recognizing human action efforts: an adaptive three-mode PCA framework. International Conference on Computer Vision 1463–1469.

[528] Troje N (2002) Decomposing biological motion: a framework for analysis and synthesis of human gait patterns. J. of Vision **2**:371–387.
[529] Davis J, Gao H (2004) Gender recognition from walking movements using adaptive three-mode PCA. IEEE Computer Vision and Pattern Recognition Workshop.
[530] Fanti C, Zelnik-Manor L, Perona P (2005) Hybrid models for human motion recognition. IEEE Computer Vision and Pattern Recognition 1166–1173.
[531] Song Y, Goncalves L, Perona P (2003) Unsupervised learning of human motion. IEEE Trans. Pattern Analysis and Machine Intelligence **25(7)**:814–827.
[532] Parameswaran V, Chellappa R (2005) Human action-recognition using mutual invariants. Computer Vision and Image Understanding **98(2)**:295–325.
[533] Yilmaz A, Shah M (2006) Matching actions in presence of camera motion. Computer Vision and Image Understanding **104(2)**:221–231.
[534] Uemura H, Ishikawa S, Mikolajczyk M (2008) Feature tracking and motion compensation for action recognition. British Machine Vision Conference.
[535] Bodor R, Jackson B, Masoud O, Papanikolopoulos N (2003) Image-based reconstruction for view-independent human motion recognition. IEEE/RSJ International Conference on Intelligent Robots and Systems 1548–1553.
[536] Rao C, Yilmaz A, Shah M (2002) View-invariant representation and recognition of actions. International J. on Computer Vision **50(2)**:203–226.
[537] Ali S, Basharat A, Shah M (2007) Chaotic invariants for human action recognition. International Conference on Computer Vision.
[538] Lai Y, Liao H (2006) Human motion recognition using clay representation of trajectories. International Conference on Intelligent Info Hiding and Multimedia Signal Processing 335–338.
[539] Dewaele G, Cani M (2003) Interactive global and local deformations for virtual clay. Pacific Conference on Computer Graphics and Applications 131–140.
[540] Zelnik-Manor L, Irani M (2006) Statistical analysis of dynamic actions. IEEE Trans. Pattern Analysis and Machine Intelligence **28(9)**:1530–1535.
[541] Loy G, Sullivan J, Carlsson S (2003) Pose-based Clustering in action sequences. IEEE International Workshop on Higher-Level Knowledge in 3D Modeling and Motion Analysis 66–73.
[542] Gorelick L, Blank M, Shechtman E, Irani M, Basri R (2007) Actions as space-time shapes. IEEE Trans. Pattern Analysis and Machine Intelligence **29(12)**:2247–2253.
[543] Blank M, Gorelick L, Shechtman E, Irani M, Basri R (2005) Actions as space-time shapes. International Conference on Computer Vision 1395–1402.
[544] Shechtman E, Irani M (2005) Space-time behavior based correlation. IEEE Computer Vision and Pattern Recognition 405–412.
[545] Viola P, Jones M, Snow D (2003) Detecting pedestrians using patterns of motion and appearance. International Conference on Computer Vision 734–742.
[546] Oikonomopoulos A, Patras I, Pantic M (2006) Spatiotemporal salient points for visual recognition of human actions. IEEE Trans. on SMC: Part B **36(3)**:710–719.
[547] Laptev I, Lindeberg T (2004) Velocity adaptation of space-time interest points. International Conference on Pattern Recognition.
[548] Rittscher J, Blake A, Roberts S (2002) Towards the automatic analysis of complex human body motions. Image and Vision Computing **20**:905–916.
[549] Yilmaz A, Shah M (2005) Actions sketch: a novel action representation. IEEE Computer Vision and Pattern Recognition 984–989.
[550] Bobick A, Wilson A (1997) A state-based approach to the representation and recognition of gesture. IEEE Trans. Pattern Analysis and Machine Intelligence **19(12)**:1325–1337.
[551] Dong Q, Wu Y, Hu Z (2006) Gesture recognition using quadratic curves. Asian Conference on Computer Vision 817–825.

[552] Shin M, Tsap L, Goldgof D (2004) Gesture recognition using Bezier curves for visualization navigation from registered 3-D data. Pattern Recognition **37(5)**:1011–1024.
[553] Wang L, Suter D (2006) Informative shape representations for human action recognition. International Conference on Pattern Recognition 1266–1269.
[554] Zhong H, Shi J, Visontai M (2004) Detecting unusual activity in video. IEEE Computer Vision and Pattern Recognition 819–826.
[555] Boiman O, Irani M (2005) Detecting irregularities in images and in video. International Conference on Computer Vision 462–469.
[556] Xiang T, Gong S (2005) Video behaviour profiling and abnormality detection without manual labelling. International Conference on Computer Vision 1238–1245.
[557] Cuntoor N, Chellappa R (2007) Epitomic representation of human activities. IEEE Computer Vision and Pattern Recognition 846–853.
[558] Harris C, Stephens M (1988) A combined corner and edge detector. Alvey Vision Conference 147–151.
[559] Lowe D (2004) Distinctive image features from scale-invariant keypoints. International J. on Computer Vision **60(2)**:91–110.
[560] Lucas B, Kanade T (1981) An iterative image registration technique with an application to stereo vision. International Joint Conference Artificial Intelligence 674–679.
[561] Dong Q, Wu Y, Hu Z (2009) Pointwise Motion Image (PMI): a novel motion representation and its applications to abnormality detection and behavior recognition. IEEE Trans. on Circuits and Systems for Video Technology **19(3)**:407–416.
[562] Cox D, Pinto N (2011) Beyond simple features: a large-scale feature search approach to unconstrained face recognition. IEEE Automatic Face and Gesture Recognition.
[563] Pinto N, Cox D, DiCarlo J (2008) Why is real-world visual object recognition hard. PLoS Computational Biology.
[564] Pinto N, DiCarlo J, Cox D (2008) Establishing good benchmarks and baselines for face recognition. European Conference on Computer Vision.
[565] Pinto N, Doukhan D, DiCarlo J, Cox D (2009) A high-throughput screening approach to discovering good forms of biologically inspired visual representation. PLoS Computational Biology.
[566] Shreve M, Godavarthy S, Goldgof D, Sarkar S (2011) Macro- and micro-expression spotting in long videos using spatio-temporal strain. IEEE Automatic Face and Gesture Recognition.
[567] Ekman P (2001) Telling lies: clues to deceit in the marketplace, politics, and marriage. W.W. Norton and Company.
[568] Ekman P, Rolls E, Perrett D, Ellis H (1992) Facial expressions of emotion: an old controversy and new findings [and discussion]. Philosophical Trans.: Biological Sciences **335**:63–69.
[569] Luu K, Bui T, Suen C (2011) Kernel spectral regression of perceived age from hybrid facial features. IEEE Automatic Face and Gesture Recognition.
[570] Tan X, Triggs B (2010) Enhanced local texture feature sets for face recognition under difficult lighting conditions. IEEE Trans. Image Processing **19(6)**:1635–1650.
[571] Ahonen T, Hadid A, Pietikainen M (2004) Face recognition with local binary patterns. European Conference on Computer Vision 469–481.
[572] Ahonen T, Hadid A, Pietikainen M (2006) Face description with local binary patterns: application to face recognition. IEEE Trans. Pattern Analysis and Machine Intelligence **28(12)**:2037–2041.
[573] Lui Y, Beveridge J (2011) Tangent bundle for human action recognition. IEEE Automatic Face and Gesture Recognition.
[574] Ben-Yosef G, Ben-Shahar O (2010) Minimum length in the tangent bundle as a model for curve completion. IEEE Computer Vision and Pattern Recognition.

[575] Conway J, Hardin R, Sloane N (1996) Packing lines, planes, etc.: Packings in grassmannian spaces. Experimental Mathematics **5(2)**:139–159.
[576] Kim T, Cipolla R (2007) Gesture recognition under small sample size. Asian Conference on Computer Vision.
[577] Kim T, Cipolla R (2009) Canonical correlation analysis of video volume tensors for action categorization and detection. IEEE Trans. Pattern Analysis and Machine Intelligence **31(8)**:1415–1428.
[578] Kovashka A, Grauman K (2010) Learning a hierarchy of discriminative space-time neighborhood features for human action recognition. IEEE Computer Vision and Pattern Recognition.
[579] Laptev I, Marszalek M, Schmid C, Rozenfield B (2008) Learning realistic human actions from movies. IEEE Computer Vision and Pattern Recognition.
[580] Li R, Chellappa R (2010) Aligning spatio-temporal signals on a special manifold. European Conference on Computer Vision.
[581] Lin Z, Jiang Z, Davis L (2009) Recognizing actions by shape-motion prototype trees. International Conference on Computer Vision.
[582] Lui Y, Beveridge J, Kirby M (2009) Canonical stiefel quotient and its application to generic face recognition in illumination spaces. IEEE International Conference Biometrics: Theory, Applications, and Systems 1–8.
[583] Lui Y, Beveridge J, Kirby M (2010) Action classification on product manifolds. IEEE Computer Vision and Pattern Recognition.
[584] Niebles J, Wang H, Fei-Fei L (2008) Unsupervised learning of human action categories using spatial-temporal words. International J. on Computer Vision **79(3)**:299–318.
[585] Silva J, Marques J, Lemos J (2005) Non-linear dimension reduction with tangent bundle approximation. ICASSP.
[586] Veeraraghavan A, Roy-Chowdhury A, Chellappa R (2005) Matching shape sequences in video with applications in human movement analysis. IEEE Trans. Pattern Analysis and Machine Intelligence **12**:1896–1909.
[587] Wang H, Ullah M, Klaser A, Laptev I, Schmid C (2009) Evaluation of local spatio-temporal features for action recognition. British machine Vision Conference.
[588] Edelman A, Arias R, Smith S (1999) The geometry of algorithms with orthogonal constraints. SIAM J. Matrix Anal. Appl. **2**:303–353.
[589] Kendall D (1984) Shape manifolds, procrustean metrics and complex projective spaces. Bull. London Math. Soc. **16**:81–121.
[590] Oshin O, Gilbert A, Bowden R (2011) Capturing the relative distribution of features for action recognition. IEEE Automatic Face and Gesture Recognition.
[591] Blake R, Shiffrar M (2007) Perception of human motion. Annual Review of Psychology **58**:47–73.
[592] Schuldt C, Laptev I, Caputo B (2004) Recognizing human actions: A local SVM approach. International Conference on Pattern Recognition.
[593] Dollar P, Rabaud V, Cottrell G, Belongie S (2005) Behavior recognition via sparse spatio-temporal features. VS-PETS.
[594] Liu J, Luo J, Shah M (2009) Recognizing realistic actions from videos. IEEE Computer Vision and Pattern Recognition.
[595] Gilbert A, Illingworth J, Bowden R (2009) Fast realistic multi-action recognition using mined dense spatio-temporal features. International Conference on Computer Vision.
[596] Laptev I, Lindeberg T (2003) Space-time interest points. International Conference on Computer Vision.
[597] Willems G, Tuytelaars T, Gool L (2008) An efficient dense and scale-invariant spatio-temporal interest point detector. European Conference on Computer Vision.

[598] Scovanner P, Ali S, Shah M (2007) A 3-dimensional sift descriptor and its application to action recognition. International Conference on Multimedia 357–360.
[599] Klaser A, Marszalek M, Schmid C (2008) A spatio-temporal descriptor based on 3D-gradients. British machine Vision Conference.
[600] Laptev I, Perez P (2007) Retrieving actions in movies. International Conference on Computer Vision.
[601] Marszalek M, Laptev I, Schmid C (2009) Actions in context. IEEE Computer Vision and Pattern Recognition.
[602] Ryoo M, Aggarwal J (2009) Spatio-temporal relationship match: video structure comparison for recognition of complex human activities. International Conference on Computer Vision.
[603] Matikainen P, Herbert M, Sukthankar R (2010) Representing pairwise spatial and temporal relations for action recognition. European Conference on Computer Vision.
[604] Savarese S, DelPozo A, Niebles J, Fei-Fei L (2008) Spatial-temporal correlatons for unsupervised action classification. WMVC.
[605] Cui Z, Shan S, Chen X, Zhang L (2011) Sparsely Encoded Local Descriptor for Face Recognition. IEEE Automatic Face and Gesture Recognition.
[606] Zhao G, Pietikinen M (2006) Local binary pattern descriptors for dynamic texture recognition. International Conference on Pattern Recognition 211–214.
[607] Zhang B, Shan S, Chen X, Gao W (2007) Histogram of Gabor phase patterns (HGPP): a novel object representation approach for face recognition. IEEE Trans. Image Processing **16(1)**:57–68.
[608] Zhang W, Shan S, Gao W, Chen X, Zhang H (2005) Local Gabor binary pattern histogram sequence (LGBPHS): a novel non-statistical model for face representation and recognition. International Conference on Computer Vision.
[609] Xie S, Shan S, Chen X, Chen J (2010) Fusing local patterns of Gabor magnitude and phase for face recognition. IEEE Trans. Image Processing **19(5)**:1349–1361.
[610] Bicego M, Lagorio A, Grosso E, Tistarelli M (2006) On the use of SIFT features for face authentication. IEEE Computer Vision and Pattern Recognition Workshop.
[611] Albiol A, Monzo D, Martin A, Sastre J, Albiol A (2008) Face recognition using HOG-EBGM. Pattern Recognition Letters **29**:1537–1543.
[612] Gorodnichy D (2005) Associative neural networks as means for low-resolution video-based recognition. International Joint Conference on Neural Networks.
[613] Kong W, Zhang D (2002) Palmprint texture analysis based on low-resolution images for personal authentication. International Conference on Pattern Recognition 807–810.
[614] Sobottka K (2000) Analysis of low-resolution range image sequences. PhD Thesis.
[615] Roh M, Christmas W, Kittler J, Lee S (2006) Robust player gesture spotting and recognition in low-resolution sports video. European Conference on Computer Vision 347–358.
[616] Lee S, Park J, Lee S (2006) Low resolution face recognition based on support vector data description. Pattern Recognition **39**:1809–1812.
[617] Yanadume S, Mekada Y, Ide I, Murase H (2004) Recognition of very low-resolution characters from motion images captured by a portable digital camera. Advances in Multimedia Information Processing 247–254.
[618] Nomura M, Yamamoto K, Ohta H, Kato K (2005) A proposal of the effective recognition method for low-resolution characters from motion images. International Conference on Document Analysis and Recognition **2**:720–724.
[619] Wu H, Chen H, Wu R, Shen D (2006) License plate extraction in low resolution video. International Conference on Pattern Recognition 824–827.
[620] Bo N, Dailey M, Uyyanonvara B (2007) Robust hand tracking in low-resolution video sequences. IASTED International Conference on Advances in Computer Science and Technology 228–233.

[621] Roh M, Christmas W, Kittler J, Lee S (2008) Gesture spotting for low-resolution sports video annotation. Pattern Recognition **41(3)**:1124–1137.
[622] Jun K, Kunihito K, Kazuhiko Y (1999) Character recognition at low resolution with video camera. J. of the Institute of Image Information and Television Engineers **53(6)**:867–872.
[623] Cutler R, Davis L (2000) Robust real-time periodic motion detection: analysis and applications. IEEE Trans. Pattern Analysis and Machine Intelligence **22**:781–796.
[624] Pittermann J, Pittermann A, Minker W (2010) Human emotions. Handling Emotions in Human-Computer Dialogues 19–45.
[625] Kim J, Hill R, Durlach P, Lane H, Forbell E, Core M, et al. (2009) BiLAT: a game-based environment for practicing negotiation in a cultural context. International J. of Artificial Intelligence in Education **19(3)**:289–308.
[626] Peursum P, Bui H, Venkatesh S, West G (2004) Human action recognition with an incomplete real-time pose skeleton. Curtin University of Technology, Australia, Tech. Report **2004/1**.
[627] Griffiths P (2001) Emotion and expression. International Encyclopedia of the Social & Behavioral Sciences 4433–4437.
[628] Baillie L, Morton L, Moffat D, Uzor S (2010) Capturing the response of players to a location-based game. Personal and Ubiquitous Computing.
[629] Wang N, Marsella S (2006) Introducing EVG: an emotion evoking game. LNCS **4133**:282–291.
[630] Baillie L, Morton L, Moffat D, Uzor S (2010) An investigation of user responses to specifically designed activities in a multimodal location based game. J. on Multimodal User Interfaces **3(3)**:179–188.
[631] Albrecht I, Schroder M, Haber J, Seidel H (2005) Mixed feelings: expression of non-basic emotions in a muscle-based talking head. Virtual Reality **8**:201–212.
[632] Ekman P, Keltner D (1997) Universal facial expressions of emotion: an old controversy and new findings. Nonverbal communication: where nature meets culture, Lawrence Erlbaum Associates Inc., Mahwah 27–46.
[633] Wang N, Marsella S, Hawkins T (2008) Individual differences in expressive response: a challenge for ECA design. International Joint Conference on Autonomous Agents and Multiagent Systems.
[634] Leite I, Martinho C, Pereira A, Paiva A (2008) iCat: an affective game buddy based on anticipatory mechanisms. International Conference on Autonomous Agents and Multiagent Systems 1229–1232.
[635] Nguyen Q, Novakowski S, Boyd J, Jacob C, Hushlak G (2006) Motion swarms: video interaction for art in complex environments. ACM International Conference Multimedia 461–469.
[636] Peursum P, Bui H, Venkatesh S, West G (2004) Classifying human actions using an incomplete real-time pose skeleton. LNCS **3157**:971–972.
[637] Fujiyoshi H, Lipton A (1999) Real-time human motion analysis by image skeletonization. Workshop on Application of Computer Vision.
[638] Li W, Zhang Z, Liu Z (2010) Action recognition based on a bag of 3D points. IEEE Computer Vision and Pattern Recognition Workshop.
[639] Wang X, Han T, Yan S (2009) An HOG-LBP human detector with partial occlusion handling. International Conference on Computer Vision.
[640] Canny J (1986) A computational approach to edge detection. IEEE Trans. Pattern Analysis and Machine Intelligence **8(6)**:679–698.
[641] Ahad A, Tan J, Kim H, Ishikawa S (2010) Motion history image: its variants and applications. Machine Vision and Applications. DOI: 10.1007/s00138-010-0298-4.
[642] Gafurov D (2007) A survey of biometric gait recognition: approaches, security and challenges. NIK Conference.
[643] Tao Y, Grosky W (1999) Object-based image retrieval using point feature maps. International Conference on Database Semantics 59–73.

[644] Shahabi C, Safar M (2006) An experimental study of alternative shape-based image retrieval techniques. Multimedia Tools and Applications. DOI 10.1007/s11042-006-0070-y.
[645] Samma A, Salam R (2009) Enhancement of shape description and representation by slope. World Academy of Science, Engineering and Technology **59**.
[646] Blostein S, Huang T (1991) Detecting small, moving objects in image sequences using sequential hypothesis testing. IEEE Trans. Signal Processing **39(7)**:1611–1629.
[647] Meir R, Ratsch G (2003) An introduction to boosting and leveraging. Advanced Lectures on Machine Learning **2600**:119–184.
[648] Freund Y (1990) Boosting a weak learning algorithm by majority. Workshop on Computational Learning Theory.
[649] Wang H (2011) Structural two-dimensional principal component analysis for image recognition. Machine Vision and Applications **22**:433–438.